William Ballantine

The Old World and the New

Being a Continuation of his 'Experiences'

William Ballantine

The Old World and the New
Being a Continuation of his 'Experiences'

ISBN/EAN: 9783744728669

Printed in Europe, USA, Canada, Australia, Japan

Cover: Foto ©ninafisch / pixelio.de

More available books at **www.hansebooks.com**

THE OLD WORLD
AND THE NEW

BY

MR SERJEANT BALLANTINE

BEING A CONTINUATION OF HIS 'EXPERIENCES'

LONDON
RICHARD BENTLEY & SON, NEW BURLINGTON STREET
Publishers in Ordinary to Her Majesty the Queen
1884

[All rights reserved]

TO

THE HON. BENJAMIN WOOD

Editor of the 'New York Daily News'
Manhattan Club, New York

I dedicate this volume, being governed by a feeling of gratitude towards one who was among the first of many to offer the hand of friendship to a stranger, and extend to him much kindness during his sojourn in the United States, and which was doubly gratifying coming from a representative of that body which in a great country forms so important and honoured an institution

WILLIAM BALLANTINE
Serjeant-at-Law

United Club
Boulogne-sur-Mer

CONTENTS.

CHAPTER I.

FIFTY YEARS AGO.

Thames police office—Description of its locality—Rotherhithe—Execution Dock—Pirates—Hanging in chains—Anecdotes of—Daring exploits of pirates—Evans—An eminent surgeon—Story of—Thames police officers—Performance of their duties—Old London Bridge—Passage under—Occasional danger—New London Bridge—Its opening—The 'Port Mahon'—Police office—Monday morning—Description—Jews—Crimping—Irish—Their description—My father the magistrate—Combativeness of the Irish—The river Thames—Rarity of steam-boats—East Indiamen—American Liners—Their disappearance—Substitution of steam—Safety of sailing-vessels—Loss of the 'President'—Tyrone Power—My interest in shipping—Vivid recollection of these days—Mr. Simmons and Mr. Fell—Angling in the Docks—The Tichborne trial—Arthur Orton—His birth and parentage . 1

CHAPTER II.

ON BOARD THE 'SERVIA.'

My youth—Recollections—Byron—Quotation—Dock-walls—The Minories—The Temple—My distaste—Future prospects—Visit to the United States determined upon—Berth taken on board the 'Servia'—Captain Theodore Cook—Embarkation—Bulk of the vessel—The machinery—Arrival at Queenstown—Favourable voyage—Meals on board—Library—Sweepstakes—Dulness of voyage—Wines and viands—Arrival at the mouth of the Hudson—Sun and icicles—Low water—Detention of vessel—Arrival off New York—The Docks—European Steam-packet Companies—Parting with fellow-passengers 10

CHAPTER III.

EARLY EXPERIENCES.

PAGE

Welcome shore—Hazy brain—Interviewed—Searching inquiry—Account of myself—Appetite for curiosity—Report of my interview—Not recognisable—Business of interviewers—Insignificant details—Genuineness of reports—Kindly spirit—Rescued—Military titles—Grand Hotel—Hotel life—Change from former days—Electricity—Elevators—Service not improved—Cooking—Wines—The Menu—Chosen guests—Ordinary dinners—Prices—Delmonico—Fifth Avenue Hotel—Entrance hall—Numerous frequenters—Energy and haste—The Saloon—*Table d'hôte* dinners—Their rapidity . 15

CHAPTER IV.

HOTELS AND COOKERY.

Sensational crimes—Stokes and Fisk—Their connection—Rivalry—Fisk's death—Public opinion—Trial—No verdict—Second trial—Verdict and sentence—Hoffman House Hotel—Works of art—A splendid painting—Statuary—The Honourable Judge Brady—Mr. Stokes—Coffee-room—Beefsteaks—Expense—The Hôtel de Paris—Celebrity of landlord—Racing successes—Generosity—Favourite dishes—Turtle—Tarrapin—Canvas-back duck—My opinion of them—Oysters—Tiernan's Eating-house—Meeting old friends—An apology 22

CHAPTER V.

STREETS OF NEW YORK.

Dickens's foreigner—My intentions—Scheme of streets—System of traffic—Overhead railway—Tramcars—Omnibuses—Quantity of passengers—Civility of conductors—Universal use of cars—General courtesy—The Stock Exchange—Visit to it—Kind reception—Compliment to Her Majesty—'God save the Queen'—Bankers—Caution—Lodgings—Situation of house—Streets of New York—Activity—Advertisements—Theatres—Mrs. Langtry—Her interviewers—A military gentleman—His description of his own proceedings—Mrs. Langtry's companion—My interviewer—Description of myself—Wallack—His father—Early remembrances—Adelina Patti—Mr. Mapleson—Soothing an angry artist—The 'Traviata'—Signor Arditi—Snowy condition of streets—Danger to pedestrians—Expenses of private vehicles 29

CHAPTER VI.

JOURNALISM AND FASHION.

Geography of streets—Clubs—Apartments—Daily papers—Every-day habits—New York journals—Their great ability—Extensive news—Trials—Lynch law—Desperate encounters—Outrages by negroes—Shipping intelligence—News from home—Accidents of voyage—Wonderful enterprise exhibited—Avidity for news—Mr. Hulbert—The Honourable Mr. Benjamin Wood—Mr. Lawson—New New York—Splendid suburb—New York season—Equipages—Mansions—Parks—A century's work 38

CHAPTER VII.

A MODERN DRAMA.

The tastes of people—Exhibited by drama—'Iolanthe' at the Standard Theatre, New York—Savoy Theatre, London—W. S. Gilbert—Sir Arthur Sullivan—Sketch of plot—Mr. Riley—Humorous performance—His account of himself—Conclusion of sketch—Popularity of this drama—Growing contempt for show—Amusing incident—Management of theatres in America—Illness of Sir Arthur Sullivan—Curious trait of Mr. Gilbert 41

CHAPTER VIII.

PLAYS AND PLAYERS.

Changes in the Drama—Opinions of society—Absence of veneration—A Chief Justice—Dramatic festival—Histrionic talent—Compliment to Mr. Irving—Irving as a manager—Stage decorations—Anecdote—Performances at New York—Miss Ellen Terry—Miss Kate Terry—Charles Kean—Anecdote—Welcome to British actors—American actors—Mr. Booth—Performance of Richelieu—Washington Irving—Rip Van Winkle—Jefferson—Admirable performance—Ben. Webster's opinion—Miss Mary Anderson at Philadelphia—Her reception in London 49

CHAPTER IX.

TWO BANQUETS.

Lord Lytton—Charles Dickens—Natural actors—Lord Lytton's public speeches—Preparation and care—Acting of Dickens—His readings—Approaching visit to America—Banquet given to him—Distinguished guests—Lord Lytton—Chairman—

Appearance of Lord Lytton and Charles Dickens—My 'Experiences'—Traits of Lord Lytton—Dickens's success in America—Generosity of Americans—Banquet to Irving—Lord Coleridge—Irving's great success 55

CHAPTER X.

GENERAL GRANT.

Insurrection of the Southern States—England and America—Change of feeling—Ignorance of each other—Exaggerated views—Running the blockade—Love of adventure—Piracy—The 'Alabama'—Its escape—Termination of the war—Increased cordiality of England and America—Deeds of heroism—General Grant—Visit to his house—Appearance of the General—His conversation—Simplicity—Orders and insignia—Mrs. Grant—Jefferson Davis—Mr. Benjamin—His escape—Called to the English Bar—Its liberal conduct—His great success—His retirement—Entertainment given—His advocacy—Meetings in Paris—Galignani—Mr. Evarts—Introduction to him—A firm of lawyers 60

CHAPTER XI.

NEW YORK SOCIETY.

Distinguished lawyers—Mr. Evarts—The Genevan Conference—Roundell Palmer—Arthur Cohen—The result—Introduction to Mr. Evarts—Description of him—The Lotus Club—Entertainment—Councillor Pleydell—The Honourable Judge Brady—A song—Mr. Justice Hayes—The result of a song—Character of Mr. Justice Hayes—His sudden death—Courtesy to English—The Century Club—Meeting of celebrities—Kindness to myself—Mr. and Mrs. Bigelow—Their receptions—Description of Mr. Bigelow—Mr., Mrs., and the Misses Mack—Their parties—Mrs. J. C. Croly—Her circle—The Sorosis Club—Her presidentship—Agreeable recollections 68

CHAPTER XII.

COURTS, CRIMES, AND PUNISHMENTS.

My professional life—Trials in the United States—Yankee stories—Not reliable—The Recorder of New York—His demeanour—The advocate—Decorum of proceedings—Other courts—The Judges—Their election—Salary—Character—

CONTENTS. xi

PAGE

Able jurists—English Judges—Selection by Chancellor—
Their character and position—English Bar—Difference from
American—A distinct body—Union of advocate and solicitor
in America—Establishment of County Courts in England—
Great changes created—Practice in police courts—Death
punishments—American system—English system—Objections to—The executioner—Execution at Liverpool—Disgraceful scene—Conduct of executioner—His associates—
Is capital punishment desirable?—Recent examples—Probable effect—Appointment of executioner—Reporters—
O'Donnell—His execution—Its probable result on others . 75

CHAPTER XIII.

THE TOMBS.

Mr. Gilbert—Conversation with—American prisons—Mr.
Howard Vincent—Arrival in New York—Visit to the Tombs
—Exterior of prison—Situation—Newgate—Its records—
Prison entrance—Youthful prisoners—Their type—Conduct
—Appearance—Mixture—The governor—Main corridor—
Prisoners under death-sentence—Their treatment—Absence
of restraint—Comfortable cells—Affecting scene—Interview with a prisoner—His crime—His appearance—Subsequent execution—Manner of governor—His appearance—
The gallows—Question of discipline—English system—
Explanation—My own experiences—Opinion as to treatment
of suspected persons—English system unjustifiable—A confession—My reading at Chickering Hall—Kindly criticism . 85

CHAPTER XIV.

LAW AND LAWYERS.

System of law—America and England—A death sentence—
Delay—Objections to—Reasons for—English system—Haste
—No Court of Appeal—Desirability of—Equity judges—Their
inexperience—Character of—Ridiculous results—Evil consequences—Criminal trial—Serious blunder—The Staunton
case—Popular indignation—Cockburn—His interference—
Modification of sentence—Release of prisoner—Question of
appeal—Necessity in capital cases—Its justice in every case—
Existence in civil cases—Sir James Fitzjames Stephen—A
criminal code—Difficulty of—Evidence of a wife—Murder
case—Rush—Another trial—Alibi proved—Position of a
wife—Influence of criminal trials—Capital punishment—My
change of opinion 93

CHAPTER XV.

BOSTON.

Boston railway—Night journey—Its discomfort—Sleeping-cars—Caution to ladies—Agreeable morning—Colonel Morse—The hotel—General Butler—Election as governor—Inauguration—Preliminary reception—Introduction to the general—His character—Division of opinion—Notables and judges present—General Butler's appearance—My surprise—His practice as an attorney—His address—Its ability—Its frankness—Its reception—Great sensation—Censure of local authorities—Mr. Warren—Renewal of acquaintance—The club—General courtesy—Regret at leaving—Unpopularity of General Butler—His subsequent defeat 101

CHAPTER XVI.

DISTINGUISHED CHARACTERS.

Philadelphia—Its beauty—Its population—Mr. Stoddart—Dinner party—Horace Furness—Shakespearian collection—An Unitarian divine—A distinguished authoress—The Penn Club—Flattering reception—Ex-Chief Justice Sharswood—Eli K. Price—The judges—Association Hall—Grand entertainment—The Bar and Bench—Eloquent speeches—Touching conclusion—Distinguished character of guests—Reflections upon the entertainment 107

CHAPTER XVII.

THE CLOVER CLUB.

Bright weather—Hospitality—Expression of thanks—The Clover Club—Its motto—Object—Monthly dinner—Qualification for membership—The Press—Representatives at dinner—Belle Vue Hotel—Guests—Speeches—Songs—Mr. Disston—Henry Philipps—Henry Russell—Barry Cornwall—Wallack—Oscar Wilde—Success of dinner—Return to New York—Its holiday appearance—Beauty of the ladies—Lord Coleridge—His opinion upon the subject—Comparison with English ladies—My opinion 120

CHAPTER XVIII.

BUFFALO, NIAGARA, AND CHICAGO.

Personal matters—My 'Experiences'—Kind reception—Mr. D'Oyly Carte—Engagement with him—Result—Mr. Phil Robinson—Journey to Salt Lake—Mr. and Mrs. Richards—

Buffalo—Falls of Niagara—Visit to—Prospect Hotel—Good living—Description of Falls—Harpies—Persecution by—Sheridan—Anecdote of—Captain Webb—His foolish attempt—Fatal result—Appearance of country—Return to Buffalo—Grand Pacific Hotel—Negro servants—Incidents of journey—Wheel on fire—Apprehension of a forger—Arrival at Chicago—Offensive interviewer—Description by him of myself 128

CHAPTER XIX.

CHICAGO AND OGDEN.

Energy of people—Departure from Chicago—The journey—Discomforts of—Heated cars—Bitter cold—Wretched food—Bills—Hints to travellers—Negligence of guards—The Rocky Mountains—The prairies—Wanting in interest—Ogden—Decent hotel—Mr. Richards—His business—Plurality of wives not universal—Sustained by persecution—Works upon the subject—Hepworth Dixon—Sir Charles Dilke—Situation of Ogden—A barber's shop—Curiosity—Departure—Arrival at Salt Lake City 134

CHAPTER XX.

THE CITY OF THE SALT LAKE.

The Mormons—Their singular position—Their belief—Plurality of wives—Patriotism—Locality of city—Fruit-trees—Streets—Other trees—Imaginary effect—Sparrows imported—Their increase—Inconvenience of—Disputes between citizens—A trial—An appeal—The judgment—Danger of collision—Lawlessness—Miners—Assemblage of—Their conduct—Scene at post office—A recollection—My impression of the miners . 139

CHAPTER XXI.

A TIDELESS SEA.

The Salt Lake—Distance from Utah—Railway—Visit to lake—Disappointment—Scenery—Banks—The pier—A steamer—Return to Utah—Dinner—The food—An Irishman's store—A good meal—Good tea—General Clawson—Extraordinary life—Journey over the plains—Successful merchant—Opposition to Government—Carriages and horses—Roads—Buildings—Tabernacle—Enterprise—Sympathy with the people . . 147

CHAPTER XXII.

WANDERINGS.

Roads—Absence of birds—A farmhouse—A Mormon emigrant—His home—His father—A strange coincidence—An optical illusion—The hospital—Sisters of Mercy—Dr. Benedict—The patients—Skilful treatment—Frost-bites—Dr. Wolcot—Habits of the Mormons—Conversation with the doctor—His opinions—The Tichborne case—A statement—An old acquaintance 152

CHAPTER XXIII.

THE PRESIDENT.

Mr. Phil Robinson—Testing his voice—Lecturing—My augury—Widows of Brigham Young—Their appearance—Mr. Clawson's wives—Heads of the community—Their views—Apostates—Ridiculous stories—Not believed—The clergy—A murder trial—One person convicted—Subsequent trials—A jury—Difficulty of obtaining one—The court—Chief Justice Hooper—Jurymen—Unwillingness to act—Fear of consequences—Unfortunate result—Much lawlessness—President Taylor—His appearance—Conversation with him—His views—The Tabernacle—Plurality of wives—Journalism—The 'Herald'—Mr. Byron Groo—Pleasant hours 160

CHAPTER XXIV.

FROM UTAH TO LIVERPOOL.

Journey to Ogden—Railway—Crowding—Miners—Appearance—Conduct—A little child—Departure from Ogden—Route—Kansas City—Denver—Unpleasant journey—Arrival at New York—Dulness—Barbers' shops—Sir Edward Archibald—His death—His brother—The post office—A bank—Steamer 'Arizona'—Departure from New York—Appearance of vessel—Its first trip—Our voyage—Fellow-passengers—Easter Sunday—Accident—Delay—Diminished speed—Similar accidents—A storm—Anxious times—Arrival at Liverpool—Reflections upon accidents—Incidents relating to them—Tremendous speed—Danger arising from . . . 169

CHAPTER XXV.

HOME AGAIN.

The Mersey—Adelphi Hotel—London—Sir James Paget—State of health—Reflections—Politics—Gladstone—The clergy—

Bishops—Curates—Science—Vivisection—Oxford Convocation—The Law—Lords Justices—Court of Appeal—Literature—Mudie—Philosophy—Science—Travels—Lyndhurst—Lytton—Biographies—Espinasse—Pomposity of—Anecdote of Lyndhurst—Traits of Lord Lytton—Gambling anecdote—Superstition of gamesters—Anecdotes of—Hope-Scott—Her Majesty 181

CHAPTER XXVI.

MEN OF MARK.

A dinner party—Editor of the 'Times'—Abraham Hayward—His appearance—Occupation—Bernal Osborne—His characteristics—Last meeting—Sir George Jessel—His ability—Self-confidence—Good-nature—Mr. Justice Byles—An Unitarian—Election failure—Anecdote of 188

CHAPTER XXVII.

SIR ALEXANDER COCKBURN.

Russell Square—Former days—Talfourd's house—Mr. Gill—Cockburn—His doctor—Latter days—Letters—His career—Medical knowledge—Symptoms—Description of—Performance of duties—Sir William Jenner—Visit to Spa—November 1880—Cockburn resumes his duties—Sudden death—His judicial character—The Queen's Bench—Extinction of name—Mellor—Lush—Anecdote of Cockburn—Kindheartedness—Anecdote of Lush—The 'Traviata'—Sir Nicholas Tindal—Erle—Sir John Jervis—Bad health—Anecdote of—Gossip—Consequences—Maule 194

CHAPTER XXVIII.

WELL-KNOWN PEOPLE.

Anthony Trollope—His life—His complaint—His own account of it—Angina pectoris—The chase—Trollope's opinion—Last meeting with him—Charles Reade—Early acquaintance—His writings—Marquis of Anglesey—A game at cribbage—Vice-Chancellor Bacon—A dinner—His caricatures—The Honourable Robert Grimstone—Westminster election—Petition—Mr. Smith—Baron Martin—Result 206

CHAPTER XXIX.

CORRESPONDENCE.

Sir Robert Phillimore—Letter from—Smethurst case—Cresswell—His character—Sir James Wilde—Anecdotes—My early days—Letter from Whitehurst—Felix Whitehurst—His early days—His death—St. Paul's School—Its masters—Empress of the French 212

CHAPTER XXX.

A RETROSPECT.

Numerous correspondents—An attack of illness—Major Bethune—His letter—An old memory—Death of a murderer—Letter from a lady—Benevolence—Lord Westbury—Anecdote of Vivisection—Ouida—Dinner with—Letter from—Editor of 'Spectator'—Quotation from—Thurtell—Trial—Anecdotes—Forbes Campbell—Letter from—Sir Robert Clifton—Alexander Mitchell—Duke of Brunswick—Mr. and Mrs. Hodgson—Milner Gibson—The 'World'—Quotation from—Dr. Elliotson 221

CHAPTER XXXI.

EASTBOURNE, PAST AND PRESENT.

Eastbourne—Present appearance—Memories—A country mansion—Charles Manby—Letter from—Mrs. Manby—Major Willard—His property—Theatrical connections—Adelphi Theatre—Honorary Canon of Rochester—Letter from—Dr. Robinson—Zadkiel—Sir Edward Belcher—Miss Bigg—Letter from—Tawell—Trial for murder—An explanation 230

CHAPTER XXXII.

EXPERIENCES VERIFIED.

Letters—Henry Spicer—Frank Burnand—Clement Scott—Watson Wood—General Marriott—Letter from—Incidents mentioned—Maidstone—Rochester—Charles Dickens—His house—Falstaff and Prince Hal—Scene of their exploits—Alexander Knox—Letter from—His retirement—Confirmatory incidents—Mrs. Knox—Conclusion of my memories . 236

CHAPTER XXXIII.

A RÉSUMÉ . 244

APPENDIX . . 257

THE OLD WORLD AND THE NEW.

CHAPTER I.

FIFTY YEARS AGO.

Thames police office—Description of its locality—Rotherhithe—Execution Dock—Pirates—Hanging in chains—Anecdotes of—Daring exploits of pirates—Evans—An eminent surgeon—Story of—Thames police officers—Performance of their duties—Old London Bridge—Passage under—Occasional danger—New London Bridge—Its opening—The 'Port Mahon'—Police office—Monday morning—Description—Jews—Crimping—Irish—Their Description—My father the magistrate—Combativeness of the Irish—The river Thames—Rarity of steam-boats—East Indiamen—American Liners—Their disappearance—Substitution of steam—Safety of sailing-vessels—Loss of the 'President'—Tyrone Power—My interest in shipping—Vivid recollection of these days—Mr. Simmons and Mr. Fell—Angling in the Docks—The Tichborne trial—Arthur Orton—His birth and parentage.

In ransacking the stores of memory, I find myself seated at a bay-window projecting over the river Thames; this appertained to a house forming the termination of a lane once famous for the evil deeds of press-gangs, and overlooking the spot celebrated by the song of 'Wapping Old Stairs.' Nothing picturesque presented itself at this point.

Thames mud rendered the approach to it dirty and slippery, and the noisy contest of watermen plying for the hire of their wherries, which still held their place upon the river in spite of the encroachments of steam, were its principal characteristics.

The opposite side of the river had been christened Rotherhithe, but was known to its inhabitants as well as the sojourners in the locality by the name of Red Riffe. I do not know whether I have spelt the pseudonym correctly, as I have never seen it written, but if a stranger had asked a boatman to take him to Rotherhithe he would have been extremely puzzled as to where his customer wanted to go. In this locality, however, and in view of the bay-window I have referred to, was a spot designated by the unsavoury title of 'Execution Dock.' This it had obtained from the fact of certain unlicensed rovers of the sea, when caught, meeting with the proper reward of their free living, and being subsequently suspended in chains with a view to prevent other navigators from indulging in similar propensities.

At the period, however, of which I am speaking these ghastly attributes had disappeared, but only recently, and were well remembered. Many a story I have listened to from the lips of the old police officers whilst they were rowing me backwards and forwards in the boats attached to the office, over which my father presided. These stories were usually related in terms that, notwithstanding the duties of the narrators, showed an evident sympathy with the heroes of them. In fact, the daring exploits of pirates and highwaymen overshadowed the deeds of atrocious cruelty which really signalised their calling, and I can well remember the chuckle with which Evans (one of the oldest and most respected of the officers) used to relate the following anecdote. If he got it from that much plundered veteran Joe Miller, I at all events got it from him.

It seems that at a date not so very long distant, when the period between conviction and execution was passed right merrily by the convict, a certain hero of the seas negotiated with an eminent surgeon for the sale of his body. The interest of science, and the fascination exercised upon the mind of an anatomist at the prospect of a healthy body, dissipated ordinary prudence, and without inquiry, having revelled in the sinews and muscles of the pirate, the surgeon paid him a liberal sum, and only learnt too late that part of his sentence condemned him to be hung in chains.

Evans was a fine, intelligent, and useful officer, and the force under him extremely well-disciplined. I have already in my former work given an account of their organisation; they were distinguished by many a deed of daring—the river-side brigands were no children to deal with, and the capture of one of them was usually attended with a perilous struggle, although generally brought about by the treachery of a comrade or the jealousy of a mistress.

Old London Bridge at this period, although doomed, still stretched its uncouth frame from the City to the Borough, and its construction rendered the passage through it, at certain conditions of the tide, dangerous to no small extent. The men who manned the police boats surmounted the difficulties with much skill, but there were times when in pursuit of a criminal they encountered considerable danger, and of course I could not allow myself to be an impediment if it so happened that I was on board. It is strange that I have entirely forgotten the external features of this once celebrated structure, and will not pirate from Harrison Ainsworth, who has I think in 'Jack Sheppard' so vividly described them.

It was a gala day in the metropolis when it was known that the New London Bridge was to be opened. The crowded streets showed the interest felt in the event; the Corporation, justly proud of having initiated the undertaking, were resplendent in their gaudy robes, and almost panted under the weight of their glittering chains; and the river, alive with thousands of boats, over which a summer sun liberally cast its rays, presented no small amount of attraction in the sample exhibited of the pretty girls of a city second to none in the beauty it displays on these occasions, decked in holiday attire, with happy, laughing faces.

My father had something to do with the show, and a dismantled ship called the 'Port Mahon,' which I fancy had been taken from the Spanish in some engagement, and lay off Arundel Street in the Strand, used generally as a police station, received a party of my father's friends, and, as I issued the invitations, I need hardly say that the occasion was one that has retained possession of my memory.

To revert, however, to the old bay-windowed room facing the Thames, in those days called an office—it would now if used for the same purpose be dignified by the name of 'Court'—let us suppose it to be upon a Monday morning. It would require the pen of a Dickens, or the pencil of a Cruikshank, to convey to the imagination of my readers the motley assemblage that presented itself upon the commencement of the proceedings: the grimy faces—the beards, unusual in those days—the cunning eyes, bleared and anxious—the tell-tale nose, and claw-like fingers that grasped the bar separating the public from the magistrate and clerks, left no mistake as to the race to which their owners belonged, and that quiet energy and determination which had secured them here, as in many a higher place, the precedence over unreasoning violence was another proof.

Dotted amongst or standing behind them, but towering inches above, were to be seen on these Monday mornings faces of a very different type, faces which, so far as black eyes and other disfigurements of a similar kind would enable a beholder to recognise their natural traits, clearly disclosed a Milesian origin. It was amongst a population mainly consisting of the above classes that my father, who held the appointment of magistrate, performed the duty of administering justice, which he had the character of doing most equitably.

It was the Israelites who represented the trading community of Wapping; they called themselves 'clothiers,' and no doubt garments of all sizes, shapes, and ages ornamented the exterior of their dwellings, and generally a black doll, slightly clad, was suspended over the doorway; what this was an emblem of I never could find out. The principal furniture of the interior was a melting-pot, which sufficiently indicated one branch of their trade, but their chief articles of sale were their fellow-creatures, which obtained for themselves the designation of 'crimps.' They were seldom present of their own

free will upon these occasions, and many a tale had
my father to hear in which their principal characteristics were developed; they were, however, good
husbands and fathers, and neither beat their wives
nor starved their children—incidents far too frequent
amongst the Christian population of the district.

The battered state of their countenances sufficiently disclosed the pugilistic propensities of the
Irish, mingling in this heterogeneous crowd. They
also were rarely willing visitors, and the narratives
of severely dilapidated policemen were not wanted to
prove the combativeness of the quarter which they
inhabited, and which rendered it by no means an
agreeable lounge for the guardians of the public
peace.

Although steam had already made its appearance, the vessels propelled by it were comparatively
rare, and the noble ships that still covered the river
trusted to the tides to take them to its mouth, and
to the winds for their passage to distant shores.
Amongst these, I well remember the 'American
Liners,' as they were usually called—of beautiful
construction, and famous for the rapidity and safety
with which they made their voyages across the
Atlantic Ocean. Where are they now? Science,
conquering nature, has substituted steam for the
elements; and the American sailing ships, following the fate of the old 'East Indiamen,' although

from different causes, have long since ended their career. Like the old East Indiamen, they were too grand to play a second part, but England can never forget the splendid game which their navies assisted to play during its country's wars.

Now the ocean is ploughed by steam, whether so safely or not can only be known by statistics that I have no means of reaching. I do not remember to have heard or read of the loss of a New York sailing-ship. There has, I fear, been more than one magnificent steamer that has left no sign behind it upon the ocean. One I remember well, it was called the 'President;' on board it were many beloved beings, amongst others one of the most popular actors of the day—poor Tyrone Power, the cheeriest of companions, and most charming of comedians. What actually happened no one lived to tell.

My boyhood, and the early scenes of my youth, had been such as threw me back a great deal upon my own thoughts, and I spent many hours in watching the life upon the river, and was greatly interested in the character and employment of the different vessels. My close acquaintance with the officers who manned the boats enabled me to learn names and destinations, as well as feats of heroism under terrible trials, that had distinguished their crews. Can it be wondered at that, even at this distance of time, I entertain a fond recollection of those glorious old ships, and a feeling almost of sorrow that their very names and history should have passed out of the knowledge of the present generation?

Before I quit the records of these days, little as it may interest my readers, I must be permitted a few words of grateful recollection in memory of two gentlemen who acted as clerks, but to whose kindness I was indebted for much that made my life comparatively pleasant—Mr. Simmons and Mr. Fell—the latter a skilful and enthusiastic angler, and in whose company I spent many hours by the side of some adjacent docks, where, strange as the fact may appear to those who know them now, there was to be found no contemptible sport. And a well-known trial, in which I was engaged, brought to my mind the fact that the father of Arthur Orton carried on business within a stone's throw of the office, and it was here that the hero of an episode in one of the most extraordinary trials of recent days first saw—I will not say the light, but prefer what was more likely—the fogs of Wapping.

CHAPTER II.

ON BOARD THE 'SERVIA.'

My youth — Recollections — Byron — Quotation — Dock-walls — The Minories — The Temple — My distaste — Future prospects — Visit to the United States determined upon — Berth taken on board the 'Servia' — Captain Theodore Cook — Embarkation — Bulk of the vessel — The machinery — Arrival at Queenstown — Favourable voyage — Meals on board — Library — Sweepstakes — Dulness of voyage — Wines and viands — Arrival at the mouth of the Hudson — Sun and icicles — Low water — Detention of vessel — Arrival off New York — The Docks — European Steam-packet Companies — Parting with fellow-passengers.

ALTHOUGH I have little to say about myself during these early days of my career that I have not already dwelt upon, and although they were not attended with any great amount of recreation, I linger over their recollection. Is it not Byron who says truthfully—

There is no joy the world can give like that it takes away,
When the early glow of youth declines in feeling's dull decay?

and I can recall the long dreary walk between dock-walls, and up the Minories to the Temple, where, far too early in life, I was supposed to read at a special pleader's chambers, and know now how the mere sensation of boyhood brightened up the monotony of the hours thus passed, and how joyously I escaped from work I hated, and from books and papers I did not understand, to my river wanderings, with their congenial associates.

Still my thoughts dwelt upon law, and my daydreams pictured happiness in forensic success, and, much as I loved an association with ships and their adventures, they were as fairy tales, and with no expectation of a life in any way connected with them. I little thought that at a future period I should visit both India and America, then presenting themselves so mistily to my imagination; and it was only at periods long afterwards, and when the pleasures both of life and memory became things of the past, that one of those epochs occurred, for which I now venture to ask the attention and favour of my readers.

A combination of incidents, a recapitulation of which would not create interest, determined me upon a trip to the United States; and having obtained some introductions, which I found everywhere warmly responded to, I secured a berth on board the 'Servia,' one of the finest of the Cunard Line of ships, 8,000 tons burden, and commanded by Captain Theodore Cook, an experienced seaman, a pleasant companion in fine weather, and under all circumstances thoroughly to be relied upon; and on Saturday, November 24, 1882, upon a dull, foggy afternoon, I took up my quarters on board.

Although I had, some ten years before, obtained a practical knowledge of the noble steamers belonging to the Peninsular and Oriental Company, on my voyage to Bombay, I was, nevertheless, almost lost in wonder, firstly, at the bulk of this vessel, the largest at the time upon the station, and at the wondrous mass of machinery by which it was propelled. Grandly we steamed out of the Mersey, and after taking in the mails, upon the following day, off Queenstown, we started upon our voyage across the Atlantic.

My experience upon the return voyage leads me to think that we had throughout an unusually favourable passage, considering the time of year. Neither ourselves nor the dishes were turned topsy-turvy, and I fancy that none of us were kept from the breakfast and dinner, liberally supplied and pleasantly shared in. Everything that could be added towards our comfort by the courtesy of both captain and crew was afforded.

There was on board a sufficient library of books, not requiring too intense a study, even for heads with a tendency not to be too steady; and much amusement was obtained amongst the passengers by their making a calculation of the number of miles likely to be run by the vessel upon the

ensuing day, sweepstakes being arranged amongst
themselves, the winner of which was the person
who had calculated most nearly the actual run,
and who, for the remainder of the day, was
looked upon as a personage. Notwithstanding,
however, these sources of amusement, I cannot
share in the opinion of those who describe charms
in these Atlantic passages, and the anxious inquiry
so often asked of our kindly captain as to what day
we were likely to arrive, pretty clearly showed the
feeling that existed in the bosom of many a passenger.

Upon the subject of wines and viands, although
abundant, I will not express any opinion, but I
have heard some of my companions declare them
to be excellent.

It was upon the morning of Monday, December
2, that we arrived at the mouth of the renowned
Hudson, and, although approaching to mid-winter,
a bright sun was shining overhead, shedding its
rays upon the sparkling icicles with which a frosty
night had ornamented the masts and sides of the
vessel. The state of tide brought us to a standstill, until there was water enough for us to reach
the Docks off New York City. The brightness of
the morning, however, had disappeared, and,
whether it was from this or other causes, the
grandeur of the river, so often celebrated in song

and story, scarcely presented to my sight a realisation of these descriptions. Certainly at this point I was disappointed with its appearance; not unlike in some of its features, it did not exhibit either so gay or busy a scene as our Thames at Gravesend, nothing that brought to the mind the power of a mercantile navy, so often claiming admiration at that locality. The wharves appeared to be principally tenanted by the different European companies, the steamers belonging to which were recognised as we moved slowly to our anchorage.

There was much shaking of hands exchanged amongst us, and kindly wishes that we might meet again—never perhaps in this world to be realised, although at the time undoubtedly sincere, for our companionship had been thoroughly sociable and good-humoured; and it was from their countrymen on this voyage that I first obtained a sample of that kindness that I met with from the population of all parts of the United States of America.

CHAPTER III.

EARLY EXPERIENCES.

Welcome shore—Hazy brain—Taken prisoner—Interviewed—Searching inquiry—Account of myself—Appetite for curiosity—Report of my interview—Not recognisable—Business of interviewers—Insignificant details—Genuineness of reports—Kindly spirit—Rescued — Military titles—Grand Hotel—Hotel life — Change from former days—Electricity—Elevators—Service not improved —Cooking—Wines—The Menu—Chosen guests—Ordinary dinners — Prices— Delmonico — Fifth Avenue Hotel - Entrance hall — Numerous frequenters—Energy and haste—The Saloon—*Table d'hôte* dinners—Their rapidity—Sancho Panza's supper.

NINE days' tumbling upon the Atlantic is calculated to produce upon the landsman a sensation of doubt as to the stability of his legs when first they touch the welcome shore, and also a decided uncertainty as to the accurate relation of those members with the brain, which itself would prefer the putting off the exercise of its own functions until a more promising opportunity for their display. This, however, was the moment selected to make me acquainted with a very pronounced specimen of American character.

I had scarcely put foot upon that glorious soil which boasts its freedom from all ordinary trammels than I was taken prisoner. It is true my bondage was unaccompanied by physical restraint and was accomplished with much politeness, but was not the less irresistible, and with shaky legs, an aching brain, and an empty stomach, I was carried off by the most affable of custodians to the hotel where quarters had been arranged for me, and there—much after the fashion in which an acute English attorney takes the examination of a witness—my general occupations and particular objects at the time were made the subject of minute and searching inquiry by this polite and kindly personage, representing, as he told me, an influential newspaper, and whose employment (a recognised profession in America) is known by the name of 'Interviewer.'

I am not aware whether these gentlemen serve any apprenticeship or have formed themselves into any guild. I know not whether there be any principles out of which they form a code, or whether each professor uses his natural powers. They possess a common object, and this is to purvey, for the apparently wonderful appetite for curiosity of the American public, the minutest of information—a strange characteristic of a people whose history is distinguished by such features of grandeur, and from whose shores have emanated such schemes of magnitude.

On the following morning I met in one of the

newspapers an account that purported to be a description of this interview, but, if this was in truth an accurate detail of what really came from my lips, it disclosed the muddle into which my own senses had been shaken, rather than any clear idea of what my outer organs might have conveyed after the administration of a dinner and a night's rest.

It must I think be admitted that throughout the United States there is a large amount of interest exhibited upon comparatively trifling matters, and which renders the business of their supply extremely profitable; and it cannot be wondered at if sometimes the highest journals are made the medium by which gossip of no public importance, but, on the contrary, of a strictly private character, is circulated. I wish, however, most emphatically to add that, whilst dwelling upon this curious passion for small details upon comparatively insignificant subjects, and which I think no one who reads the journals published daily in all the cities of the United States will deny to be a prominent feature, I do not impute to the gentlemen who furnish the supply any manufacture of news or unwarranted bitterness of spirit; their intention, with rare exceptions, is to put the public in possession of the truth and to report exactly the facts, and thus to cater for its amusement; and, as far as I am personally concerned, I have every reason to be grateful for the kindly spirit in which they have upon *nearly* every occasion performed their functions.

After about an hour of this duress—and it was no fault of mine that my captor had caught a subject so little worthy of the patience and perseverance he expended upon it—I was rescued by my friend Colonel Morse, and under his auspices repaired my bodily wants with an excellent dinner. And here I may mention that in this country, which makes equality one of its proudest boasts, it is very rarely that you are introduced to anyone under the simple designation of Mister; and although dukes, earls, marquises, and barons, whose grand attribute is to have nothing to do, are not to be found, the army supplies titles to numbers of the community, who are by no means ashamed of working hard at occupations of anything but a military character.

Colonel Morse was assisting in the management of a theatrical establishment; but he was exceptionally entitled to his military dignity, having attained it by services in the United States army, during the Southern insurrection, and where also he had obtained a by no means unfrequent accompaniment to glory in the shape of an ague, which gave him no chance of forgetting some of the incidents of his former profession. He introduced me to the Grand Hotel, where I took up my quarters for my first night in America. I need not pause to describe hotel life as it exists in the States. This institution with similar characteristics is now developed all over Europe. England has numerous specimens of it. Boniface has disappeared, with his good and evil doings. I fancy the glory of his days recorded in many an old play, and other works of almost forgotten fiction—the foaming ale, and crusted port—disappeared with the Rovers and Rangers of fashion, and the highwaymen and bagmen of the road.

Now towering edifices invite into noble halls, where people are ticketed off without being looked at, and deposited in rooms at different altitudes, and which have been assigned to them by means of electricity; the transmission is effected by what in this country are called lifts, and in the United States—elevators. If any improvement has been discovered by some fortunate individual in the fare afforded in these gilded palaces, I am not the person. My experience—and it has not been small in Europe, and not insufficient in America to form a judgment—is that, whilst called upon to pay exorbitant prices for the show with which you are surrounded, the material comforts of life have been greatly diminished. The cooking generally is vile, and wines, except being profanely christened with the sacred titles of a former age, bear no relationship to their ancestors. Do not let the noble race of cooks imagine that I intend any slur upon their talent. All I venture to affirm is that we—the 'Oi Polloi'—are rarely given the benefit of it. The 'Menu,' into which the old 'Bill of Fare' has been transformed, is a wonderful piece of literature, but I venture to think that the numerous 'la's,' giving grace to every dish, have but few representatives which are permitted to appear before the vulgar. I was told only the other day by a great railway director and chairman, that he had recently a perfect dinner at Delmonico's, and I have no doubt that the guests at the Ministerial banquet at Greenwich would (conscience permitting) thoroughly enjoy the cooking. But I appeal to those who have experience either in Paris, New York, or London, to confirm my assertion, that a guest unknown to proprietor or waiters has small chance of an adequate dinner. The Delmonico is a splendid building, and was at one time, and may be now, one of the most celebrated taverns in the city, and famous for launching happy couples into the whirlpool of life.[1]

I am inclined to think that the Fifth Avenue Hotel (so called from a thoroughfare bearing that name) has been one of the most talked of in the city of New York, and I have heard it described

[1] Marriage breakfasts are frequently celebrated at this tavern.

as a 'wonder of the world.' No doubt, externally and internally it is very magnificent. The entrance hall is extensive, and a congregation of the male sex seems always present, although changing in its component parts; groups seem engrossed in discussing vital affairs—eagerly talking. Haste and energy are the ever-prevailing features of the scene, and the impression is created that life is too short for the work to be performed. A splendid saloon above affords, from the hours of five to eight o'clock, the opportunity for a *table d'hôte* dinner, served at different tables to both sexes, with astonishing rapidity, and at a reasonable price, and if the people really eat what is served to them they must possess wonderful organs of mastication, and ought to have unlimited digestion.

I only dined there upon one occasion, and have a very hazy recollection of the ceremony. I found myself in the presence of various dishes, and although I have no doubt that I was given sufficient time to master their contents, they seem to my memory to have disappeared as did the dishes at Sancho Panza's supper, recorded by Cervantes in that wonderful work of romance, philosophy, and truth, 'The History of Don Quixote.'

CHAPTER IV.

HOTELS AND COOKERY.

Sensational crimes—Stokes and Fisk—Their connection—Rivalry—Fisk's death—Public opinion—Trial—No verdict—Second trial—Verdict and sentence—Hoffman House Hotel—Works of art—A splendid painting—Statuary—The Honourable Judge Brady—Stokes landlord—Coffee-room—Impression of Stokes—Beef-steaks—Expense—The Hôtel de Paris—Celebrity of landlord—Racing successes—Generosity—Favourite dishes—Turtle—Tarrapin—Canvas-back duck—My opinion of them—Oysters—Tiernan' Eating-house—Meeting old friends—Middlesex magistracy—An apology.

CRIMES, sensational and romantic, are by no means of rare occurrence in the United States of America, and New York not many years ago was the scene of one that caused great excitement. E. S. Stokes and Jem Fisk were associated in financial matters, and there was a suggestion, generally believed, and certainly not improbable, that a rivalry existed in connection with a lady. Fisk was successful in the pounds, shillings, and pence part of the business, and was accused of having over-reached his associate, who also found, as might have been expected of a lady young, fair, and frail, that her affections followed the money. These combined causes seem to have had an unfortunate effect upon Stokes's mind, and as his old comrade and friend, Fisk, was walking up the stairs at the house of an acquaintance in front of him, that gentleman took the opportunity of drilling a hole through his body with the bullet of a revolver. There could be no doubt of the deliberation with which the act was committed, but popular feeling, influenced by what was generally believed to have been the transactions between the parties, pronounced an informal verdict of 'serve him right,' and the jury impannelled to try him would not come to any conclusion, and were discharged without giving a verdict. A second jury, however, found him guilty, under extenuating circumstances, and he was sentenced to a long term of imprisonment.

This, as related to me, is the outline of a story, which I do not present to my readers as anything wonderful, either in its facts or its surroundings. Verdicts in free countries will always be affected, more or less, by the outside opinion formed by the masses, and justice in the very teeth of law is not unfrequently thus attained; but it is the circumstance that I am about to mention that has induced me to relate this illustration of its having done so.

At a not very long distance from the Fifth Avenue Hotel stands another house of public entertainment, worthy of a place in the finest quarter of any city in the world. It is called the Hoffman House. A magnificent entrance hall contains many very exquisite works of art—amongst others, a large picture of modern date by a native artist, representing a mythological old gentleman, who has apparently given offence to a number of nymphs, who are about to execute 'Lynch Law' by consigning him to a pool of neighbouring water; really, as far as I am able to judge, it is a very fine work, and is an object of interest both to the citizens and to strangers. There are several statues, and also other paintings exciting admiration, and making the hall itself an object well worthy of interest. The coffee-room, which leads out of it, is richly ornamented, and nothing can be better than the attendance, and it is a *sine quâ non* for the waiters to be without beards.

I was indebted to a gentleman (whom I am not sorry thus early to mention) for being taken to this gorgeous hotel—the Honourable Judge Brady, one of the members of the Supreme Court. I presume him to be of Irish extraction, and he possesses all the genial humour justly attributable to the gentlemen of that country, with other qualities which have during the many years that he has been a judge obtained for him the character of being unsurpassed in that office by any of the members of a truly distinguished Bench.

It was upon an occasion when I was lunching with this gentleman in the coffee-room that I was introduced to the proprietor [1]—a middle-aged, gentlemanly man, giving somewhat the impression of the well-to-do vicar of an English village. Nothing could exceed the quiet, sedate manner in which he moved amongst his customers, by whom he was received as if he deserved respect and consideration, and it was some time afterwards, and after I had availed myself of his chaperonage through the artistic beauties of his establishment, that I learnt (I confess with astonishment) that he was the hero of a tragedy so serious in its details—E. S. Stokes.

The establishment of the Hoffman House, like that of the Fifth Avenue Hotel, consists also of sleeping accommodation, but has no *table d'hôte*, and is conducted purely upon the café principle, and is in very excellent style. Their preparations of 'beef-steaks' in different forms, and under different names, are really good, and partake of the character of old English cookery. Of course everything is expensive, and *l'addition* proclaims in no un-

---

[1] Since I wrote the above I have learnt, through the report of some legal proceedings in an American journal, that he had partners in the establishment.

mistakable language that its recipient has been dining in the midst of gilt and looking-glass.

Next to the Hoffman House is a comparatively small establishment—the Hôtel de Paris; if I remember rightly, it is less gorgeous, but certainly quite as elegant as any of the others, and indeed, I think, is ornamented in better taste. The landlord of it is a celebrity, having acquired fame in the English sporting world. He is credited with carrying off great prizes and much money in the equestrian contests of our shores. His generosity to our jockeys excited more attention than approval.

The dishes upon which an American citizen chiefly bases the culinary honour of his country are turtle, tarrapin, and canvas-back duck. Now, with regard to the first of these, I have had several opportunities of trying it, and the only time upon which I was on the verge of a quarrel whilst in the States was with a fellow-passenger in a railway car, when I ventured to assert that his countrymen did not know how to cook it—and they do not.

With regard to tarrapin, I should not have attempted to express upon the other side of the Atlantic any doubt of its perfection, but upon the occasions when I enjoyed it, I recognised the cook, and not the reptile.

The canvas-back duck has a world-wide celebrity, but it was usually served in such a state of rawness that to me it was repulsive.

Oysters can contest the palm with our natives, and are much cheaper; and in the interest of that large portion of my friends to whom economy is an object, I will give them an address where oysters, good and cheap, chops and steaks, fresh off the gridiron, and excellent bitter ale may be had at a moderate price.

It is a very unpretentious-looking house, situated next to the Bijou Theatre, and the name of the proprietor is Tiernan. Do not let my readers be horrified at hearing that there are neither table-cloths nor napkins for the male guests, unless accompanied by one of the opposite sex, when there is admission to an inner room, containing tables with their usual accompaniments, denied to those without such insignia of respectability.

Both rooms were crowded after the theatre, and many an old acquaintance with whom, in the mother country, I have shared my Welsh rare-bit and tankard of stout, did I meet during my nightly visits, flourishing under the liberal encouragement given in New York, and elsewhere throughout America, to the British actor, and, thank Heaven! there did not exist the nuisance of a Middlesex magistracy to interfere with our natural wants, and curtail the time necessary to digest our food.

There are some strong-minded people, especially of the fair sex, who do not sacrifice to creature comforts, after the selfish manner of man, and who may object to the foregoing pages upon the ground of their triviality; but I trust they will recognise the fact that hotels and their appurtenances form a very important element in the life of the traveller. 'What sort of hotel?' is not unfrequently asked, even before any question is put about the churches of the locality, and it might sometimes be thought that its cookery is of more importance than its creed. Thus, being obliged to admit that bodily comforts do take up an important portion of public thought, I must throw myself upon the merciful consideration of those who prefer and practise lives of self-denial.

CHAPTER V.

STREETS OF NEW YORK.

Dickens's foreigner—My intentions—Scheme of streets—System of traffic—Overhead railway—Tramcars—Omnibuses—Quantity of passengers—Civility of conductors—Universal use of cars—Civility of population—The Stock Exchange—Visit to it—Kind reception—Compliment to Her Majesty—'God Save the Queen'—Bankers—Caution—Lodgings—Situation of house—Streets of New York—Activity—Advertisements—Theatres—Mrs. Langtry—Her interviewers—A military gentleman—His description of his own proceedings—Mrs. Langtry's companion—My interviewer—Description of myself—Wallack—His father—Early remembrances—Adelina Patti—Mr. Mapleson—Soothing an angry artist—The 'Traviata'—Signor Arditi—Snowy condition of streets—Danger to pedestrians—Expenses of private vehicles.

As my experiences of New York are confined to a period of two months, I shall not follow the example of the foreigner, so graphically described by Dickens in one of his novels, who, note-book in hand and spectacles on nose, has, during a visit extending to about that time, prepared a full account of the laws, habits, institutions, and probable future destiny of our country, but shall confine myself to describing a few features, the knowledge of which may be useful, and certainly are reliable. In the first place, let me advise the visitor to render himself a master (if he can) of the scheme of the streets, and to learn the system of traffic by which they are worked.

The entire length of one of the main arteries of the city is traversed by a railway which passes over the passengers' heads, upon a level with the first floor of its houses. Other of the great thoroughfares are traversed upon the level roadways by tramcars passing in quick succession. Omnibuses of an ordinary kind convey the traffic through the less important localities. All classes use them, and both sexes. A remarkable phenomenon pervades them all—they always appear full, and yet never refuse a fare, and somehow or another the passenger becomes amalgamated with a mass of humanity, the car continues its journey, and the conductor his invitations in the most emphatic manner. The civility and attention of all the servants, and the good taste prevailing amongst the miscellaneous mass who mingle in the vehicles, renders the absence of all restriction as to numbers compatible with comfort. Ladies habitually use them; indeed, as far as my observation went, the fair sex require no protection, either in the public conveyances or the public streets, beyond what is afforded by the good taste of the population.

Whilst I am upon the subject of the streets of New York and their occupants, I cannot forbear recording with gratitude a trait which I most peculiarly appreciated in the obliging civility and good nature shown invariably to myself and, I assume, generally to the puzzled strangers in the city, by affording them information and the necessary directions as to the localities they are in search of. The following incident will, I am sure, be read with pleasure by the English public.

A visit to the Stock Exchange under very favourable auspices was secured to me by a gentleman holding the position of president of that institution. He occupied a sort of rostrum, upon which I was seated beside him. There seemed an awful noise, analogous to what distinguishes the similar establishment in our capital. It soon became known that an Englishman was present, the crowd, a very large one, gathered round us, and a section of them sung very admirably ' God Save the Queen,' accompanied with vehement cheering from the entire throng. I felt personally much gratified, but it was impossible, if I had desired to do so, to disguise the fact that the enthusiasm was attributable to the respect and admiration entertained through the length and breadth of America, by its real natives, for the character and virtues of our Queen.

As I am wishing in the observations I offer (although many of them may be of a trifling character) to be of some service to visitors to this great city, there will be no harm in mentioning a circumstance, my ignorance of which very nearly lost me an important engagement. None of the banks will cash a cheque unless the bearer of it is known, and upon the occasion I allude to, although I trust I presented a tolerably decent appearance, I was looked over and over by one clerk and another, until I really began to doubt whether I was myself, or some one else not favourably regarded in the city. Just at this moment a member of the American Bar addressed me by name, and all civility and every attention was then afforded me. I found afterwards that caution so exhibited was universal throughout the banking establishments.

I have anticipated the experiences which exhausted several days' wandering, but must now return to the time of my arrival in New York.

Hotel life is both expensive and uncomfortable, and I sought and obtained most agreeable apartments in the house of Madame Galliard, the widow of a gentleman, once a wealthy planter, but who, like many other citizens of the Southern States, was a victim to their collapse. This lady was thoroughly a gentlewoman, and my relations with her were entirely friendly, and in many respects serviceable to myself. Her house was situated in a locality described as Twenty-seventh Street, a situation bearing in relation to New York a similar

position as the streets bordering upon Hanover and
Cavendish Squares do to London. A thorough
rest had enabled me to recognise my legs as
belonging to myself, and I then began to take in
the features presented by New York city.

Movement unceasing, faces with a stamp of
thought upon them, fill the thoroughfare, and yet
the notices upon the walls tell the searcher after
amusement that there is no dearth of it, and
theatres (which I generally found full) offered
abundant scenes wherein to pass the evening hours.
During my sojourn in the city the beautiful Mrs.
Langtry was the rage. In the profession she so
gallantly adopted, she has obtained a distinguished
success, and it must be admitted that she has not
contented herself with saying, 'My face is my
fortune,' but has applied herself diligently to the
study of the art in which she has sought the favour
of the public. My friends the interviewers ought
to erect a monument to her memory. From the
time that she landed in America she afforded
scope for their industry, and proved their devotion
to their calling. One of these (a military gentleman of distinguished ancestry, he styled himself)
considered that he was called upon to serve his
country by overcoming the outworks, and entering,
against every opposition, the apartment at an hotel
where Mrs. Langtry vainly imagined she would

D

be able to lunch in privacy. According to this gallant officer, he had a perfect right to ascertain the minutest particulars of her habits, and he was very indignant that this intrusion, which he considered complimentary, should have been resented, 'and wondered greatly at the want of taste that prevented the favourable appreciation of his good taste and gentlemanly feeling.'

I quote from his own description, appearing in a St. Louis journal, at which town the lady was at that time staying; and, whatever may be thought of the affair by others, the major appeared to be fully satisfied that he had done his duty.

Mrs. Langtry was accompanied to America by a lady, a very old acquaintance of mine, who had obtained much fame in England as an actress, but having formed a matrimonial connection which rendered following her profession unnecessary, she had quitted the stage. She also was an object of most excited inquiries, and it being known that I had the pleasure of her acquaintance, I was saluted in the streets of Philadelphia upon one occasion by a very gentlemanly-looking personage, whom to my knowledge had never seen before, and was asked some question relating to this lady's movements.

By this time, however, I had learnt wisdom, and all that resulted from this interview was a description of myself in a morning journal, in which the principal feature was that I wore my hat on one side. But I have wandered away from New York and its streets—to them I must now return.

Upon the walls a familiar name greeted my eyes—that of Wallack.[1] His father was an idol of my childhood; his personation of Alessandro Masaroni, the brigand-chief, equalled (in my youthful judgment) the grandest efforts of histrionic art. Of his son I had still a vivid recollection. When first I knew him he was a curly-haired boy, living with his family, as I was with mine, at Hampstead. He has pitched his tent in the United States, where he is deservedly popular. He has done good service to the histrionic art in America, and, as far as I know, cultivated the legitimate drama; he has also built a theatre, but I fear that this has somewhat overweighted him. I had met him once or

[1] Mr. Wallack, the father of this gentleman, and I believe also of a brother who appeared upon the stage, was one of the handsomest men I ever saw, and his wife also, whom I well recollect, was a beautiful woman. She was the daughter of a gentleman extremely popular in a foregone generation. The name he was known by was 'Irish Johnstone,' and I have frequently heard him spoken of in the circle which in my *Experiences* I have described, consisting of Mr. Const, Billy Dunn, and others more or less connected with theatrical pursuits. He was an exquisite singer. I cannot recall whether he was the composer or only the singer of the charming drinking-song ending with the refrain:—

And that I say is a reason fair
To fill the glass again!

twice since the days of our childhood, and was delighted to see him again, and to find that he was thoroughly appreciated in the United States.

The name of 'Patti' induced me to seek the den of Mr. Mapleson. I found that well-known *impresario* soothing in his blandest tones an angry lady whom, whilst he admitted her appreciation of herself to be correct, he had named for a part much lower in the operatic scale than her own estimate. Her voice, if I could judge by its compass in the room, would certainly have filled the theatre, but as he explained to herself and a husband of most brigand-like appearance, who was silently scowling by her side, he could not give good taste to the public, who preferred Patti. In the evening I listened to a performance of the 'Traviata,' which I thought surpassed everything that I had ever heard, even from this wonderful artist, and it gave me great pleasure to meet upon a subsequent occasion the charming *prima donna*, and also my old friend Signor Arditi, who was conducting the orchestra, under Mapleson's management, at New York. It is very pleasant to meet old friends in a strange country, and many were the happy recollections, though not unmingled with sad thoughts, brought back to my mind by this meeting.

In describing my first impressions of the streets

of New York, I must not forget that there was
thick snow upon the ground, and it behoved the
foot passenger to keep his mind upon the pavement, and enclose his feet in clogs ; and even then
he might not escape an ignominious exhibition of
himself at full length ; and, as I have already hinted,
unless his finances are very flourishing, do not let
him venture upon the close boxes that hold the
place of cabs, as the smallest charge known to the
autocrats who own them is a dollar, representing
four shillings of English money.

CHAPTER VI.

JOURNALISM AND FASHION.

Geography of streets — Clubs — Apartments — Daily papers — Everyday habits — New York journals — Their great ability — Extensive news — Trials — Lynch law — Desperate encounters — Outrages by negroes — Shipping intelligence — News from home — Accidents of voyage — Wonderful enterprise exhibited — Avidity for news — Mr. Hulbert — The Honourable Mr. Benjamin Wood — Mr. Lawson — New New York — Splendid suburb — New York season — Equipages — Mansions — Parks — A century's work.

December 10.—I have now passed several days in New York, and have made some progress in the geography of the streets, and the habits of the people. I have been most generously received in several of the clubs, which, although most comfortable, do not present such gorgeous exteriors as our own. I have become associated with my apartments, and feel myself at home. A blazing fire in my grate contrasts agreeably with the thick persistent snow presenting itself outside, and a stalwart, good-humoured Irish 'help' has just brought me in an excellent cup of tea, and a collection of newspapers fresh from the press.

Amongst our habits there is none more fixed than that which an English gentleman contracts from the daily perusal of his favourite newspaper. He knows exactly the spot to look for each piece of desired information, and until he has grasped the topics of interest to himself, and learnt perchance some of the business of his neighbours, figuratively speaking he is not dressed for the day. Each topic has its own place, and he knows where to find a birth, marriage, or death —a trial, an inquest, or the utterances of the editorial sages. He knows also where to discover the locality of a convenient house, and learns where a horse is to be picked up, a great bargain, and without a blemish.

It was only by close application that I was able to wend my way through the mazes of the American press, and become capable of appreciating the wonderful ability which distinguishes its principal journals, certainly not surpassed by that of any country in the world. One impression took hold of my mind when reading the contents of the 'Herald,' 'New York World,' 'New York Daily News,' the 'Tribune,' and other of the chief papers —that they could not be recording the events of a single country, or even those of one generation.

There is an infinity of space included in their columns positively bewildering, and so astounding a difference of habits and incidents that it might be supposed that a century of years instead of the time occupied by the diurnal revolution of the earth had been ransacked for their production. In one column will be met the account of a trial conducted with all the decorum of Westminster Hall, and in the next, in a tone expressive of no surprise, one learns that half-a-dozen costermongers have constituted themselves into a jury, and settled the fate of a fellow-creature, who is exhibited some few minutes after this informal meeting dangling from the nearest tree. This is called 'Lynch Law,' and scarcely a day passes without either an instance of it being related, or a desperate encounter between the sheriff of a district and a mob for the possession of an individual, who probably would not find any improvement in his condition whichever party got possession of him, unless a more formal hangman and experienced performer could be so considered.

Such events as these would, if indeed they could occur in our country, occupy days of discussion and elaborate reports in the daily papers, but they are only used to fill up some little corner in an American journal. Outrages by negroes appear very frequent, and, as described, are of a very atrocious character; but although, from what I saw of the administration of the criminal law in New York, I am sure that justice was administered impartially, I cannot help thinking that in some of the far-away localities the 'nigger' met with a somewhat short 'shrift.'

Amongst the objects of interest that were the first to command my attention in the morning papers was the shipping intelligence. This is natural for a stranger, as upon the arrival of the different packets depends his news from home, and the incidents of the voyage, accurately described, including only too frequently the picture of machinery injured, and the very unpleasant struggles, in consequence, with the winds and waves. Friends may have been on board, and reflections are forced upon him about his own chances during the voyage back. The possibility that instead of eight days he may be tossing about the Atlantic for sixteen is no joke, and during my stay in America there were many catastrophes related involving delay, great inconvenience, and necessarily some danger. An instance of such an occurrence it was my fate to experience, but of this I shall hereafter give an account.

I soon acquired sufficient knowledge of the arrangement of the papers to find easily the topics interesting to myself, and somewhat, if not adequately, to appreciate the wonderful enterprise that has encompassed, and occupied by its energy, the immense space extending between the two oceans; and I think I ought to add that the avidity for news fully equals the power of supply. I had the pleasure of being acquainted with the editors of two of the influential papers in New York—Mr. Hulbert, the editor of the 'World,' and the Honourable Mr. Benjamin Wood, the editor of the 'New York Daily News.' To the former I was introduced by my friend Mr. Lawson, the proprietor of our 'Daily Telegraph.' Mr. Hulbert was a gentleman who had mixed much in English society, and the rooms he occupied in New York were adorned with works of art of great value. From him I received many acts of attention and kindness.

I enjoyed and thoroughly appreciated much hospitality from the Honourable Mr. Benjamin Wood, and it was his cook who so transformed tarrapin that I found it really most enjoyable.

I need hardly mention that in the same imperfect way in which I have endeavoured to give a sketch of certain features of New York city, so in what I have said about the journalism — do not affect to exhaust a subject upon which a volume might be written by abler pens than mine; and up to the present, in recording my impressions of New York, I have dealt only with the busy streets, thronged with people, intent upon the labours of life.

I have not invited my reader's company to what will ere long justify the name of 'New New York.' With almost incredible rapidity a suburb has sprung up, and is daily enlarging. Mansions, well worthy of a place in Belgravia or the Champs-Elysées, are, as speedily as erected, occupied by citizens possessing, according to reputation, enormous wealth.

Well-appointed equipages are to be seen in all the fashionable quarters, the occupants of which, clad in Parisian costumes, challenge comparison with their fair cousins who are seen in Hyde Park or Bond Street,[1] and although no amount of ingenuity can furnish the appearance of antiquity which gives grandeur to many of the private mansions of our gentry, and to places of public resort, parks have been laid out that exhibit in their construction the most perfect taste and elegance.

In fact, in whatever aspect New York is viewed, the mind is bewildered by the evidence of what has been done during the space of a single century by the indomitable energy of man.

[1] The period of my visit to New York has obliged me to accept the account of a friend respecting the appearance presented in the fashionable quarters of the city during the season.

CHAPTER VII.

A MODERN DRAMA.

The tastes of people — Exhibited by drama—' Iolanthe ' at the Standard Theatre, New York—Savoy Theatre, London—W. S. Gilbert—Sir Arthur Sullivan— Sketch of plot—Mr. Riley—Humorous performance—His account of himself—Conclusion of sketch—Popularity of this drama—Growing contempt for show—Amusing incident—Management of theatres in America—Illness of Sir Arthur Sullivan—Curious trait of Mr. Gilbert.

OF the tastes of the inhabitants of any great city, a judgment can be formed with tolerable accuracy by their patronage of the drama, and I think it will not be uninteresting to refer to a performance that seems to have been equally appreciated by the audiences of England and America, not only by those of London and New York, but in the provinces of both countries.

This, to which I can give no classification, as it is unlike anything I ever saw before, is called 'Iolanthe.' Whilst I was in New York it was running at the Standard Theatre, under the able management of Miss Lenoir, and at the same time in London at the Savoy, under Mr. D'Oyly Carte, and with various companies throughout both England and the United States. The words of

the drama, which are the composition of W. S.
Gilbert, are very smart and epigrammatic, and the
music, full of life and brilliancy, is the production
of Sir Arthur Sullivan.

I will endeavour to give a sketch of the plot.
A lovely fairy, bearing the name of Iolanthe,
yielding to the fascinations of an earth-born
mortal—not possessing the romantic charms
usually assigned to the heroes of romance, but
the more substantial one of a flourishing business
as a special pleader and equity draughtsman—
becomes his wife, and thus loses her position in
fairy-land, but still remains as young and as beautiful as she was before she linked her fate with the
successful lawyer. No account is given of the
married life of the parties, and no cause assigned
for their separation, which has occurred before
the drama commences. In the meanwhile, notwithstanding a *mésalliance* which might have injured his prospects, the lady's husband mounts to
the highest step in his professional career, and becomes Lord High Chancellor of England. A period
of some years is supposed to elapse. Iolanthe is
restored to the society of her fairy-sisters, and
finds it somewhat inconvenient when she meets a
young gentleman entitled to call her mama.

And now occurs an incident that must be
recognised as strange amongst all the vagaries

attributed to the British House of Lords. The peers, headed by their Chancellor, start upon a picnic tour, and find themselves amongst the fairies; they excite not unnaturally the admiration of these slightly clad personages, being themselves arrayed in the full robes, including coronets, of their respective orders. They on their part profess, with great *empressement*, exhibited in excellent choruses, honourable intentions toward their entertainers.

At the New York Theatre a gentleman named Riley performed the character of Chancellor with admirable humour. He had evidently studied some original whose appearance he had closely copied, and when, in robes exactly similar to those worn by that dignitary, he first made his appearance, his solemn gravity, exhibiting a mixture of pride and humility, was simply perfection.

He gives an account of himself to his brother peers in the following lines, which add to the truthfulness of his appearance:—

> 'The Law is the true embodiment
> Of everything that's excellent;
> It has no kind of fault or flaw—
> And I, my Lords, embody the Law.'

The effect of a can-can (into which with the accompaniment of singing he suddenly burst) was exceedingly funny, and was repeatedly encored by the audience. He is represented as having been somewhat gay in his younger days, and is by no means sorry to find that his fairy-wife still retains her youth and beauty.

The young gentleman who can boast a descent from such a combination of prose and poetry as a lawyer and a fairy forms a respectable alliance, and the noble aristocrats, after much singing and dancing, avail themselves of the chance that has so opportunely presented itself of following his example—upon which the curtain drops.

As I have already intimated, this piece of somewhat strong buffoonery was in New York, as I hear it was also in London, most admirably put upon the stage, and held a place in the lengthened patronage of two of the most prosaic people in the world. England joined with America in enjoying the ridicule cast upon the House of Peers, and the outward show and parade of the woolsack is in our country rapidly taking place with the Lord Mayor's coach; and there can be no doubt that the sterling merit, moral and intellectual, usually possessed by the holders of the Seals, would be far better appreciated if their possessors were not disfigured by these baubles.

There was a very amusing incident connected with the production of this piece, in a gallant battle fought by Miss Lenoir with the Customs authorities, as to whether ballet dresses could be brought into New York duty free. She contended that they were articles of trade, and ultimately, after much learned argument, succeeded in her contention.

The theatre under the management of the above lady was admirably conducted, but, as I believe such is the case with all of these establishments in New York, I do not mention it as any exception.

Sir Arthur Sullivan and Mr. Gilbert were gentlemen well known to me in England. The former is an example of conscientious hard work, which gave a shock to his constitution, from which I fear he is still suffering.

Mr. Gilbert told me a very curious trait in connection with himself, which he was quite unable to struggle against — he was incapable of being present before the curtain at any of his own pieces, and once, when the Prince of Wales, who occupied a box in a theatre during the performance of one of them, desired his presence, he was obliged, after remaining a short time, to beg the permission of His Royal Highness to retire.

CHAPTER VIII.

PLAYS AND PLAYERS.

Changes in the Drama—Opinions of society—Absence of veneration—A Chief Justice—Dramatic festival—Lord Coleridge—Histrionic talent—Compliment to Mr. Irving—Irving as a manager—Stage decorations—Anecdote—Performances at New York—Miss Ellen Terry—Miss Kate Terry—Charles Kean—Anecdote—Welcome to British actors—American actors—Mr. Booth—Performance of Richelieu—Washington Irving—Rip Van Winkle—Jefferson—Admirable performance—Ben. Webster's opinion—Miss Mary Anderson at Philadelphia—Her reception in London.

THE little sketch with which I concluded my last chapter suggests reflections upon the Drama, and the many happy days it has afforded me make it a pleasant subject to dwell upon.

Many and prominent are the changes in the feelings of the public, of which it is the exponent. It must be felt that the organ of veneration is fast disappearing from society when the sacred precincts of the Court of Chancery are invaded, and a Lord Chancellor, of an apparently solemn type, is introduced in company with the young ladies of the ballet, himself dancing a *can-can*. And how the old ladies (of both sexes) belonging to a former generation would shake their solemn heads if they could hear (as happened recently) that a real Lord Chief Justice had presided over what *they* would have termed the orgies of a dramatic festival!

Times are indeed changed, and I do not despair of living to see an Archbishop sending over to the American shores a popular actor, laden with his benediction. I never heard that the noble president of Mr. Irving's entertainment had been much given to theatrical society, although doubtless in his wild youth he may have been a welcome guest in many a green-room, and there can be no doubt that Lord Coleridge, having undertaken the task, possessed all the knowledge necessary to perform it with success.

Society of the present day is only too glad to discard the prejudices of a former age, and to enrol amongst their number a class that, in addition to their estimable qualities (and in the works of humanity and charity none exceed it), supplies so much amusement and information.

Although the presence of the Lord Chief Justice was no doubt a compliment to Mr. Irving, it was not required to secure him a hearty welcome in the United States, where, independent of his professional powers, the estimation in which his character is held, and the generous qualities which he is known to possess, would of themselves have made him a highly appreciated visitor.

This gentleman has been so indefatigable a

worker in his profession, that he is necessarily associated with the changes in the decoration of the stage and the costumes of the performers; and I believe that the British Museum has been ransacked for illustrations to assist in the correct delineation of the scenes and dresses of the period intended to be portrayed in the different old dramas. There is a story extant, that the *artiste* who composed and executed the dress of a beautiful and favourite actress of our day, and achieved a wonderful success, was obliged to take a month's repose to recruit herself after the thought and labour she had expended upon it.

The performances now going on under the management of Mr. Irving, and which I presume to be similar to those exhibited by him at the Lyceum Theatre in London, exhaust every means known to modern taste and research in a correct representation of the scenes; and the costumes of the different characters are in perfect keeping. He has had also the good fortune to secure, as representative of his heroines, a lady who belongs to a race of actresses, and whose impersonations seem scarcely attributable to art. Miss Ellen Terry will always be associated with the splendid success that has so deservedly followed the undertakings of Henry Irving, both in this country and the United States.

I have frequently witnessed the performances of

the eldest sister of this young lady when she was playing at the Princess's Theatre, under the management of Charles Kean—Miss Kate Terry. She is now married to a wealthy gentleman, and many years have passed since I saw her. I think that the last time was when she performed with great success the part of Marguerite, in an extravaganza founded upon the legend of 'Faust,' and upon which occasion that most correct of managers—Charles Kean—playing the character of 'Mephistopheles,' is said to have shocked Her Majesty (who was present) by offering to bet—' Two to one in Bishops.'

Another of the Misses Terry is playing successfully in London.

The well-assorted company, in which no trace is discoverable of the jealousy which has sometimes been too justly attributed to managers in making a selection of brother-performers, will be regarded as having materially assisted in the great success of this undertaking.

The hearty welcome, however, given by the American public to all those English actors who possess merit is by no means through any dearth of its own native talent, and I cannot forbear recording the pleasure that I have derived from the performances of some of them—one of the most prominent being Mr. Booth.

This gentleman appeared to me not only to possess many natural qualities for the stage, but also to have given most careful study to the parts he undertook. He played the same class of characters as those selected by Mr. Irving, who gave him the opportunity of exhibiting them at his theatre in London, where they appeared together in a friendly and generous rivalry. I leave more learned and experienced critics than myself to deal with their comparative merits, but I cannot help expressing the delight I derived from the performance by Mr. Booth of Richelieu in Lord Lytton's drama of that name.

I had seen Macready, Phelps, and others who had played successfully in the same rôle, but certainly none ever surpassed Booth. I will not recapitulate many other performances of like excellence.

In the whole range of English fiction there are probably no two works that take such permanent possession of the youthful mind as 'Robinson Crusoe' and the 'Travels of Gulliver.' These two wonderful creations of Defoe and Jonathan Swift find rivals in the charming tales of Washington Irving. Few there are who have not acknowledged the realism of the idle, good-natured, hen-pecked Dutchman, Rip Van Winkle, only too glad to exchange the company of a scolding wife for a carouse with the apparently hospitable inhabitants of the mountain. With such a temptation, he was very little likely to investigate the character of his hosts.

Was there ever a piece of dramatic art that surpassed the impersonation by Jefferson, the great American actor, of the deluded victim? If possible, he gave even more life to the legend than the author himself had done. It is many years since I saw him play this part at the Adelphi Theatre to an enthusiastic audience, and I remember Ben. Webster, then amongst the best of living actors, expressing the opinion that I now repeat—that he had never seen a finer performance.

Whilst in the States, I endeavoured to see the young actress who has since created a great sensation in London. She was then playing at Philadelphia, but, unfortunately for me, the theatre was very large, and so crowded that I could only get a glimpse of the figure, and obtain a very imperfect hearing of the words. She struck me as being singularly graceful in her movements, and statuesque in repose. But the British public has shown, in its reception of Miss Mary Anderson, that it is as ready to recognise and appreciate merit as the Americans have so constantly done in their reception of those from our shores, and signally of Henry Irving.

CHAPTER IX.

TWO BANQUETS.

Lord Lytton—Charles Dickens—Natural actors—Lord Lytton's public speeches—Preparation and care- Acting of Dickens--His readings —Approaching visit to America—Banquet given to him—Distinguished guests—Lord Lytton—Chairman—Appearance of Lord Lytton and Charles Dickens—My 'Experiences'—Traits of Lord Lytton—Dickens's success in America—Generosity of Americans —Banquet to Irving—Lord Coleridge—Irving's great success.

IN the 'Experiences,' which have been so kindly received by the public in my own country, and likewise met with an extensive circulation in the United States, I have dwelt with much pleasure upon my acquaintanceship with two gentlemen, whom the topics I have been discussing bring back forcibly to my memory—Lord Lytton and Charles Dickens. They are each an example of an actor born; they both took an intense interest in the profession, and the skilfully constructed plays of the former could never have been written unless his mind had been very appreciative of dramatic effect.

I am not aware that Lord Lytton ever essayed his powers in amateur representation, but in private life, although most agreeable, he never entirely threw aside a certain study for effect. He was never caught out in a jagged or disjointed sentence. His public speeches were evidently the result of great preparation, and were delivered with consummate care, and if fate, instead of having made him a distinguished member of the Legislature, had forced him upon his own natural tastes and resources, I can imagine him pronouncing before an admiring audience the monologue out of some Shakespearian drama.

Charles Dickens was an actor, not only by nature but in practice. His performance in private theatricals rivalled that of many a professional actor. His mobile features and sympathetic voice charmed and entranced the hearer, and his 'Readings' (as he modestly called them) were the works of his own mind expanded into life.

The incident which I am about to mention will, I trust, excuse my recurrence to these two distinguished men. Charles Dickens, many years ago, like Mr. Irving recently, having revelled in the fame that attended him in this country, announced his intention of submitting himself to an American audience, and his friends and admirers, which constituted the entire British public, felt a common desire to wish him 'God speed.' And thus it came to pass that Lord Lytton was selected as the exponent of public opinion towards the man it wished to honour, and who seemed to be in the nature of things the very individual for that office. The banquet given upon this occasion was distinguished by the presence of all who were at that time celebrated in literature, art, and the professions.

How sad it is to think of the gaps that have been made in this gathering! My memory recalls only too many personal friends, and our country has to regret the death of both those who were the principal objects of attraction upon this occasion. Charles Dickens must have felt the compliment, not as coming from the statesman, nobleman, and man of fashion, but from his illustrious brother-author.

The banquet is one not to be forgotten, and I remember distinctly these two men of the age seated next each other, and it appeared to me that there was a similarity of feature, but a difference in the expression of face and character of dress.

Both would, even when unknown, have commanded attention; the elder, elaborately dressed, somewhat after the style in which he was wont to figure when Count D'Orsay led the fashion, and in whose company he was often to be seen. At the period I am speaking of, the deafness with which he suffered in the latter days of his life had commenced, and probably occasioned a gravity of countenance scarcely natural. He possessed a very fine head, exhibiting power and kindness. The author of 'Boz,' still handsome, seemed as full of animation and brightness as a boy home for his holidays; and, as to dress, I do not suppose he ever studied any fashion but his own liking.

I have ventured upon a former occasion to describe what I knew of Lord Lytton and some of the traits which had come under my observation, and it has been with satisfaction that I find from the elaborate and interesting biography lately published by his son that, upon the very few matters I ventured to refer to, I have not fallen into any error.

I parted with Dickens after the dinner with sincere affection, and was pleased, though not surprised, to find that he passed through a series of triumphs in the States never before equalled, and which not only added to the proofs of his genius, but also exhibited the generosity of a people about whom, some years before, he had written an ill-considered opinion. I happen to know that he greatly regretted having done so, but in truth the Americans are by no means so sensitive as they are given credit for, and are certainly very forgiving.

I very much regret that illness prevented me from joining in the entertainment given to Irving upon similar grounds to the one which was given to Dickens, at which I shared. Social popularity, joined to his singular and well-deserved professional success, not unnaturally suggested that his visit to America should be preceded, as was that of the great novelist, by a cordial and hearty farewell, and he was entertained at a dinner in which the representatives of every class took their part. A very distinguished nobleman presided. I read with interest the speech he made upon this occasion, and doubtless his own subsequent appearance in America was calculated to add to the value of his warm panegyrics upon the popular actor who was the guest of the evening.

CHAPTER X.

GENERAL GRANT.

Insurrection of the Southern States—England and America—Change of feeling—Ignorance of each other—Exaggerated views—Running the blockade—Love of adventure—Piracy—The 'Alabama'—Its escape—Termination of the war—Increased cordiality of England and America—Deeds of heroism—General Grant—Visit to his house—Appearance of the General—His conversation—Simplicity—Orders and insignia—Mrs. Grant—Jefferson Davis—Mr. Benjamin—His escape—Called to the English Bar—Its liberal conduct—His great success—His retirement—Entertainment given—His advocacy—Meetings in Paris—Galignani—Mr. Evarts—Introduction to him—A firm of lawyers.

YEARS have elapsed, how many I do not remember, since the period of what must now be called the 'Insurrection of the Southern States of America,' and the disastrous result to the Southerners is still felt, and a natural soreness exists in the minds of the sufferers themselves, and their descendants. It is admitted on all hands that the decree is irrevocable; and it is also well worthy of observation how great a change of feeling has sprung up between our country and the United States since the termination of the war.

The truth is that the people of the two countries were comparatively unknown to each other, and

English travellers in America had seized upon superficial features, exaggerated, and turned them into ridicule; whilst the Americans, not indulging largely in foreign travel, entertained very narrow views of the people who inhabited other countries.

On our side of the Atlantic nothing certainly was known of the real merits of the dispute between the North and South; but unreasoning sympathy followed what was believed to be a struggle against oppression and tyranny, and the feeling was by no means confined to the unreasoning masses. The combined influences of avarice and love of adventure seized upon the blockade of the Southern coast to gratify both passions, and running the blockade was eagerly engaged in by many for the mere love of adventure. Sympathy also, for which our country has been obliged to pay pretty dearly, was largely given to the piratical adventurers who scoured the seas, plundering the vessels of the North.

It is admitted by all constitutional lawyers that affording assistance to the enemies of a friendly country is a breach of the law of nations, and this question had to be considered at the time the well-remembered 'Alabama' was lying in the Liverpool Dock. The American Government had furnished ours with due notice, and upon this, it is now conceded, we were bound to have prevented its exit. The legal question had been submitted to the law officers of the Crown, and it was the duty of one of them to furnish an opinion.

I happen to know that this gentleman broke down under the great pressure his mind was subjected to at this period, that a delay in consequence took place in the opinion reaching the proper quarter, and that before it arrived the vessel had succeeded in escaping.[1] Whether this was so or not I am unable to say, and I fear that the general satisfaction exhibited at this result gives some cause for thinking that there was scarcely sufficient care taken to prevent it.

After the repression of the rebellion our two countries became more cordial; the deeds of heroism recorded upon each side had created an admiration that extended to both equally. Now even the Northerners feel pride in the deeds of their fellow-countrymen—rebels as they esteemed them to have been. From this time the traffic and intercourse between America and England has largely increased, and their social relations cemented. Our cousins compete with ourselves in their wanderings, and, as I discovered in every

---

[1] I avoid giving the name of this gentleman, but I know the fact of his illness, and also know that to this cause was attributed the inaction of the Government. Those interested in the matter may consult Captain Bullock's *Secret Service of the Confederate States in Europe*, which has been recently published.

quarter in which I moved, the most kindly and hospitable feeling is exhibited to English people travelling in the States.

Prominent amongst the heroes of this war, and one who in England was credited in no small degree with its successful termination, was General Grant, and I presume that to his conduct is attributable his double election to the Presidentship of the States. To him I had received introductions of which I very gladly availed myself, and it was with much pleasure I received an invitation to his house. I felt great curiosity to see the man whose career had filled so large a space in the world's history.

I accompanied some ladies, to whom I was much indebted for many acts of courtesy during the time I was in New York—Mrs. and the Misses Mack. There was a large party—I suppose the proper name for it was 'a conversazione.' Handsome rooms were filled with a distinguished company—the gentlemen doubtless deserving attention, the ladies commanding it—and it is no compliment to say that no assembly could have exhibited more beauty or better taste. A young lady, a niece, as I understood, of the General's, who presided with much grace at a tea-table, rendered this homely occupation the centre of much attraction.

If I enlarge upon this agreeable topic I shall

be accused of my natural predilections carrying away my thoughts from the 'man of many fields.' I was duly introduced to him. There was nothing in demeanour that pointed him out—his appearance and manners were simple and unpretending. In an English party I should have set him down as a County Member, and for a time it was difficult to imagine that he could be the real General Grant. His conversation was on ordinary topics, and not a word escaped his lips that could lead the listener to imagine the exploits he had performed, and the varied and interesting scenes through which he had passed. The only proof that he valued the honours that had been heaped upon him was to be found in cabinets filled with the orders and insignia that had been conferred upon him from various sources.

I met him upon one ether occasion at Mrs. Mack's, where he exhibited the same simplicity. I had also the pleasure of an introduction to Mrs. Grant, and she seemed as little spoilt as I judged her husband to be from the amount of attention and consideration that must have been her lot during the many years she held the distinguished position of wife to the President of one of the greatest countries in the world.

It seems strange that the exploits of the Northern generals, and their success in crushing out the resistance of the Southern States, should have created an incident having any bearing upon the English legal profession, and that a Confederate statesman should have found a haven, and obtained distinguished success as a lawyer and advocate, before the highest tribunals in Great Britain—and yet such was the case.

Amongst the most trusted Ministers of Mr. Jefferson Davis—the short-lived President of the Confederate States—was a gentleman named Benjamin, and no doubt he was in that position credited with possessing considerable influence in the insurrectionary movement. When it collapsed his situation was by no means a pleasant one, for although nothing could be less bloodthirsty than the conquerors, he would if caught have had no small chance of being exalted in a fashion very different from that which has ultimately become his fate.

He contrived to escape, and after many adventures, which would make an amusing story, succeeded in reaching the shores of one of our colonies, thence found his way to England, and began life again as a law-student. He received from the hands of the English profession, most creditably to itself, not only a cordial welcome, but unusual facilities for pursuing his career. He very early obtained a patent of precedence, and

F

conducted with distinguished ability causes against the most eminent of our lawyers, until last year, when, to the regret of all his friends, he was obliged through ill-health to give up the profession.

He then received a proof of the high estimate in which his legal talent and kindly nature were held, in a meeting of the Bar, presided over by Sir Henry James, the Attorney-General, and which in the warmest terms conveyed towards him their sympathy and good wishes.[1]

The character of his advocacy was very different from that of which I had the opportunity of judging amongst American lawyers generally. I should say that its characteristics were unimpassioned reasoning, and immovable persistence in enforcing his argument. He had great powers of endurance, and he would never have been taken from a good rubber of whist through any fear of not being up in time the next morning. His wife was a French lady; and he usually spent his vacations in Paris, and there, at Galignani's Newsroom, we were frequently wont to meet.[2]

---

[1] I was myself prevented by illness from being present.

[2] Since the above lines were written the subject of them has passed away, greatly to my grief, but not to my surprise.

I have read with interest the articles which have appeared in the principal journals referring to this event, and although they add much information, they substantially confirm the views that my acquaint-

I was favoured by him with a very kind letter of introduction to different gentlemen in New York, amongst others, to Mr. Evarts, well known as one of the most distinguished advocates of the American Bar, and also to an eminent firm, combining both advocate and solicitor, one of whom had for many years filled the office of judge—a combination worthy of reflection, and to which I shall hereafter have occasion to refer.

anceship with him had led me to form. One inaccuracy has crept into the details of his professional career. He never was, as stated in a paper remarkable for its usual accuracy, 'A Queen's Counsel.' The rank he held was that of 'Patent of precedence;' this placed him for all practical purposes of the profession in the same position, but it gave the Crown no *exclusive* claim upon his services, which it does upon those who hold the former rank.

I have reason to believe that it was through some feeling that he had himself upon the subject that he selected the patent.

The last time I saw this distinguished and kindly gentleman was in Paris, in his accustomed seat at Galignani's.

CHAPTER XI.

NEW YORK SOCIETY.

Distinguished lawyers—Mr. Evarts—The Genevan Conference—
Roundell Palmer—Arthur Cohen—The result—Introduction to
Mr. Evarts—Description of him—The Lotus Club—Entertainment
—Councillor Pleydell—The Honourable Judge Brady—A song—
Mr. Justice Hayes—The result of a song—Its effect upon Lord
Campbell—Character of Mr. Justice Hayes—His sudden death
—Courtesy to English—The Century Club—Meeting of celebrities
—Kindness to myself—Mr. and Mrs. Bigelow—Their receptions
—Description of Mr. Bigelow—Mr., Mrs., and the Misses Mack—
Their parties—Mrs. J. C. Croly—Her circle—The Sorosis Club
—Her presidentship—Agreeable recollections.

As the names of illustrious American generals became known in our country through their military achievements, so in a peaceful combat with ourselves, amongst other distinguished lawyers the name of Mr. Evarts became very generally known, and although connected with an episode in our history of which we have no reason to be proud, this gentleman has always been regarded with respect and honour. At the Genevan Conference he met, as antagonists, Roundell Palmer, now Lord Chancellor of England, and Mr. Arthur Cohen. All that learning could bring to bear on both sides of the question was exhausted, and, as I have already intimated, we have had to pay pretty handsomely for our predilection for Captain Semmes and his companions.

I was very pleased to obtain an introduction to the famous American lawyer, and was received by him with much cordiality, and at his own table I had an opportunity of appreciating the charms of his conversation, and also the company of other great lawyers and judges whose names have escaped my memory, leaving only the impression upon it of general brilliancy. I knew but one of the guests—the Honourable Judge Brady, of whom I have before made mention.

But to return to my host. Mr. Evarts is, I believe, considerably past sixty years of age, but would not be thought nearly so old. He is tall, and somewhat stooping in his gait, but is singularly active, and possesses features youthful, very mobile, and capable of much expression. He is good-tempered, unaffected, and full of fun.

I met him upon another occasion at a well-known club called the 'Lotus,' at an entertainment to which I am unable to give a name. As far as I know, it began at one o'clock (it might have done so earlier), and certainly lasted until six in the evening. During all these hours Mr. Evarts maintained his seat, delighting everyone with anecdote and repartee, and whilst showing the infinite knowledge obtained by experience, seemed to possess the exhilaration of a boy.

I feel sure that his dignity will not be offended, when I say that he forcibly reminded me of a character in one of the most charming works of our great novelist Sir Walter Scott, and I could almost imagine him like that most learned, generous, and acute of advocates described in 'Guy Mannering'—Councillor Pleydell—indulging in 'high jinks' amongst the roystering boys of Edinburgh.

At both the above parties the Honourable Judge Brady was a prominent figure. I have already dwelt upon his social characteristics, which were fully exhibited upon these occasions. May I venture to record that this learned judge indulged the company with a song? and I trust that the fact of his possessing no inconsiderable musical taste will not detract from the estimate entertained of his judicial qualifications. I am, at all events, able to furnish him with a companion not unworthy of his association.

Amongst the most learned, industrious, and painstaking of lawyers was my dear and valued friend Mr. Serjeant Hayes. He worked and laboured in vain, neglected and unrewarded, until upon one occasion, fortunately for him, Lord Campbell, the grimmest of English Chancellors, was pre-

sent, when he sang a song of his own composition.
It was entitled 'The Dog and Duck,' and was
founded upon a defence made by a member of the
circuit—the pride of the Rope-Walk[1]—Mr. Miller.
It tickled the risible faculties of the Chancellor:
he was convulsed with laughter, and what learning, industry, and perseverance had failed to
accomplish, yielded to the poetic legend of 'The
Dog and Duck.'

The promotion, however, came too late. He
was an example not of a heart sick from hope
deferred, but of a constitution broken, and he
died suddenly a very short time after he had
reached the Bench. His gaiety, however, continued to the last, and I have heard him, when a
judge, sing the song at Serjeants' Inn that had
made him one of its members, with the same
humour that had distinguished his performance
before he had attained the ermine.

I should have been very glad if my stay in
America had enabled me to enjoy more meetings
including the members of my own profession.
They would, I am sure, have made a most agreeable addition to my 'Experiences,' which, as my
readers will understand, is all that I profess to

[1] To the unlearned in circuit phraseology, it may be necessary to
mention that this term is applied to Counsel principally engaged in
criminal cases.

give, and certainly with no assumption of infallibility of judgment.

If I affected to write an account of any section of American society, I should most properly lay myself open to the charge of presumption in doing so upon such slender opportunities as those afforded me. What I have undertaken to do, and hope to have done successfully, is to show the general tone of feeling towards our country and the universal courtesy exhibited to English visitors.

Amongst other marks of attention that I received was a very gratifying one at the Century Club, of which I had been elected an honorary member. This club comprises men of eminence of all classes, and it is customary for a large gathering to take place on a Saturday evening. Upon one of these occasions I was presented to what I will venture to describe as a thoroughly representative body, and I shall never forget the kindness which was extended to me. My name was not unknown, and my humble attempt at literature had been circulated largely in the States, and I could not but feel that much more was made of both topics than I merited through the generous feelings of my entertainers.

It happened that, shortly after my arrival in America, events of a private character occurred in England causing me much anxiety, and involving a great deal of troublesome correspondence, and this circumstance prevented my availing myself of many kindly opportunities given me of mixing in New York society.

Amongst those, however, with whom I became early acquainted were the Honourable Mr. and Mrs. Bigelow, whose receptions were very pleasant. I was delighted with the opportunity afforded me at a family dinner of having a talk with this gentleman. He doubtless is a representative man, has figured largely in affairs of State, and for a time held the distinguished office of Minister at the Court of France.

I do not think I am mistaken in supposing him to be a fair type of the class to which he belongs. He seemed to possess a large fund of general knowledge, exhibited naturally, and without the slightest trace of affectation, remarkably free from egotism, and simple both in tastes and manner. I regret very much that at the time I did not know of the position he had held in France, as the acquaintanceship I had with Prince Louis Napoleon in certain business matters whilst he was in England, and which I have related in my former book, would have given any views arrived at by the acute and practical mind of the American statesman very great interest.

Mrs. John Bigelow was a charming hostess, and

I am not likely to forget the pleasant opportunities she gave me of mixing in American society.

I also availed myself of invitations from Mrs. Mack, whose handsome house in the most fashionable quarter of the city was rendered attractive by the cordial hospitality of herself and husband, fully aided by their accomplished daughters.

In the rooms of Mrs. J. C. Croly, at her Sunday evening receptions, I met the representatives of all that was distinguished in art and literature in New York, Mrs. Croly moving in literary circles, and taking no unimportant place in their ranks. This lady is president of a club, which is, I am told, famous; it is called the Sorosis, and, as it includes in its members the principal authoresses in the United States, I have no doubt it possesses extensive influence; and the welcome given me by Mrs. Croly forms no insignificant item in the grateful recollections I carried away with me from America.

CHAPTER XII.

COURTS, CRIMES, AND PUNISHMENTS.

My professional life—Trials in the United States—Yankee stories—Not reliable—The Recorder of New York—His demeanour—The advocate—Decorum of proceedings—Other courts—The Judges—Their election—Salary—Character—Able jurists—English Judges—Selection by Chancellor—Their character and position—English Bar—Difference from American—A distinct body—Union of advocate and solicitor in America—Establishment of County Courts in England—Great changes created—Practice in police courts—Death punishments—American system—English system—Objections to—The executioner—Execution at Liverpool—Disgraceful scene—Cruelty to prisoner—Conduct of executioner—His associates—Is capital punishment desirable?—Recent examples—Probable effect—Appointment of executioner—Reporters—O'Donnell—His execution—Its probable result on others.

My readers will quite understand, from the nature of my own professional life in England, that I was glad to avail myself of the opportunity of witnessing the mode in which trials were conducted in the United States; and although I had been but a few days in the country, it was quite long enough for any amount of credit I may have given to the Yankee stories circulated by smart writers in our country to have disappeared. I did not picture the judge in a monkey-jacket with his hat cocked on one side, and pipe in mouth, nor the advocates in similar costumes, and giving an occasional spur to their eloquence by 'liquoring up.'

I found in every court I visited that the utmost decorum prevailed; and this does not apply to New York only, but to other districts not supposed to be so far advanced in civilisation. Indeed, I did not discover any of those marked peculiarities that are attributed by some writers to these tribunals. I daresay there are plenty of sayings that might be caught hold of and noted down, and which to English ears may have a strange effect. I, for one, think it a great pity that visitors to America cannot find better employment.

Amongst other courts I visited was that of the Recorder of the city, where I had the opportunity of hearing a criminal trial. The judge, although not habited in robes, nor his head adorned with a wig, exhibited dignity, patience, and impartiality; and the advocate, equally unencumbered, performed his duty with zeal and ability; whilst courtesy from the Bench, and respect towards it, were as fully marked as they habitually are in Westminster Hall or the new Palace of Justice.

On subsequent occasions, in New York and elsewhere, I have noticed the same propriety throughout the proceedings, and although, unfortunately, I was unable to be present at any great trials, I think I had abundant means of forming an opinion, and that which I have described is, I believe, a fair type of others. The results also, as far as I observed, were sensible and proper.

It is a common subject of remark that the majority, if not the whole, of the judges are elected by public vote, and that with few exceptions they are subject to re-election, and that their stipends are ridiculously small. Frequently they return to the Bar, where even moderate success secures a large income. I myself met with one of the partners in a solicitors' firm who had seceded from the Bench, and was making 5,000*l*. per annum, his income from his judicial position not having exceeded that number of hundreds.

However, in the very varied companies into which I went, and where there certainly was no lack of freedom in the expression of opinion, I never heard any want of confidence in the judges expressed, or the slightest slur upon their integrity; and it must be conceded that the Bench includes many most able and learned jurists and lawyers.

By a very different method the selection of judges takes place in our country, and a result equally honourable is obtained, although many would be inclined to consider that evils of much gravity might arise from its nature.

The selection of all the judges of the High Court in England, as well as those of the County

Courts, being vested in the Lord Chancellor, himself a successful lawyer,[1] and a strong political partisan, it says much for the character of the material out of which judgeships are created, as well as the high sense of duty on the part of those who select them, that amongst the admitted features of our law, and the many grounds there are for complaining of its enactments, the character of the Bench is rarely challenged, either by its own countrymen or by foreigners, who of whatever nation readily place themselves under its protection.

The salary of the judges is fully equal to all ordinary demands, although in many instances less than the income they were making at the Bar.

There is another institution in America connected with the administration of the law which differs from ours. This consists of the fact that the Bar is not, as with us, a distinct body, holding an important social grade, as well as possessing special privileges. In the United States the profession of the law is not divided by the formal distinction of barrister and solicitor, but each is competent to perform the duties of every legal character.

Practically, however, partnerships generally exist, each member of which confines himself to a particular line; and thus it happens that whilst one

---

[1] The appointment of the Lord Chief Justice is an exception. This functionary is selected by the Cabinet.

of the partners draws the brief in a cause, another accepts the duty of bringing the facts before the court, and generally acting as advocate.

Really, however, except so far as the maintenance of a grade, which is the receptacle of the offshoots of distinguished families, and contains many members who scarcely pretend to lay themselves out for work, the difference between the institutions in the two countries exists more in form than substance, and is confined entirely to practice in the higher courts.

In an earlier age there was, in my opinion, a substantial reason for its existence. It was thought desirable that the counsel who had to conduct the cause in court should have no communication previously with the witnesses whom it would be his duty to examine, and a very strict rule exists down to the present time against the presence of any of them at preliminary consultations. It was thought that the words from a counsel's mouth would furnish hints that, intentionally or otherwise, would bias the evidence subsequently given by those who had heard them.

But it is obvious that if this be, as I think it is, a valid ground, it would be more likely to operate amongst the lower class of witnesses and causes than in those of a higher order and before more experienced tribunals.

But now County Courts are established, in which

the vast majority of causes involving the justice of the country are conducted, and solicitors habitually conduct them. They also practise in the tribunals before which minor criminal cases are tried, and all preliminary inquiries are made preparatory to their ultimate investigation. It cannot be contended that, if there be evil existing in consequence of the conjunction of barrister and solicitor, it ought to be permitted to exist in one class of tribunal and forbidden in another. In truth, the American system is much more simple and logical, as well as much better adapted to the present state of society.

In the administration of the criminal law there is another difference from the mode adopted in our country, and which is worthy of remark. It is well known that the punishment of death exists as with ourselves, and also that it is inflicted in comparative privacy; but the length of time that intervenes between sentence and execution strikes the minds of Englishmen as being remarkable. Doubtless one of the reasons is that, although there is no court of appeal in which the case of a convict can be argued, every capital sentence is reviewed before a legal tribunal, the case relied upon is considered by one of the judges, and before execution takes place it is reported upon to a full Bench.

This is certainly a more humane and rational course where the life of a fellow-creature is concerned, than that pursued in our country of leaving a very short interval between sentence and its execution, although the latter is doubtless more convenient, and prevents the continuance of an excitement which is usually more morbid than rational; but it forces upon the consideration of thinking minds whether there are not objections to a legalised system of death punishments. They are now carried out, as I have mentioned above, in comparative privacy, but I, for one, have always doubted whether this does not destroy one of the reasons for its own existence.[1]

It is a matter of pride with us that publicity surrounds all inquiry, and is prominent in every tribunal, and its results, for good or evil, guide the opinion of the masses, whilst at the same time the opinion of the masses greatly affects their conduct. It was said that a public execution brutalised the spectators, and a description of great force and power, given by a popular author,[2] of the scenes surrounding one of them which he witnessed, added to the prevailing feeling.

Once only I was present at one of these spectacles, and I found, mixed with much that was reckless, coarse, and ruffianly, that there was

---

[1] Upon the Committee that sat upon the subject of abolishing the publicity of death punishment there was a great difference of opinion, many able statesmen and lawyers being opposed to the change.

[2] Charles Dickens.

a feeling of intense and not thoughtless or unreflective horror. Now in England, at all events, this ceremony is arranged and carried out in a small family party, and which the public eye is not present to control.

This observation is forced upon me by a proceeding that occurred upon one of these hole-and-corner occasions in the North of England. The wretched culprit stood, the rope round his neck, the hangman by his side—waiting—either for the stroke of a neighbouring clock (which might have stopped), or for a signal from the governor, and when at last the victim was cast suspended from the gallows, eight minutes of torture intervened before the soul was forced from its earthly tenement.[1] Was the hangman drunk? Was the governor ignorant or neglectful? If this scene had occurred in public, the former would have run a chance of being torn to pieces by an indignant mob.

In all countries where death has existed as a penalty for crime, the office of the executioner

[1] Since the above lines were written, another scene has been enacted upon another wretched criminal, at the same place and by the same actors as upon that which I have related. Perchance the cord was too long! or, as was intimated by the governor, the 'Officer of the Law'—pseudonym for hangman—had taken a drop too much! On the former occasion this functionary accused the governor. Who knows? The result in both instances was illegal torture upon one of our fellow-creatures.

has been looked upon with aversion and horror. Does it exhibit an improvement in the tastes of a people when a section of them can be found to seek his society, revel in the anecdotes of his foul calling, gloat over the exhibition of the instruments by which he has strangled human beings, and possibly send him fresh from the orgies of some low pot-house, in a half-drunken state, to execute the last solemn bidding of the law? The answer I imagine to this question is clear.

Then what is the conclusion? If public executions were a source from which brutality grew up, and private executions are attended with scenes which would not bear the presence of the public, and a morbid feeling of interest is created with the most loathsome of human occupations—surely it is that death penalties should perish at the shrine of civilisation.

Let us look by the light of late examples at other possible results from this privacy, and I venture to think it is by no means unimportant. I speak from the information afforded by the public journals of another recent event—the execution of O'Donnell. At this, gentlemen who are described as the representatives of the press were alone admitted. By what rule they are selected by the Sheriffs of London and Middlesex, who perform their duty of executioners through the medium of the hangman they hire for the purpose, I have no means of knowing, and whilst I do not intend to cast the slightest slur upon the gentlemen in this instance, who doubtless performed their task honourably, they are not officers connected with justice, nor can they be said to satisfy the conditions of that reliance which the people entertain for a public press.

It does not appear from their account that any resistance took place; the criminal performed the *rôle* of a Christian martyr, and was strangled with a smile upon his countenance. According to all accounts he was a totally ignorant peasant, believing he had a mission to avenge the wrongs of his country; and the description of the mode in which he met his death will serve rather to encourage than deter the deceived and benighted beings of his class, whilst the miscreants who use them as tools will revel in immunity, and obtain fresh power to initiate further crimes.

CHAPTER XIII.

THE TOMBS.

Mr. Gilbert—Conversation with—American prisons—Mr. Howard Vincent—Arrival in New York—Visit to the Tombs—Exterior of prison—Situation—Newgate—Its records—Prison entrance—Youthful prisoners—Their type—Conduct—Appearance—Mixture—The governor—Main corridor—Cells—Prisoners under death-sentence—Their treatment—Absence of restraint—Comfortable cells—Affecting scene—Interview with a prisoner—His crime—His appearance—Subsequent execution—Manner of governor—His appearance—The gallows—Question of discipline—More humane than in England—Explanation—My own experiences—Opinion as to treatment of suspected persons—English system unjustifiable—A confession—My reading at Chickering Hall—Kindly criticism.

It is strange to reflect upon the circumstances through which ideas are implanted in the human mind, and certainly it would scarcely be imagined that the curiosity excited by a conversation I had with Mr. Gilbert, the eminent author, greatly affected my desire to visit America. It occurred at a party at the house of my friend Mr. Howard Vincent, the late intelligent and able head of the London Detective Police, and it is not improbable that the occupation of our host led to the conversation in question.

Mr. Gilbert described to me very vividly

scenes he had witnessed in American prisons, and his account of the discipline prevailing in them certainly excited my wonder, and, but for their coming from such a source, I should scarcely have accorded my belief. They were, however, fully supported by my subsequent observations.

Very shortly after my arrival in New York, I availed myself of the services of Judge Brady to enable me to visit the principal prison of the city, and which I imagine to be the one chiefly referred to by Mr. Gilbert. Like 'our Newgate' (it is customary to speak of it in this affectionate style, almost as if it were a beloved institution), the New York receptacle for great criminals is situated in the very heart of the city. It does not present any exterior signs, that I can remember, that, as with our prison, bring to the imagination of the beholder the terrible scenes that have been enacted within its walls, and the appalling sights that have issued from them. Newgate is indeed a page written in the history of our country, and one which, for the credit of it, would be well erased.[1]

Although presenting no exterior signs that distinguished the purposes for which it was used, the

[1] I have recently read a most carefully written and highly interesting work by Colonel Arthur Griffiths called the *Chronicles of Newgate*, from its most early date down to the present moment, and even I, not unconversant with its history, read almost with incredulity the account of the tortures inflicted under the name of justice.

prison of New York—a comparatively modern one I assume—bears the ghastly title of 'The Tombs.' I was received by the governor with the utmost politeness, and enabled to inspect the different arrangements of the gaol.

I was surprised to find that the portion of it which formed a sort of entrance hall was tenanted by boys of different ages, charged with trifling offences. They were of the type to be seen in the London streets.

Poor lads! What other result can be expected from their gutter life?—and babyhood reaching childhood without one feeling of that unreasoning joyousness, which even amongst the most gently nurtured is never felt in after life.

There was the hardened, impudent *gamin*, who rather delighted in an imprisonment which secured him food and warmth ; and there were specimens of those out of whom shame had not been extinguished, and their present position only a commencement of the process.

After some conversation with the governor, in which I expressed my surprise at the mixture that seemed to be unchecked, and in the justice of which he apparently agreed, I was conducted by him to that portion of the prison mainly occupied by persons under sentence of death. This consisted of a corridor sufficient to contain some seven or eight cells of reasonable dimensions, which were ranged upon one of its sides, and opened out upon it, to which corridor the occupants of the cells (all of the male sex) had access.

Those whom I saw were dressed in their ordinary costumes, lounging in different a'titudes, and some of them conversing together. There was no apparent restriction upon their movements or actions, and they were permitted to receive visitors, two or three of whom, as I was told, being there at this time; and it did not appear that any control or supervision was exercised over them, although there were doubtless officers within reach.

The cells, open at this time of day, presented every appearance of comfort, and in some of them were indications of the employments upon which the convicts were permitted to occupy themselves; in one I noticed a palette and paints, and some of the work of a not altogether contemptible artist. The cases of all these prisoners were under consideration, and they were awaiting the result.

One scene I witnessed of a singularly affecting character. A woman, not devoid of good looks, had been allowed by the kind-hearted governor to carry to her husband the news that his death-sentence had been commuted, and, clasped in each other's arms, the interview affected the hardened criminals around. I heard afterwards that upon more than one occasion she had nearly perished through the man's brutality.

I noticed, when the poor woman was approaching the cell in which her husband was at that time sitting, a young man of not more than nineteen years of age, with a somewhat pleasant countenance, moved out of her way, raising his hat as she passed. I had been prepared to see him, and knew that his case had been reported upon by Judge Brady, and that he would be left for execution. His crime had created some sensation in New York from its singular brutality. He had been engaged in a burglary, and when quitting the house, without the slightest provocation or necessity, had shot the owner, who was endeavouring to get out of the way.

The appearance and demeanour of this lad excited my sympathy, and it was with much surprise that I heard from Judge Brady the history of his crime, and also that he was associated with a gang of the worst ruffians in the city, to become a member of which it was a necessary qualification to have committed a murder. He was an example of the length of time allowed to exist between sentence and its execution, he having been convicted some months before.

I made some casual remark to him which led to a further conversation. He told me he was waiting to see his lawyer. I remarked that I supposed he had been visited by a clergyman. 'Ah!' he said, 'you think that I have no chance?' I made no answer. After a pause, during which I fancied he was struggling to control his feelings, he said in a low voice, 'Will you shake hands with me?' I held mine out; he did little more than touch it, but a cold shudder ran through my frame at the thought that, perhaps, in a few hours he would be a corpse. He was subsequently executed, and I heard bore his fate with firmness.

I could not avoid noticing the gentle tone of the governor towards all the inmates. He was, however, a very fine, resolute-looking man, and appeared equal to any ordinary emergency; and I presumed that, in his management of the prisoners under his care, he was the representative of the system by which persons under charge for grave offences are treated by the law of America.

As I was leaving the prison accompanied by him, I called his attention to some iron gratings, at one end of the corridor nearest to the entrance hall, and asked what they were, and was prepared to learn that they contained the grim instruments of justice.

Now, although I can quite conceive objections of a grave character attending what undoubtedly would be considered the lax discipline of this prison, it must be remembered that the men confined in it, although their doom was generally only too certain, had still the possibility of a reversal of sentence; and surely punishment should not (as it does in our country) commence until guilt is humanly certain, and persons charged with crime ought not to be subjected to any inconvenience, except such as is necessary for their safe custody.

In the administration of the law in England, although we are apt to enunciate the principle that everyone is esteemed to be innocent until proved guilty, punishment begins with the accusation, and the hardships and degradation to which alleged offenders are exposed, even before trial, do little credit to the civilisation of which we are proud.

I make no apology for many of the above observations appertaining to my own land. In the title I have given to these pages, I intended to prepare my readers for any digression of this character, and although I wished, and do wish, my trip to the United States to form a material feature, I did not intend to exclude other experiences of my own, and reflections upon them. It is not unnatural that my visit to the courts of justice in New York, and to the remarkable prison I have endeavoured to describe, should have induced me to enlarge upon the subject, and refer to the knowledge acquired during my past professional life; and in the next chapter I shall venture upon the ventilation of views that in a former work I have mentioned, and which recent observations have materially strengthened.

This will, I think, be a convenient opportunity for referring to a personal matter which, probably from a sense of its not being calculated (at all events in my mind) to afford unqualified satisfaction, I have hitherto neglected to do. When I went over to the States, I had made an arrangement with a gentleman, whose representative in New York was Colonel Morse, to give some description of scenes in my career, and I imagined I could furnish an agreeable entertainment to an American audience.

I first essayed to do so on December 15, 1882, at Chickering Hall, the great arena for such exhibitions. Upon this occasion I was introduced to those assembled in complimentary terms by Judge Brady, which gentleman also proved his sincerity as well as kindness by making no comments upon the performance. My venture proved the old adage, 'Ne sutor ultra crepidam.' The critics treated my attempt with much more humanity than I felt it to deserve, and I conclude this chapter by thanking them for their mercy.

CHAPTER XIV.

LAW AND LAWYERS.

System of law—America and England—A death sentence—Delay —Objections to—Reasons for—English system—Haste—No court of appeal—Desirability of—Equity judges—Their inexperience— Character of—Ridiculous results—Evil consequences—Criminal trial—Serious blunder—The Staunton case—Popular indignation —Cockburn—His interference—Modification of sentence—Release of prisoner—Question of appeal—Necessity in capital cases—Its justice in every case—Existence in civil cases—Sir James Fitzjames Stephen—A criminal code—Difficulty of—Evidence of a wife—Murder case—Rush—Another trial—Alibi proved—Position of a wife—Influence of criminal trials—Capital punishment—My change of opinion.

In my last chapter I have brought to the notice of my readers so much of the system of criminal jurisprudence in the United States as came within my cognisance, and am thus enabled to consider the action of the law, in two countries of a high state of civilisation, upon an essentially important subject.

There are many obvious objections to the length of time intervening between a death sentence and its execution; a very prominent one is that the crime itself has passed from the public mind before the penalty is paid, and thus the excuse for capital punishment—that it acts as a deterrent warning—is materially weakened. On the other hand, it gives opportunity for inquiry of the most comprehensive and searching kind, which surely is a duty before human life is sacrificed.

In England, the execution of a convicted person follows with comparative rapidity upon the death sentence, and this, as it appears to me, renders it almost barbarous that there should exist no court with powers to review the circumstances of the case, and any errors that may have occurred upon the trial. Infallibility upon the part either of juries or judges is not to be expected, and an additional element of uncertainty has been introduced in our country, of late years, by the appointment of men without experience to preside in criminal courts. Equity judges in these courts are more or less bad, but it is pure nonsense to say that they can be filled by intuition with a knowledge of the procedure, at total variance with all their preceding experience.

Let me do these gentlemen justice. They have generally been selected from the most learned and distinguished men in their branch of the profession, and I have never heard a word whispered against their care, industry, and humanity; but the very conscientiousness that they doubtless possess must weaken their powers in the novel task they are called upon to perform; and although it is far better that justice should fail than that an improper conviction should take place, it is a very serious evil when such occurs through the inexperience of a judge.

Already stories have been circulated which, if they have left no stain upon the ermine, have certainly covered it with ridicule; and one very worthy gentleman, showing a profound ignorance of the unworthy use to which the vulgar apply perfectly innocent terms, has furnished a subject for laughter at every mess-table in the United Kingdom. As the law now exists, there is no appeal from any verdict, however presided over, upon a criminal trial.

The following instance, which appears to me to illustrate the necessity of a court of appeal in a very remarkable manner, was not tried before any of the learned judges selected from the Court of Chancery, but before a judge of very varied and extensive experience in criminal law. Four persons—three men (I believe) of the name of Staunton, and a young woman—were indicted at the Central Criminal Court for the murder of the wife of one of the men. There were circumstances that gave rise to strong prejudice against them, and the case was ushered to trial with all the babble of an excited coroner's jury.

There was absolutely not a shadow of case

against the young woman, and it ought not to have been allowed to go to the jury. With regard to the others, there was evidence that would have warranted a verdict of manslaughter. They were *all* four found guilty of murder, and sentenced to death. Amongst lawyers, and all men of sense and humanity, the result created a feeling of indignation. I know from his own lips that this was the case with Sir Alexander Cockburn, and I have reason to believe that some representation emanated from him to the Home Secretary.

The young woman was at once discharged, and the sentence of the men commuted into one of imprisonment. It is quite superfluous to mention that this is not a solitary instance of the possibility of innocent people suffering through the erroneous result of a trial.

I have intimated more than once that it is undesirable that a long interval should exist between a death sentence and its fulfilment, and if an appeal was confined to capital cases alone, the present staff of judges, with some additional powers, could be made available for such a court. But if, as it seems to me to be the reasonable conclusion, in criminal as in civil cases, that a person against whom a verdict has been given is entitled to have the evidence reviewed, then doubtless a material addition must be made to the number of judges, but these, if properly utilised, need not add substantially to the charge upon the country.

The mode to be adopted I have considered and explained in my former experiences, and, with all humility and deference to greater men, I see no reason for altering my opinion of the efficacy of the plan I have there suggested.

Sir James Fitzjames Stephen has applied his great mind and matured experience to the creation of a criminal code, and favoured me with a copy of its proposed enactments; but, whilst admiring much of his work, I believe the result he has endeavoured to attain is perfectly impossible. I, however, fully appreciate many of the changes suggested, and do not doubt that very great improvements might be made in the present provisions of the law, which would tend much to facilitate the labours of a court of appeal.

There are anomalies existing between the law applicable to civil proceedings and those that exist in reference to criminals, in addition to the rights denied to the latter of an appeal, that ought to command alteration. In the most trivial, as well as the most important, of civil suits the evidence of a wife is admissible both for and against her husband, whilst a person charged with a criminal offence does not possess such a right, and yet it can well be imagined that, in many instances, she alone could prove his innocence. The Crown also being incompetent to call her, public justice may seriously suffer.

Two instances occur to my memory which strongly illustrate the mischief that may easily arise from such a restriction. A murder of a most atrocious kind was committed many years since, and a man named Rush was charged with it. It appeared that, at some period previous to the charge, he had become connected with a woman who lived with him as his wife, and who had been very urgent with him to marry her. He had promised but had not done so, and by her evidence he was convicted and hanged. Had she been his wife he must have escaped.

The other instance presents somewhat different moral features. A young tradesman was prosecuted by the South-Western Railway Company for an offence committed upon their premises. I was the counsel concerned for the prosecution. His identity was sworn to by numerous witnesses. He was a married man, and nothing was suggested prejudicial to his character. Still the evidence against him was overwhelming. It appeared, however, as I believe to have been the case, his defence was true: he had on the day of the alleged occurrence gone to Epsom Races in company with a young woman, not his wife, and who entered the witness-box, and gave a detailed account of his movements during the whole of the period in question. He was acquitted. If he had taken his wife to the races, nothing could have saved him.

I hope that in the observations I have ventured to make, in this and former chapters, upon crime and punishment, I may not be deemed presumptuous. I am entitled to claim as some justification the lengthened experience I possess, and in my opinion it is impossible to exaggerate the enormous influence that the details affecting these questions exercise upon the public mind. A case in the House of Lords, involving millions, interests but a very small section of the public, but a trial in the Crown Court at the Assizes is read and commented upon by the entire country.

Upon the subject of capital punishment my opinion has wavered. I confess that now I advocate its abolition, but feel it impossible to assert too emphatically that a court of appeal is an absolute necessity in connection with its existence. Having delivered myself of opinions which are the result of mature thought, and which I venture to think are not without some application to the procedure in the United States, as well as in my own country, I will now ask my readers to accompany me on a visit to Boston, of which I propose to give some of the details in the next chapter.[1]

[1] A Bill is now being carried by Sir Henry James before the House of Commons, in which many improvements are being introduced, upon the above subject, and in which I perceive that the question above referred to has been discussed, and possibly an alteration in the law may be effected before these pages make their appearance.

101

CHAPTER XV.

BOSTON.

Boston railway—Night journey—Its discomfort—Sleeping-cars—
Caution to ladies—Agreeable morning—Colonel Morse—The
hotel—General Butler—Election as governor—Inauguration—
Preliminary reception—Introduction to the general—His character
—Division of opinion—Notables and judges present—General
Butler's appearance—My surprise—His practice as an attorney—
His address—Its ability—Its frankness—Its reception—Great
sensation—Censure of local authorities—Mr. Warren—Renewal
of acquaintance—The club—General courtesy—Regret at leaving
—Unpopularity of General Butler—His defeat.

In recording the short visit I paid to Boston I cannot pretend to introduce any novelty. Its history — so gratifying to American pride — is stamped upon its monuments, and the city itself furnishes an example of taste and beauty not to be surpassed. From New York it is reached by a railway, and as I travelled by night I endured my first introduction to the sleeping cars.

I use the word endured deliberately; the berths, like those in a ship, are ranged upon each side of a long passage, and the narrow hole into which a passenger is poked was in my case planted immediately over a hot-air pipe, by which

I was nearly baked, whilst outside there was a fair chance of being smothered. And let me caution ladies against night-travelling in America. There is no separate sleeping compartment provided for their accommodation, and, with the male sex surrounding them, they must tumble into the berth assigned them as best they can, and, as the berths are constructed one above another, the amount of unpleasantness to ladies may be easily conceived.

The miserable night, however, came to an end, and a bright, keen, winter morning ushered us into the beautiful city of Boston.

I was in the company of Colonel Morse, who knew the locality well, and under his agreeable guardianship was soon settled in one of its magnificent hotels. I forget its name, but it matters little—they are all alike, and I was duly ticketed off to a bedroom without being looked at. I have found the sleeping arrangements at American hotels invariably good, the culinary department indifferent, and the hurried service and want of all cosiness thoroughly distasteful to those unaccustomed to the habits of these caravanserais.

I arrived in Boston immediately after the election of General Butler as governor of the State, and, through the introduction of Colonel Morse, I was favoured with an invitation to be present at the inauguration ceremony attending his reception.

There is, I imagine, no public man in the United States who has made for himself warmer friends or more bitter enemies than General Butler. Colonel Morse entertained for him strong feelings of friendship, and his career was favourably represented to me. Of course it is not likely that any man whose life has been divided between the bitterest scenes of an internecine war and a political atmosphere almost as bitter and exciting, can hope to escape without some pretty strong adjectives being applied to his name, and what I saw of him and his proceedings certainly led me to feel no surprise at such a result.

The ceremony was held in a magnificent hall, which upon the occasion in question was densely filled. All the notables of the State, including the judges, were present. Upon my arrival a reception was being held of the private friends, male and female, of the governor, and at this I was presented to him. Previously to being so, I knew nothing of him except by repute of having been an officer of rank in the United States army during the Southern insurrection, and distinguished for the strictness of his discipline.

I had pictured to myself a dashing-looking soldier, with the military attributes more than

usually pronounced. Much was my surprise when
I beheld a short, stout, ordinarily dressed individual, with a singularly inexpressive face, and a
soft, unassuming manner; and my surprise was not
diminished when I learnt that since the war he had
practised most successfully as a lawyer, that he
was a favourite advocate in desperate cases, and
had pulled many an awful rogue out of a dilemma.

After an hour or so, engaged in receiving his
friends, he ascended the tribune. I had been
introduced to the judges, and was seated in their
company immediately adjacent to where the general
stood. The change that came over him was remarkable: his face lighted up, and showed indications of brightness and intelligence, and, as he
proceeded with a written oration, he exhibited
great mastery of the subject and thorough confidence in himself. I could not entirely appreciate
the application of his address, as the subjects and
the people dealt with were unknown to me, but
the sensation created was quite unmistakable. He
referred to different institutions and their management, which in every case he denounced and
declared that he should amend.

I suppose that the body of the hall contained
many of the managers of these institutions, and
as each criticism was in the most straightforward
fashion pronounced by the governor, a movement

was discoverable in the section referred to ; and the assembly continued in a state of ferment from the commencement of the address until I, with much difficulty, extricated myself from the crowd by which I was wedged in—with the conclusion forced upon my mind that, if General Butler's survey of the holders of office in the State was a correct one, its glorious memories were by no means faithfully represented by those who conducted the affairs of its local institutions.

I can imagine some such effect as I witnessed being produced by an oration of a similar character addressed to a collection of the select vestries of Great Britain.

I had come to Boston for the purpose of giving one of the Readings that I had essayed at New York, and was listened to by an audience rather select than numerous, with attention and kindness.

I certainly have, in this respect, no ground for regretting my visit, and with the city itself, its stately terraces and noble memorials of past triumphs, seen under a cloudless sky, and with the keen, invigorating air of December prevailing, it was impossible not to be delighted.

I also had great pleasure in renewing an acquaintance I had formed on board the 'Servia' with Mr. Warren, who was then coming over with his wife (I believe a bride) from a visit to England.

This gentleman's family are, I understood, the sole proprietors of one of the great lines of Atlantic steamers, and also influential citizens of Boston. I need hardly say that I received from him every attention, and was introduced to the principal club, where I met several other gentlemen with whom I passed a most agreeable evening, which added to my regret at being obliged to limit my visit to the city to so short a period.

The auguries I formed upon hearing the governor's address have since been verified. The task which he had undertaken, and exhibited so much frankness in disclosing, was not one calculated to render his position a bed of roses whilst he continued to retain it, or a permanent one if dependent upon the majority of his inauguration audience. I know nothing of the merits of the many questions he ventilated, but, as his re-election depended upon many of those whose conduct he attacked, it is not wonderful that he failed to obtain the means of carrying out his views, and was defeated upon the next occasion in the contest for governorship.

CHAPTER XVI.

DISTINGUISHED CHARACTERS.

Philadelphia—Its beauty—Its population—Mr. Stoddart—Dinner party—Horace Furness—Shakespearian collection—A Unitarian divine—A distinguished authoress—The Penn Club—Flattering reception—Ex-Chief Justice Sharswood—Eli K. Price—The judges—Association Hall—Grand entertainment—The Bar and Bench—Eloquent speeches—Touching conclusion—Distinguished character of guests—Reflections upon the entertainment.

PHILADELPHIA—an hour before sunset on a winter afternoon. How exactly I came here I am scarcely able to tell, but I imagine after being partially baked and suffocated in a night train, a process which affects all the organs of the brain, including memory.

However, here I am, the rays of the sun lighting up the shops dressed with all their Christmas novelties, splendid hotels worthy of any capital in the world, the streets clearly defined, and the population crowding them, the happiness that a holiday, a bright sun, and a crisp, pure air are certain to create stamped upon their faces.

And surely, whether the objects were animate or inanimate, there could not be found any more worthy to be shone upon than those presented by

Philadelphia. The city is beautiful, its buildings interesting, its shops handsome, its population cheerful, and the female portion of it singularly attractive; and I have much reason to remember with gratitude the cordial welcome extended to me from all quarters.

Upon the day of my arrival I received through Mr. Stoddart—a well-known gentleman, the proprietor of an extensive printing establishment in this city, and also in New York, and who had published a very elegant edition of my 'Experiences' —an invitation to dine with Mr. Furness, an influential inhabitant. Of this I availed myself, and have seldom had an opportunity of enjoying a greater intellectual treat.

Horace Furness, my host, is a European as well as an American celebrity. He has devoted much time, industry, and labour to investigations and criticisms of the works of Shakespeare. He possesses every edition of our great author worthy of being studied, and has himself produced a volume commanding much attention. His library contains editions and treatises that must have taken many years and much judgment to collect.

I wished I could have transported into the cosy room where these treasures were exhibited, and have introduced my valued old friend Frank

Fladgate to the possessor of them. It would have been an intellectual treat, rarely equalled, to have listened to these two profound worshippers of the same divinity.

My host's father, a Unitarian divine, was one of the party. He presented a very venerable appearance and must have been of advanced age, but the brightness of his intellect was in no respect affected by his years. Sound common sense, liberality of views, and entire freedom from bigotry distinguished his conversation, and I was told that he was one of the most eloquent and popular preachers in the United States.

I was also charmed with the conversation of Mrs. ——, a lady of very varied attainments, celebrated as an original author, and also as the translator of well-known German works. I was very glad that, in listening admiringly to her conversation, and availing myself of the knowledge she displayed upon numerous subjects, I was spared the chance of my own superficiality being exposed to dissection by so acute a mind.

After this very agreeable dinner, I attended a reception given in compliment to myself at the Penn Club, an institution of a similar character to the 'Century' at New York, and partaking in its constitution of similar elements to those of the Athenæum in London. The most distinguished literary and professional men of Pennsylvania belonged to it, and none amongst them possessed higher claims to eminence than a gentleman who had recently retired from the presidency of the State Judicial Bench, Chief Justice Sharswood; and at a complimentary dinner given to whom by members of the profession I had afterwards the privilege of being present, and of which I propose shortly to give some account. I was much struck with the appearance of the learned gentleman, who seemed to bear his years and honours right well, but who, I deeply regretted learning, has since departed this life, probably sinking under the weight of ceasing to be useful.

To revert, however, to the reception at the Penn Club. Other judges were present, a former governor of Pennsylvania, the mayor of the city, and—by no means the least respected—Mr. Eli K. Price, who bore ninety-nine years on his shoulders, and was still an active practising lawyer, apparently greatly respected. My name seemed to have reached the assemblage under kindly auspices, and I received a most hearty and flattering welcome from all present.

Upon the following evening I addressed an audience at the Association Hall. I was received very kindly, but I believe, if natural politeness and a sense of hospitality had not largely prevailed, I might have been addressed in the not very complimentary quotation, 'It's not your vocation, Hal.'

'*On Wednesday evening, December* 20, 1882, *about three hundred members of the Philadelphia Bar, together with the entire local judiciary* (*invited guests*), *assembled in the lobby of the Academy of Music, adjoining the* foyer, *where a reception was held in honour of the Honourable George Sharswood.*'

I copy the above announcement from an account published of an entertainment given to the above gentleman upon his retirement from the Bench as Chief Justice of Pennsylvania, and at which upon a very complimentary invitation I was present. From signs not to be mistaken, the recipient of this honour was beloved and esteemed by every member of the Bar and Bench present, and I listened with pleasure to a long and interesting speech in which he recorded the experiences of upwards of half a century; and those who remember or have heard related the incidents of a legal life embracing the same period in our own country, with the change of habits that has followed, and the alteration of travelling, can imagine the 'circuits' accomplished 'somehow' across houseless deserts.

His descriptions, enlivened with sparks of bright humour, were, notwithstanding their technical nature, listened to with great and engrossing interest. He himself, admittedly a splendid jurist and profound lawyer, undervalued his attainments in the following remarks, which I cannot, even at the risk of being egotistical, forbear from quoting:—

'Perhaps after all Lord Chancellor Lyndhurst's rule for the selection of a judge is the best one. "I look around," said he, "for a gentleman, and if he knows a little law, so much the better."' Judge Sharswood then proceeded to say—'I am indebted for this anecdote to the very entertaining reminiscences of the distinguished member of the English Bar who has favoured us with his company this evening.'

The whole of the speech delivered by him is worthy of being read, and was doubly interesting to me from the knowledge it exhibited of English law and lawyers; and probably the following observations founded upon so lengthened an experience will meet amongst our body a cordial concurrence, and I hope that my professional brethren, at all events, will feel that I am not unduly exhausting their patience in quoting verbatim the quaint but graphic description given by the ex-Chief Justice of some recollections of former days :—

'It is now more than half a century since I was enrolled in your number. It has been a great period in the history of this country, and of the world; of great improvements in every department of life, of marvels—I had almost said of miracles. There have been great changes in the law, in the Bar, in the courts, in the administration of justice. Soon after my admission I was retained to appear before the Board of Property at Harrisburg. It took me seventeen long hours of hard staging, by the way of Reading, to get there; and when I came back in thirteen hours,[1] through Lancaster, in a swift mail-coach, with seats for only four passengers, it was thought wonderful. Such was the rapid transit of that day. Lawsuits and everything else were conducted with stage-coach slowness.

'Yet we should not disparage the methods of our predecessors; even stage-coach travelling had some decided advantages. An old driver on the road from Chambersburg to Bedford, which I always used to take by choice on account of the beautiful scenery of that mountain region, used to say: "Give me a good turnpike, and a quiet team going at the rate of six miles an hour, and if the coach breaks down, or anything happens, *there* you are! But if you are going on one of these railroads at the rate of thirty or forty miles an hour, and anything happens, *where* are you?"

'I have sometimes thought that if one of those

---

[1] Not being acquainted with the relative distances of the localities referred to, I must leave them to the imagination of my readers.

stately and dignified gentlemen to whom, in my early professional life, I used to look up with so much respect—nay, with so much awe—the leaders of the Bar—" sad and reverend apprentices" my Lord Coke would have called them—I say, if one of them should now reappear in our court-rooms, he would be as much astonished and bewildered as at the sight of a locomotive, with a long train of crowded passenger cars, flying over an iron road at the rate of fifty miles an hour. The locomotive he would doubtless consider as a demon broken loose from the lower regions, and the court-room as a demon also, " whose name was Legion!"

'The mills of justice, like those of the gods, then " ground slowly but surely." Attorneys, especially the older ones, who had got over the ambition of seeing their name on the trial list, were not in the habit of ordering cases on the trial lists inside of two years. There was very little or no chance of cases being reached in less time; and in the meantime clients and witnesses were subject to the expense and trouble of attending court every term at least for a week, from day to day. Many cases went, of course, through the alembic of compulsory arbitration, either for the sake of securing the lien of an early judgment or award, or of getting a look into the hand of the other side. The arbitration system was introduced for the purpose of dispensing with attorneys, making every man his own lawyer; and it ended, as all such schemes invariably do, in a great increase of business and income to the profession. Everything then moved with the greatest deliberation. It was an age of long trials, long speeches, long arguments, long everything.

'About two years before I was admitted, while I was in the junior class at college, I obtained leave from the kind-hearted old gentleman who was then the provost to attend a celebrated trial going on at *Nisi Prius*. Four of the most eminent counsel were engaged and each spoke for five hours; and what will strike you as remarkable, although it was not unusual then, all their speeches were written out in full and read to the jury. You can easily perceive what injustice was done to suitors, "clamouring for justice" as the old books have it, by such interminable delays, and how often "hope deferred" made "the heart sick." I saw many sad instances of it in my brief practice, and carried a deep sense of it with me when I went on the Bench. It was a common saying among business men, that "it was better for a man to abandon a cause, however good, than to go to law."'

Another observation I will venture to quote of this great and truly conscientious judge:—

'I have sometimes been haunted with the fear

that in riding this hobby so hard—driving trials so fast—injustice must have been done to suitors in many cases. It was, however, a choice between two evils; for it is with the administration of justice as with everything else, "there is nothing perfect under the sun." It is, indeed, a most difficult problem with any court to reconcile that speed which is necessary to prevent such delay as practically amounts to a denial of justice with the care, study, and deliberation required to arrive at the proper determination of important questions. *Festina lente* is the simple rule; but, in its application, *Hic labor, hoc opus est*.'

In speaking of Mr. Eli Price he said :—' He was Chairman of the Committee by whom I was examined for admission to the Bar, fifty-one years ago.'

The Chief Justice then went on to describe Price's various claims to distinction in the following terms :—

'I doubt if he could tell us, even by approximation, how many titles in this large city, which he has seen grow almost from a village to its present proportions, have passed under his cautious and scrutinising eyes. Mr. Price has not been what we term a conveyancer, but in England he would have stood in the same rank which is adorned by the names of Booth and Butler, Fearne and Preston.'

He then quoted an epitaph upon the last of these distinguished conveyancers, very little known beyond English legal circles.[1]

In an affecting conclusion the honourable gentleman recognised with evident feeling a number of his former pupils, many having attained distinction at the Bar, some having reached the Bench, and one who was about to succeed him as Chief Justice.

Mr. Justice Paxson, one of the judges of the Supreme Court of Pennsylvania, responded to the toast of that court. His observations also were full of interest, and I think the following are so completely in accord with the views of our own profession that I require no apology for quoting them:—

'The character of the Supreme Court, as well as of all other courts, must depend in a great measure upon the Bar. An able and high-toned Bar will seldom have an inferior Bench, and it will never tolerate a bad one. An able, courteous, and dignified Bench will never have an unruly Bar;

---

[1] 'Stern death has cast into *abeyance* here
    A most renowned conveyancer.
    Then lightly on his head be laid
    The *sod* that he so oft *conveyed*.
    In constant faith and hope he sure is,
    His soul like a *scintilla juris*,
In nubibus, expectant lies,
    To raise a *freehold* in the skies.'

they naturally assist and strengthen each other, and out of this condition of mutual dependence spring all that is honourable and useful to either. The inspired writer was evidently defining the qualifications for judicial station when he said, "Let every man be swift to hear, slow to speak, slow to wrath." The judge who adopts this as his rule of conduct will never have reason to complain of his Bar.'

The following, being his concluding words, were uttered with an intensity of tone that carried his hearers by storm :—

'The retirement of the Chief Justice is a sore subject with me, and will leave its scar; next to my own kin, there is no one for whom I feel a greater affection than I do for him. I would gladly have avoided these personal allusions, but I could not. There are moments when a man must speak, or the very stones would cry out. I should dishonour my manhood were I to fail to give utterance to-night to the love I feel for George Sharswood. May the Lord bless and keep him in sickness and in health, and envelop him in the folds of His everlasting love !'

I will not risk wearying my readers by giving other details of this truly interesting occasion, but I am bound to say that it was impossible to be present without recognising the high tone that prevailed throughout, and my reflections afterwards were, that I had been in the presence of a Bench and Bar in every respect calculated to confer honour upon any State; and I am proud to say that I recognised in its tone and sentiments exactly those traits that I have often witnessed in gatherings of a somewhat similar character amongst my own professional brethren.

CHAPTER XVII.

THE CLOVER CLUB.

Bright weather—Hospitality—Expression of thanks—The Clover Club
—Its motto—Object—Monthly dinner—Qualification for membership—The Press—Representatives at dinner—Belle Vue Hotel—
Guests—Speeches—Songs—Mr. Disston—Henry Philipps--Henry
Russell—Barry Cornwall—Wallack—Oscar Wille—Success of
dinner--Return to New York—Its holiday appearance—Beauty of
the ladies—Lord Coleridge—His opinion upon the subject—Comparison with English ladies—My opinion.

It gives me great pleasure to recall the days I passed in Philadelphia. As I have stated, this beautiful city was clad in holiday garb, and the brightness of the weather brought out in the fullest relief its characteristics; and I cannot (even at the risk of being accused of needless repetition) help dwelling upon the hearty greeting extended from all quarters to myself. My time would not allow me to avail myself of numerous offers of hospitality, but I hope that if these lines should be fortunate enough to meet the eyes of those whom I will venture to call my kind friends, that they will accept with trust my expression of warm and lasting gratitude.

Amongst the numerous invitations to which

I have referred was one from the members of the 'Clover Club' to a dinner. As the name did not at the time convey any information to my mind as to its character and purposes, I will quote them from a programme with which I have since been favoured, and which is headed by a design representing a quill pen and a gridiron, with the motto contained in a somewhat mysterious scroll:

'"Whilst we live, we live in clover." The principal object of this club is to meet monthly for a dinner, at which the members endeavour to entertain such notable persons as may be sojourning in the city at the time. It is composed mostly of newspaper men, with a sprinkling of other professions—the chief requisite in a candidate for membership being good fellowship.'

As far as a judgment formed upon a single opportunity is of value, this requisite had been fully complied with. An excellent dinner, one of the best I had partaken of in America, was given at a splendid hotel called 'The Belle Vue.' I cannot attempt to designate the entertainers—representatives, as I was told, of all the principal journals, managers, actors, artists, at least one Attorney-General, and officers in mufti, formed altogether an assembly not too large for every-one to be a sharer in its conviviality. How thoroughly I recognised the type! and how strange it seemed to me, who in England have so often revelled in such parties, scarcely to recognise a single face! Everyone was in good humour, and the spirit of fun pervaded the table.

I think it was at this dinner that I again met my old friend Wallack, still the graceful and polished representative of light comedy. Oscar Wilde was also one of the guests. He had concluded his lectures, and doffed the costume with which he had astonished American audiences, but failed to convert them.

Speeches not too long, recitations never tedious, and songs always amusing, made the evening gallop. Amongst the latter, how delighted I was to hear Barry Cornwall's celebrated song of 'The Sea' given by Mr. Disston. This was a great favourite with me in early days—it exactly accomplished my ideas of melody—and the admirable rendering of it by this gentleman brought vividly to my recollection two celebrated vocalists and personal acquaintances, both of whom I had heard sing it in days gone by: Henry Philipps, who will be remembered by old English play-goers as performing a principal character in Weber's noble opera of 'Der Freischütz,' after its translation into English; and Henry Russell, whose musical compositions and repertory of songs have long been a source of delight both to Americans and English.

Barry Cornwall was a *nom de plume*, his real name was Procter, and he was by profession a banker. This song lighted up a train of memories —of happy hours passed amongst kind friends, when life was young, fresh, and hopeful, and with the thoughts thus engendered I will conclude my sketch of the entertainment, adding thanks to my hosts for what in my mind's calendar will be marked as a 'red-letter day.'

I returned to New York upon the following day, leaving Philadelphia with regret. I suppose that at other periods of the year the city would be clad in a more business-like costume, and present a more sedate appearance. At this time everyone seemed arrayed in holiday garb, and certainly I never saw fairer specimens of beauty than were displayed in the streets by American ladies. It must have been after such an opportunity of enjoyment that the natural eloquence of our Lord Chief Justice, and his vivid appreciation of female loveliness, led him to do some injustice to his fair countrywomen in his comparison of English and American beauty, and which occasioned much comment in the States. I copy a paragraph from the 'Washington Post:'—

'His expressions regarding the American ladies

have imperilled the Lord Chief Justice's chances of ever again finding favour in the eyes of English beauty. An absence of only two months from his native land has served, he says, to win him from the standard of English loveliness, and he can conscientiously challenge only the American type of beauty;[1] wherever he went the American lady was the same charming personage, and the American girl the same self-possessed compound of independent anomalies. He could not sufficiently praise the fresh complexions, the charming manners, and the independence that marked the ladies he counted himself fortunate in meeting, and—fairly turning against his own countrywomen—he unhesitatingly admitted that in his eyes the American women were the more attractive.'

And, if we are to rely upon a correspondent of the 'New York World,' who claimed to have interviewed Lord Coleridge on the steamer that took him to England, his lordship said 'he thought the American women far excelled their English cousins both in beauty and intellect, and he should not be backward to say so on his native soil.'

Now, although I cannot claim either the judgment or experience of Lord Coleridge upon the beauty and fascinations of the fair sex, and pro-

[1] This sentence does not convey so clear a meaning as is usual in the utterances of the noble lord, and probably has arisen from a mistake of the reporter.

bably not his susceptibility to their influence, and although my admiration whilst in the United States was constantly excited, I cannot follow even so great a leader in these opinions; but I am confident that the American ladies will be quite contented, and their countrymen will not be displeased, at the place I assign to them of equality with their English cousins. I am not surprised that Lord Coleridge should have been somewhat ecstatic in his praises, as I myself feel some difficulty in speaking in terms of moderation of a people from whom I received so much kindness, and I am afraid that sometimes the last beauties we meet do appear with the fairest features.

CHAPTER XVIII.

BUFFALO, NIAGARA, AND CHICAGO.

Personal matters—My 'Experiences'—Kind reception—Mr. D'Oyly Carte—Engagement with him—Result—Mr. Phil Robinson—Journey to Salt Lake—Mr. and Mrs. Richards—Buffalo—Falls of Niagara—Visit to—Prospect Hotel—Good living—Description of Falls—Harpies—Persecution by—Sheridan—Anecdote of—Captain Webb—His foolish attempt—Fatal result—Appearance of country—Return to Buffalo—Grand Pacific Hotel—Negro servants—Incidents of journey—Wheel on fire—Apprehension of a forger—Arrival at Chicago—Offensive interviewer—Description by him.

I HAVE not thought it would interest my readers to dwell upon certain matters of a purely personal character, although to a great extent they induced my visit to the United States. I had led an active professional life—somewhat irregular, and broken by the visit to India, which in a former series of my experiences I have described; it was not unnatural, and certainly not a thing of which I had a right to complain, that the clients I had left gathered round me but slowly upon my return, and, whilst I was conducting a case of some notoriety a fit of illness, which became the following day the world's property, shook to their foundation the claims I had upon my former *clientèle*. In truth, I was much affected by the shock, and remained for many months certainly unequal to any serious pressure of work.

I brought out my 'Experiences'—my first literary attempt. They were kindly received, and my mind was inoculated with the idea that I might add something to an exchequer, not over-burdened, by 'Readings' in the United States. My desultory professional career had not given me a claim to the higher honours of the profession, and I was not offered one of those which I might have accepted without loss of position, and so, under the auspices of Mr. D'Oyly Carte, I entered into an engagement to give a certain number of readings in the New World; and the introductions I received from many kind friends in England secured for me the hearty reception from all classes that I have already mentioned.

As a matter of business, I have previously intimated, my adventure was a comparative failure. But whilst I was staying in New York I became acquainted with Mr. Phil Robinson, well known in literary circles both in England and America, and it was considered that I might be useful in some business in which he was engaged, and which rendered a journey to the City of the Mormons necessary. I accepted the offer made me, provided that I was released from my engagement with Mr.

D'Oyly Carte. This gentleman, through his agent, behaved with the greatest liberality and gentlemanly feeling, and I was thus enabled to arrange to start on February 18, 1883, for the Salt Lake City.

Our party consisted, in addition to myself, of Mr. Robinson, a friend of his connected with a London journal, Mr. Richards, a solicitor by profession and a Mormon by religion, and his *only* wife, an accomplished lady, to whose care and management throughout the journey we were much indebted for whatever comfort we enjoyed.

In due time (I forget what length) we reached Buffalo, where we stayed for the night, and, learning that the divergence from our main road to the Falls of Niagara would not occupy more than a few hours, we determined to make the excursion, and accordingly on the following morning started for this celebrated locality, arriving there towards the close of a gray wintry day.

It is well known that a portion of these Falls are presented from the American bank, and another portion from the Canadian, and it was to the latter, through various extortions in the way of tolls, we made our way, and put up at the Prospect Hotel. It is pleasant to record, amongst the vile food that usually signalised our meals during our journey to Utah, one decent dinner, under the auspices of a civil proprietor, and his obliging, pretty wife; and in addition to this, which English travellers will acknowledge to be no small recommendation, the house itself is certainly the best situated at the Falls.

These wonderful products of nature, or its disruption, were clad in winter garb. Huge blocks of overhanging ice impeded, but did not prevent, the descent of the still unfrozen torrents of water. Grandeur, sublime and bewildering, was the impression produced upon my mind at the time. The weather rendered the fur coat, in which I had wrapped myself, a most desirable companion in my wanderings in the locality, of which the general effect was by no means improved by our being pounced upon, from caves which we unwarily approached, by unearthly-looking specimens of the nuisances that beset travellers in Europe, and who profess to exhibit to their unwilling victims the beauties of cathedrals and show-houses. These creatures urged us in scarcely intelligible and half-frozen *patois* to climb to some point or another, at the risk of breaking our necks, or at least of spraining our ankles, entreating us to encompass our legs with boots having huge spikes at the bottom, and looking like instruments of torture, and encase our bodies in garments of many shapes and sizes, dirty, draggled, and torn.

K

Such persecution as this would turn Heaven into a place requiring patience to put up with it, and certainly Niagara in the winter season is not Heaven. I thought of the immoral but practical advice of Sheridan to his son, who had half-killed himself going down into a coal-pit. 'Why did you go?' asked the father. 'One likes to say that one has been,' answered the son. 'Why did you not say so then?' was the wondering suggestion of the unscrupulous parent.

The scene was brought back to my recollection when reading of the insane attempt made by poor Webb to swim across the Falls. I knew something of him in years gone by, through a reckless scrape he got into, and from the consequences of which I believe I rescued him. He must have known the almost hopelessness of the attempt, however sanguine his nature. It was said that there had been a subscription got up for him. Was it poverty that made him feel that the eddies into which he cast himself were not worse than those by which he was already encompassed, and that by a miracle he might escape from both? I suppose that in summer the neighbourhood of the Falls, which is pretty, would enhance their grandeur, although this is much disfigured by buildings of a truly Cockney type.

After passing one night at our comfortable

hotel, we returned to Buffalo. Of this city I have nothing to record. I found the same uncomfortable mode of serving out provisions, and the indifferent character of what was served, the same excellent, cleanly, and well-managed sleeping arrangements, and on the following day we started *en route* for Chicago.

We speedily found ourselves in an immense caravanserai, entitled the 'Grand Pacific Hotel,' where a poor dinner, badly cooked, made a reasonably delicate person regret the necessity for eating. The service was entirely conducted by blacks, and what I thought was the idiotic mummery of the nigger melodists who favour us with their entertainments in England, I found to be the perfectly natural characteristics of the species. Excellent discipline prevailed, and nothing could be better than the bedroom arrangements.

In our journey out there were two incidents worth mentioning, although neither of them appeared to excite any astonishment amongst our fellow-passengers. One was, that a wheel of the carriage in which we were travelling caught fire; this was apparently viewed by the officials of the railway with profound philosophy, and at each station they gathered round the burning wheel, looked with some interest at the progress the fire was making, and threw three or four buckets of water over it. The whistle was heard, and off started the train, jumping and rolling, the wheel emitting sparks, as if it thought it great fun, and so on for some fifty miles, when I suppose conveniences occurred for our changing the carriage, and we were relieved from what was imminent peril.

The other incident we were observers of, although not near enough to join in the evident amusement it excited. A forger had located himself with his wife in one of the carriages. Just as the train was about to start a couple of policemen appeared, who proceeded to perform their duty. Like the wheel on fire it seemed to excite no surprise, and as the train passed on I caught just a glimpse of the felon and his wife, the two policemen, and some mutual friends of both sexes, liquoring up at the bar of the railway restaurant.

At Chicago I met for the first time a specimen of the interviewing community thoroughly offensive. On all other occasions, although I sometimes groaned over their translation of my remarks, I found them courteous, and certainly fair in intention. I had been for a ramble in the streets, and upon my return found that an individual, who reminded me forcibly of Quilp,

[1] This scene reminded me of the well-known picture of 'The Railway Station' by my old friend Mr. Frith.

had taken possession of my room. No apology or excuse seemed to be necessary. Patient waiting had enabled him to catch his fish, and a complacent smile did not add attraction to his countenance, whilst he proceeded to examine me.

Wearily I sat answering questions; I saw no escape, except in his getting fatigued, which appeared impossible. On, on, continued the wearisome, silly, meaningless questions, and although I knew, of course, that he did end at last, I have not the slightest conception how it came to pass, unless indeed I fell asleep, and even his grating voice did not succeed in waking me. I found him gone; it was like recovering from a nightmare.

I forget in what paper an account of this interview appeared, but I remember that I was described as a wretched object, with a worn-out, wearied expression of face, which was, I am sure, after our interview had proceeded a short time, literally true; and, with regard to my person, that I unfortunately laboured under a hump-back, which I assure those readers who have not seen me is not one of my personal characteristics.

CHAPTER XIX.

CHICAGO AND OGDEN.

Energy of people—Departure from Chicago—The journey—Discomforts of—Heated cars—Bitter cold—Wretched food—Bills—Hints to travellers—Negligence of guards—The Rocky Mountains—The prairies—Wanting in interest—Ogden—Decent hotel—Mr. Richards—His business—Plurality of wives not universal—Sustained by persecution—Works upon the subject—Hepworth Dixon—Sir Charles Dilke—Situation of Ogden—A barber's shop—Curiosity—Departure—Arrival at Salt Lake City.

CHICAGO is the centre of much wealth, and one of the most remarkable examples of the energy of the people of the United States, and of the rapidity with which, under their hands, vast plains are metamorphosed into populous cities. It would, however, be foreign to the intention of these pages to dwell upon its history, in which there has been much to command admiration, and I intend no disrespect in saying that its surface presented no features of attraction to the casual visitor; and I was glad, after a two days' sojourn, to quit its grimy streets, and proceed onwards upon my journey.

So again I found my body submitting with such philosophy as was contained in my mind

to the jolting of the train, sometimes going at a
speed which threatened the imminent probability
of its separation from the line, and at other times
dragging on so lazily that hope of reaching the
end of the journey was nearly extinguished—
turned out at intervals from the over-heated cars
into an atmosphere of bitter cold, on the plea of
either breakfast or dinner (Heaven save the
mark!)—ushered into a room sparsely furnished,
huddled together at tables, spread with cloths of
more than doubtful hue, and waiters or waitresses
(they might have been either as far as their
appearance went) rushing at you, and dabbing
down before you in quick succession various extraordinary messes, supposed to be food; then called
upon to pay an extortionate bill, which if you
stopped to investigate you would risk losing your
seat in the machine in which you had to endure
life for the next few hours.

And it is a fact, that ought to be known to
travellers in America, that no notice whatever is
given to them by the guards when the trains
are about to start, and therefore let them, if they
seek the so-called restaurant, or leave their place
for a breath of fresh air, keep their eyes sedu-
lously upon their carriage, or they will run the
risk of being left in an even more abominable
situation than that which they hope will take

them to the end of their journey. To me this seemed interminable, and I shall never forget the wretched nights I passed. On a former page I have given a description of American sleeping-cars, which it is not necessary here to repeat.

On we moved towards the Rocky Mountains, over immense tracts of prairies, within the period of little more than a generation traversed by savages alone. A wonderful sight they are to look upon! so vast! so utterly bewildering! Neither man, beast, nor bird to be seen through the wearisome days of travel. We reached, and we passed over these mountains. Sportsmen and tourists can tell of wild scenes and daring exploits amongst their recesses, but the traveller by rail sees and feels nothing to create either amusement or interest.

At last—and how welcome was the sight!—we reached Ogden, a town at the foot of the range upon the further side. Here for a short time we abode in an hotel, which had more pretensions to comfort in its culinary arrangements than any that recently it had been our fortune to meet with.

Our kind friends Mr. and Mrs. Richards resided in a comfortable house in the town, where the gentleman carried on business as a solicitor, and I believe he was the most confidential adviser of the Mormon association. From conversations I had with his wife, she had apparently no dread of their matrimonial establishment being added to; and I may mention here that plurality of wives is by no means universal amongst members of the sect, nor do I think that the practice is looked upon with favour by many of the more intelligent professors of the religion.

This, however, like so many of the habits and ordinances, with examples of which the history of all ages abounds, is sustained by the persecution to which it has been exposed, and it is the pivot upon which persecution mainly turns. It is defended by its adherents upon religious grounds, whilst the professors of the very various systems of religion which certainly prevail in the United States, however different they may be from each other, unite in a common warfare against the daring innovators of all their systems.

Many works well worthy of being read have been written upon the social phenomenon of the Mormon Pilgrims. Hepworth Dixon has published treatises of much labour and great interest upon the subject, and Sir Charles Dilke has brought all the resources of his mind to its consideration. What I observed I will relate when giving an account of the Salt Lake City, without any pretence of offering a solution of the problem. This, however, I will say, that unless I have greatly mistaken the character of the Americans, nothing bearing the shape of tyranny will ever prevail against a section of their citizens.

Ogden is very beautifully situated in the midst of mountain scenery; the air is bracing and healthy, the shops apparently good, and the people very polite, but possessing the inquiring disposition of Americans generally. And of this I had a vivid example in a barber's shop, where I deposited myself to get shaved. The town is, I should think, little frequented by travellers, and I suspect it got wind that a 'real Britisher' was to be found under circumstances which would make it difficult for him to escape. The proprietor of the shop certainly appeared *this* morning to be much patronised, but it really afforded me great pleasure, after the operation upon me was concluded, to answer the questions, civilly, although without apology, asked me by the people of various denominations, collected together upon this occasion.

We parted from our kind friends with much regret and, after a day journey of a few hours by rail, arrived without incident of any sort at the Salt Lake City, and took up our quarters at the Continental Hotel in that famous town.

CHAPTER XX.

THE CITY OF THE SALT LAKE.

The Mormons—Their singular position—Their belief—Plurality of wives — Patriotism — Locality of city — Fruit-trees—Streets — Other trees—Imaginary effect—Sparrows imported- Their increase —Inconvenience of—Disputes between citizens—A trial—An appeal — The judgment — Danger of collision — Lawlessness — Miners—Assemblage of—Their conduct—Scene at post-office—A recollection—My impression of the miners.

WHAT do I think of Utah, the City of the Dead Lake?—the last encampment of a wandering tribe, hated by the million, and yet possessing an almost supernatural power of resistance against every combination, hourly and daily gaining wealth and influence.

Are they really bigoted believers in a revelation? and is Joe Smith, according to an honest conviction, a successor to Moses and Christ, and one whose words are stamped with the holiness of the Almighty?

These are questions forced upon the mind of every intelligent individual who is brought into contact with this remarkable sect. Since the period that Hepworth Dixon and Sir Charles Dilke dealt with the question, its difficulties have increased rather than exhibited any diminution. The rancour against them seems intensified, whilst it is perfectly clear they will resist to the utmost any endeavour to crush them. And thus exists in the very heart of the United States a sort of *imperium in imperio*, consisting of a people governing themselves by their own laws and religious faith, and in many respects, notably in that of plurality of wives, acting in direct antagonism to the laws of the State of which they are the subjects; and yet American to the backbone, yielding to none in any matter that would be calculated to affect its honour or independence.

Before, however, I proceed to offer, as I do with the greatest diffidence, my impressions of the people, let me endeavour to give my readers some idea of the locality itself. This cannot be done by a description of the scene, presented as it was to my vision in a winter garb, for, bright as was the sun, clear the atmosphere, and invigorating the air, the beauty of the country required the early months of summer to be really appreciated.

Although the city itself appeared to consist only of three or four long and uninteresting streets, it was in point of fact a portion of a square, made up of villas and cottage residences, and every inch of ground was utilised by a fruit tree, apple and peach being the most prominent. The surface of

the land was undulating, and at the period of
the year to which I want the imagination to be
directed, the eye would be met on all sides with
the exquisite colouring of an orchard, and all its
varied hues burnished by the beautiful sunlight
that prevails, whilst the heavy morning dews,
drawn from the boughs by the rising luminary,
would add to the view a perfume that requires to
be experienced, for words are too feeble to describe
it. This flight of imagination is fully justified by
the description of many persons who have witnessed and appreciated the glorious scene.

I ought in mentioning all the open spaces as
being filled by fruit trees to have excepted the
two or three main streets, the one especially in
which the principal hotels were situated. These
were planted with other trees, the names and
nature of which I really do not remember, forming
walks similar to the Boulevards in Paris, and in
the summer time affording agreeable shade for
the passengers, and under most of them seats are
conveniently arranged. The soil was, I imagine,
favourable to the growth of every kind of tree, for
in the town itself, as well as in the surrounding
country, they were extremely luxuriant.

By some unlucky impulse, an inhabitant had
introduced from the mother country a being
previously unknown to the Salt Lake, in the

shape of the genuine, twittering, audacious London sparrow, and it has increased and multiplied to such an extent that the inhabitants are almost prevented from occupying the seats by the noisy possessors of the branches overhead. From the multiplication of the species one is inclined to think they were feathered Mormons that this unlucky importer introduced; they have, in point of fact, become almost unbearable.

Sparrow clubs have been tried, but in vain; the impudent little wretches, like the owners of the soil, seem to flourish the more they are persecuted, and I believe that at last the unhappy citizens will have to apply to the wisdom of the Legislature to find a remedy for the plague. I confess that I used to be rather glad to hear the well-known twitter upon my window-sill, with the remembrance it brought to me of Cockneydom, and committed what was high treason in Utah by throwing to them a few crumbs of bread.

The people in Salt Lake City are divided between those who are Mormons and those who are not; and the former are looked upon with envious eyes, not I imagine for their property in wives, but because they possess loaves and fishes of a real marketable value. In fact they have got hold of the plurality of offices and employments of any importance; and whilst I was staying in the city a cause was going on in the Court of Appeal, upon a question whether they, being outside the State, were capable of holding them. It was on appeal from a decision of a single judge adverse to them, and who was also one of three judges constituting the court; and it was believed that if the judgment had been sustained a very serious and probably sanguinary disturbance would have been the consequence, as the appellants were prepared to resist by force any attempts to carry it out, and there was no doubt that those who would have benefited by the decision were equally determined to support it.

Of course the result could not be predicted, but the Mormons had no reason to despair, since by some means or another they might have succeeded in defying authority. Fortunately, however, the decision was the other way, and the bowie-knives and revolvers were laid aside for another occasion. My informant was the senior judge who gave the casting vote, and who told me that an opposite judgment was looked upon as matter for the gravest dread by the more peaceful citizens.

There can be little doubt that the element of lawlessness does exist to a considerable extent, under a generally peaceful exterior. One day my landlord was kind enough to suggest to me that it was not very desirable to wander about the streets that afternoon, as there would be a large irruption of miners from the neighbouring works, and, although they were not usually aggressive, their society was not of a strictly agreeable character beyond the range of their own circle, and that their play-things were not selected simply for amusement. I was, however, curious to see the workers whom history and fiction had surrounded with so much romantic incident, and the sight was certainly well worthy of the very small amount of trouble it occasioned.

A large crowd environed and occupied the lower part of the main street—I was told upwards of a thousand. I wandered amongst them, not without difficulty, but never meeting the slightest discourtesy or molestation; and yet what an atom I was beside even one of these underground giants, for so they appeared to me, and I really think their average height warrants this expression. Great, broad, muscular, and bronzed almost to blackness; their clothing beggars all power I possess of description—necessity was evidently the only tailor of the mines, and chance the only store.

I remember, I think it was at Bradford, now many years ago, that I was conducting an election petition for my old friend Mr. Forster, now the sitting member. He was Liberal and popular. The neighbouring coal-pits disgorged their contents, who crowded the court and its approaches in a dense mass of robust, powerful forms. I was a favourite as representing the member whom they had assisted in sending to Parliament, and my egress from court was a scene which at the time my modesty would have induced me to avoid, but I remember now *without pain* the grasps of their large, honest hands. The crowd around me *this* afternoon in Salt Lake City brought back a recollection not unpleasing of the cordial welcome of the Yorkshire miners.

At the end of the town where there was this assemblage the post office was situated. It was besieged by many of them inquiring for letters. I expected one and made my way to the box, where I found a stalwart miner in energetic discussion with the clerk, who was unwilling to give him a letter which he claimed as intended for him. I was appealed to, to decipher the address, and fortunately did so in a way to satisfy all scruples. My friend, with a good-natured nod to me and a smile upon his swarthy countenance, wandered off to read what was probably the effusion of a far-distant sweetheart.

I say emphatically that, whatever may be the

L

habits of these exiles from the beaten tracks of society, their physiognomy betrayed no ferocity. They seemed, upon the occasion I have so imperfectly sketched, like a parcel of great boys out for a holiday—noisy, boisterous, and good-humoured; and, upon inquiring on the following day, I learnt that their visit was attended with no scenes that would contradict the view I formed.

CHAPTER XXI.

A TIDELESS SEA.

The Salt Lake—Distance from Utah—Railway—Visit to lake—Disappointment — Scenery — Banks — The pier — A steamer — Return to Utah—Dinner—The food—An Irishman's store—A good meal—Good tea—General Clawson—Extraordinary life—Journey over the plains—Successful merchant—Opposition to government—Successful—Carriages and horses—Roads—Buildings—Tabernacle—Enterprise—Sympathy with the people.

I HAD sojourned for some days in Utah before the question arose in my mind as to why it was called the Salt Lake City. Nothing in the shape of a body of water had presented itself during my wanderings, but I learnt upon inquiry that the lake upon which the name was founded was distant from the city some twenty miles, and was at this period reached by a railway; and our party were kindly given an opportunity of visiting the locality, a train being provided for the transit, and an excellent lunch at the termination of the journey, which was performed with more deliberation than usually attends American proceedings.

I must lay myself open to the charge of ingratitude, by admitting that I do not remember to which of the many friends from whom we met with kindnesses we were indebted for this welcome attention, and I must own that I brought away from the scene itself a sense of disappointment. I am told by visitors to the Holy Land that this feeling usually attends their first visit to places celebrated in Scripture, and I suppose that my imagination had promised a scene of grandeur which the appearance of the lake and its surroundings certainly did not warrant.

Space there undoubtedly was—an expanse of water presented itself, tideless, and so impregnated with salt that no living creature could exist in it, bounded by banks so low as to be scarcely distinguishable. Some feeble attempts had been made to utilise it. A pier of very humble pretensions had been erected upon its margin, and once, as I was told, a steamer had traversed its waters. The immediate country around presented no features whatever of interest—no standpoint from which any view could be obtained. It is sometimes called the Dead Lake, and that appellation suits well my impression of it.

We returned to our hotel in time for what was ludicrously termed dinner at that establishment— in fact, the proprietor used the Old World names, and we were supposed to indulge in breakfast, luncheon, and dinner, but of what the viands were composed no speculation on my part enabled me to arrive at even a proximate conclusion. I saw no strange animals wandering about, and therefore suppose that oxen, sheep, and pigs were utilised for the purpose, but I must leave future travellers who are fond of solving mysteries to discover in what manner.

I remember with gratitude one good meal— this was at a store, which unfortunately I did not discover until about to leave. It was kept by an Irishman, whom I had known something of in the old country—at least, he said so; I had no recollection of the fact. The meal in question consisted of an antique loaf of bread and piece of cheese, which it was easy to see had already been fully appreciated by other animals than bipeds; but I thoroughly enjoyed it, seated upon a beer-barrel, and I must not forget the accompaniment of some good British beer.

Throughout the States—and according to my recollection at the Salt Lake also—tea is reasonably good; milk may always be procured, and I had every reason, here as elsewhere, to be thoroughly satisfied with the sleeping apartments.

Many were the overtures of kindness that our party received whilst staying in the city, and some very substantial proofs were given of it by a gentleman named Clawson, whose career, if all recorded of him be true, would make a very interesting romance. Few, in the history of real life, could recall incidents more varied and adventurous. At Utah he was reputed to be amongst the most wealthy of the Mormons. I do not think that he was owner of more than ten or a dozen wives.

This gentleman, under pressure from the United States Government, was obliged to quit the original settlement of the Mormons, and by the manual labour of himself, wives, and family, struggled over vast plains, inhabited only by savages, dragging with them the waggon containing their goods and chattels, and ultimately succeeded in reaching the spot pointed out by the prophet of his tribe as a future resting-place—the Jerusalem of his people—and here he and his followers have thrived and prospered. A raid was threatened upon the colony by the United States Government, and my friend, equal to all occasions, doffed the garments of peace and arrayed himself in the symbols of war. He became generalissimo of a united and resolute band of fellow-citizens, determined to resist with their lives, if necessary, the attack upon their property and religion.

The elements, however, worked in their favour, and their enemies—as happened in the case of a certain king, who marched up a hill with ten thousand men—marched back again, and thus my friend, who for energy, courage, and perseverance as a civilian, was never surpassed, was dubbed ever after with the title of General.

His business, whatever it was—and I fancy that the merchandise he dealt in might be described by the word 'legion'—was apparently carried on in a shed of most unpretentious appearance and dimensions; but he was the possessor of traps and horses, the former innocent of springs, the latter well bred, but not over well educated. These he very liberally placed at my disposal, and although my arms were nearly strained out of their sockets, and what are called roads in Utah nearly dislocated my bones, I felt very grateful for the opportunity given me of a drive.

Without assuming that my wishes and sympathy can be of value, I do confess that when I looked around this city, and learned that it was the result of Mormon enterprise, and was shown the Tabernacle, and other splendid buildings—the offerings to the belief they have adopted and the God of their imagination—I did most fervently and truly hope that they might be left in peace, and that time and experience might be trusted to abolish excrescences which may now be thought to deface an otherwise noble history.

CHAPTER XXII.

WANDERINGS.

Roads—Absence of birds—A farmhouse—A Mormon emigrant—
His home—His father—A strange coincidence—An optical illusion
—The hospital—Sisters of Mercy—Dr. Benedict—The patients
—Skilful treatment—Frost-bites—Dr. Wolcot—Habits of the
Mormons—Conversation with the doctor—His opinions—The
Tichborne case—A statement—An old acquaintance.

THE weather during my stay at Salt Lake was very beautiful, clear, and invigorating, and, being an early riser, I used to make my way out of the immediate purlieus of the city by one of the two or three roads that were sufficiently civilized for passengers. These were not very good, nor did they extend far.

One feature of the country I thought strange. With the exception of my old friends the sparrows, who evidently preferred a town life, I never saw a bird of any description. I listened in vain for a chirrup that would give life to the surrounding country, and should have welcomed with pleasure the cawing of a crow. On one of my rambles, however, I met with a familiar sight. I had walked a mile or so from the town, when I came upon some farm-buildings, presenting the pleasant features of an English homestead. I cannot attribute to myself any feelings more romantic than a strong desire for fresh milk, and, opening the outer gate, I passed beside familiar cocks and hens, and revelled in a refreshing view of pigs enjoying themselves in manure and a dirty pond, very much as British swine are wont to do, whilst more than one rosy-faced child ceased from similar occupations to look at an object evidently strange.

At the door of the house a decent-looking man ushered me into what might have been the familiar Old World kitchen of a farmhouse. There were four or five respectable-looking females, two or three labourers, and some urchins of more advanced age than those I had already seen. I met with a kindly welcome, and my wants were at once supplied.

My host accompanied me for two or three miles upon my walk, and I learnt from him that he had emigrated from England twenty-five years before, had become a Mormon, possessed more wives than one, was tolerably prosperous, and not discontented with his lot. He had not heard of his family for some years, and his reference to them brought to light a strange coincidence. His father had been one of my father's boatmen, and had obtained through him the post of gatekeeper at the St. Katharine Dock. I remembered him from the description perfectly as one of those who had so often rowed me during my passages up and down Old Father Thames. Thus it happened that my name was an honoured one amongst these boundless plains.

The farmer kept no servants; his wives and elder children assisted him in the cultivation of the farm—a portion of which consisted of apple and peach trees, which were reasonably prolific. I remarked to him on the absence of birds, and he confirmed my observation, but told me that about twenty miles to the south there was a valley in which singing birds, including canaries, abounded. Of this I had no confirmation.

This *rencontre*, and the gossip about the domestic life of a Mormon farmer, greatly interested me, as did also the recollections that his origin brought to my memory of my early days, and I trust the details will not be considered too trivial to be presented to my reader's attention.

Upon one of my matutinal wanderings a strange incident occurred to me; whether attributable to the state of my brain or to some atmospheric phenomenon I am unable to say. I had wandered some yards out of the main road, and seated myself upon a piece of rock which formed a convenient projection. It was at the conjunction of two pathways, one leading upwards to the hills, the other straightforward, and the former pathway rose very gradually.

At this point a foot-passenger came up; we exchanged some few words, and he proceeded to follow the lower road. As I watched him, there appeared with equal distinctness to my vision two forms of the same person—the one proceeding on the lower, and the other upon the upper pathway. Which was the true Simon? I could only determine by having seen him take the lower path. Both forms disappeared at the same time, but the illusion was the most complete that it is possible to imagine, and served me for reflection, not without a little apprehension upon the subject of the state of my organs, for at least the remainder of the day.

About a mile distant from the city, upon one of these roads, perched upon a slight eminence, stands a building of more pretensions than any of those dotted about its neighbourhood. It is a hospital, supported, as I understood, by the liberal aid of all classes of the community, Mormons and Gentiles equally, and open without restriction to everyone who requires aid. I was taken over it by the medical attendant, Dr. Benedict. All the female assistants, including the matron, are members of a religious body of the Roman Catholic persuasion. I went through the different wards, and certainly the self-imposed duties seemed to be admirably performed.

There were no cases that warranted fear of a fatal result, although there were some that excited sympathy for the sufferers. These arose from exposure to the cold upon the neighbouring plains, and in many cases resulted in the loss of one or more limbs—a terrible calamity to poor boys whose only means of living is daily labour. These frost-bites are impossible to be guarded against. One poor fellow, who had lost a hand and foot, told me that he had had the care of a few sheep, and had fallen asleep, only as he thought for a minute or two, and upon waking had found himself frost-bitten, and some operations of a very complicated and difficult nature had been performed by the surgeon. It was easy to see, by the mode in which the eyes of the patient lighted up at this gentleman's approach, how kindly were his ministrations; whilst the Sisters, moving noiselessly from ward to ward, seemed to bring a feeling of happiness to those for whom, without hope of reward on this earth, they sacrifice their days. These exiles in a comparative wilderness are indeed good women.

When I learnt that Dr. Benedict resided and practised in the Salt Lake City, I could not help thinking of the story told by that old libeller, Dr. Wolcot, of our George the Third, who, upon seeing an apple-dumpling upon a cottager's table, exclaimed, 'God bless my soul! how came the apple inside?'

The doctor was a bright, intelligent Irishman, and exactly the personage to create confidence. He certainly impressed me with a belief that he was thoroughly master of his profession. There never was a cheerier face for a sick-room, and how he happened to be encased in the 'crust' of the Salt Lake City was as much a puzzle to me as the apple in the dumpling to the monarch.

I took advantage of the very pleasurable interview I had with him to learn what I could of the habits of the Mormon people. His opinion was most favourable—no instances of cruelty to women, no beggary, and, unless the plurality of wives be a crime, a singular absence of such vices as usually prevail in towns. He remarked upon a fact that I had myself noticed, that the children were very kindly, judiciously, and healthily nurtured. He was not himself a Mormon, nor did it appear to me that he troubled himself much about any doctrinal matters.

It so happened that, amongst other subjects of conversation, my connection with the Tichborne case was mentioned. He told me that the Claimant had many votaries in the neighbourhood, and that there was a person residing in the city who asserted that he was in the boat that rescued the crew of the 'Bella,' and amongst them the Claimant. I understood from the doctor, and also from others, that the man who made this statement was quite respectable, and had been settled for several years where he was at the present time.

I had no particular curiosity upon the subject, and should have thought no more about it if the person in question had not introduced himself to me; and I certainly heard the account he gave with great interest, and I tested his relation in every way that my own memory of the facts deposed to upon the trial would enable me to do, and saw no reason to doubt the intended truth of the story.

He told me that he was at the time the steward of the vessel that had picked up the wrecked crew of the 'Bella,' that he had himself first settled at Melbourne, and afterward made his way to the Salt Lake; and he further added that two of his comrades who were present at the rescue were working in a neighbouring mine.

This narrative is only one of many circumstances that lead me to believe that, about the time of the Tichborne adventure, there must have happened some of the incidents related, and that probably a shipwrecked crew was picked up;

but whether such a solution accounts for the stories, some of them wild enough, but some clothed with an air of probability, surrounding this extraordinary case I will not pretend to say. Certainly from some cause or another there exists in the Salt Lake City an intense curiosity and interest upon the subject.

At one of those melancholy farces described by our worthy host as a dinner I recognised a face that I thought was familiar to me, and found that it appertained to a gentleman who, some years ago, was well known in London society, and was at one period a member for an English borough. I do not suppose that he would have the slightest objection to his name being mentioned, but, not having his sanction, I avoid doing so. He had become largely interested, whilst in England, in mining speculations, and had taken up his abode in the Salt Lake City that he might superintend the works of a particular mine, and I gathered from him that he was likely to remain a long time in the neighbourhood.

He mingled his groans with mine about the provisions, but bore with resignation a state of things that presented no single ray of hope for its improvement. To my great regret he was called away suddenly, and had not returned before my departure.

CHAPTER XXIII.

THE PRESIDENT.

Mr. Phil Robinson—Testing his voice—Lecturing—My augury—Widows of Brigham Young—Their appearance—Mr. Clawson's wives—Heads of the community—Their views—Apostates—Ridiculous stories—Not believed—The clergy—A murder trial One person convicted—Subsequent trials—A jury—Difficulty of obtaining one—The court—Chief Justice Hooper—Jurymen—Unwillingness to act—Fear of consequences—Unfortunate result—Much lawlessness—President Taylor—His appearance—Conversation with him—His views—The Tabernacle—Plurality of wives—Journalism—The 'Herald'—Mr. Byron Groo—Pleasant hours.

Mr. Phil Robinson, who had written an interesting book upon the Mormon community, and was also well known for other works both in England and America, was, during our stay in Utah, solicited to give a course of lectures, and was advised before doing so to try the compass and management of his voice in some large space; and accordingly, the theatre, an extensive and handsome building, being placed at his disposal, he made the experiment in the presence of a party of friends. I augured favourably, and I believe correctly, of his probable success.

Amongst those who were present to hear him were some half-dozen wives, or I suppose I ought to call them widows, of the late Brigham Young, a former President of the Mormon community. They occupied what with us would be called the proscenium box. I was duly introduced, and I suppose they were a fair example of the ladies who are contented with divided husbands. I should have been glad to have been able to discover something to distinguish them from the ordinary British wife, but really they seemed to me an assemblage of nicely dressed, quiet ladies, and apparently upon very sociable terms with each other.

I was presented to some of Mr. Clawson's wives, who gave me the same impression. I had several opportunities of conversing with some of the principal members of the persuasion, including the President himself. There never appeared the slightest objection to afford information, or to discuss the theory and practice of their religion. They alleged that they had by their perseverance and industry made a wilderness into a flourishing community, and thus obtained into their hands the control and management of many of the offices of emolument and trust in the city—that those who had done nothing now endeavoured to despoil them—that plurality of wives was a mere stalking-horse, and that they might have just as many as they pleased, without censure, if they would only

M

part with certain possessions, much more appreciated by the Gentiles.

There have been apostates from the body, women generally, who have circulated stories about supposed Mormon ceremonies and rites of a very similar character to those attributed in the middle ages to the Jews; but the good sound sense of the Americans, even if it does not prevent some of them coveting their neighbour's goods, have estimated such romances at their proper value. My informants asserted that what is only an attack upon their temporal position is supported and embittered by the clergy of all denominations; and this statement can readily be believed by those who have watched the habits of Churches in all ages, and in every country.

It is very long before legal machinery can in a new country be got into working order, and the following instance is an example of its incapacity at Utah to deal with certain exigencies liable to occur. Some two years before I visited the Salt Lake City a murder had been committed, the details of which are unimportant. As however I understood, there had been a trial, and one of two persons charged with the crime had been convicted. The jury having disagreed about the case of the other, were consequently discharged, and he since that period had remained in custody.

There had been periodical attempts to try him, but it was found impossible to obtain a jury within the limited jurisdiction of the court. Another attempt was to be made, and on the day fixed for its coming on I was accommodated with a seat upon the Bench (to use the phraseology adopted in our papers upon these occasions), beside the learned Chief Justice Hooper. All the persons competent to be jurymen had been summoned; they presented the appearance of substantial yeomen.

The prisoner, well dressed, and quite at his ease, was standing in the dock, but, as was intimated to me by the judge, everyone knew beforehand that the whole affair was a mere farce, and that a jury would never be obtained. Some of those called were challenged by the prisoner—others on the part of the prosecution—some declared that they were biassed, and others begged themselves off on the plea of health. There were seven, however, who were passed, and I, not being behind the scenes, imagined that the requisite number would be reached, but the judge smiled at my delusion.

'Oh,' said he, 'they' (speaking of those who had answered) 'know all about it, and if they had thought there was any chance of a trial we should not have seen one of them. The fact is, no one doubts the prisoner's guilt, but he has a great many friends, and the jury feel too much regard for their own lives to risk finding the fact.'

The result of the failure on this occasion was to postpone the attempt for another six months, and in the meanwhile the accused would be comfortably lodged and fed in gaol.

The impression of the Chief Justice was that the man who *had* been convicted was innocent; he, however, had been condemned to hard labour for life, and was depending for his release upon the conviction of his alleged associate.

This is a wild state of things—certainly not attributable to the judge, of whom everyone spoke as a learned, firm, and conscientious exponent of the law—of which also the community of the Mormons were innocent, for they formed no part of the machinery of the court. It was the Chief Justice whose casting vote I have already alluded to as having established, for the time at all events, the privileges of the Mormons. But I am very much mistaken if there is not a slumbering mass of lawlessness throughout the district, which only wants a match applied to it to burst into a flame; but what ultimate result it will bring about would require much wiser and better-informed men than myself to form the most remote conclusion.

I have postponed until nearly the last of the details of my visit the most interesting circumstance that occurred to me. This was my introduction to President Taylor, High Priest (I use my own expression), head man, and ruler of the Mormon host; and as upon the Pope are supposed to be descended the powers of the Saviour, so in this personage the powers of Joe Smith, the great Prophet of Mormonism, and his authority, are vested.

Involving as this belief does the existence of supernatural power in an individual, and whose authority is more or less dependent upon the belief, there can be no doubt that in these times of scepticism upon all dogmatic questions it is most interesting to come into contact with a person supposed to be so endowed.

The first time I saw him was at his own house, at a sort of reception, and I naturally observed closely his appearance and manner. As far as these went he wanted nothing but the 'apron and lawn sleeves' to make a model for an English bishop. It was difficult to define his age, but it must have been much over sixty; his countenance was pleasing and benevolent, and he reminded me very forcibly of the late Lord Chancellor Hatherley. He talked with the air of confidence which is apt to distinguish those who are not subject to contradiction—slowly, and as if his words were to be collected and treasured.

I had, of course, no opportunity of private conversation with him at this interview, but upon a subsequent occasion he did me the honour to invite me to drive with him. He took me over the Tabernacle, which is capable of holding several thousand persons, and said to be remarkable for its acoustic qualities; certainly it was impossible not to be convinced of the untiring industry and energy of the people. He did not avoid the questions respecting the plurality of wives, which he justified for reasons that can scarcely be discussed in a work of so little pretension as mine, and also upon the ground—which is certainly intelligible enough— that one of the objects in view was a speedy increase of population when making a settlement upon hitherto uninhabited plains.

He professed himself a firm believer in the Scriptures, in their entirety and literal sense. Agnosticism was a word that had not yet reached Utah. He said there was nothing in Holy Writ inconsistent with subsequent revelation, and such revelation had been made to Joe Smith, and the Mormon community was ordained and governed under its provisions.

During this interview I scarcely opened my lips. The words flowed from his naturally, and with a certain amount of smooth eloquence, dictatorial rather than persuasive. I cannot think he was a man of high mental powers or enlarged grasp, and he did not disclose much, and certainly not deep, reading. From what I heard of his predecessor the Prophet, that individual possessed the attributes of a politician, and the tact of a man of the world; and much regret was felt by many of the body that, in the troublous times that were threatened, a ruler of greater energy did not govern the action of affairs, instead of one amiable, kindly, beloved, and respected, but not credited with the force of character calculated to encounter the great emergencies which were more than dimly showing themselves in the political horizon.

If I had been writing a political treatise, or affecting to give more than a superficial view of the curious anomalies contained in the inner life of this remarkable city, I should have found much to assist such an object in its journalism. There were two leading papers, written with much ability, which sufficiently proved that, although smouldering, the elements of discord were certainly of a formidable character, and not very deeply seated below the surface; and I shall await with interest the development of a future which will probably present features of much public importance.

I had the pleasure of many an agreeable gossip with the editor of the 'Herald,'[1] Mr. Byron Groo.

[1] This journal is designated by a local name which has escaped my memory.

He allowed me the privilege of entering the editorial den at all times, and a day not always presenting features of interest in the town was much enlivened by the opportunities given me of enjoying his conversation. He was one of those men to whom one seems drawn instinctively, and in saying good-bye to, probably for ever, one element of pleasure is withdrawn from your life.

CHAPTER XXIV.

FROM UTAH TO LIVERPOOL.

Journey to Ogden — Railway— Crowding — Miners—Appearance - Conduct—A little child—Departure from Ogden—Route—Kansas City—Denver—Unpleasant journey—Arrival at New York—Dulness—Barbers' shops—Sir Edward Archibald—His death—His brother—The post office—A bank—Steamer 'Arizona '—Departure from New York—Appearance of vessel—Its first trip—Our voyage — Fellow-passengers -- Easter Sunday — Accident — Delay — Diminished speed—Similar accidents—A storm—Anxious times-- Arrival at Liverpool—Reflections upon accidents — Incidents relating to them—Tremendous speed—Danger arising from.

On the 12th or 13th of March, A.D. 1883, I took my final leave of the Salt Lake City, availing myself of a local train which stopped at Ogden, a journey of a few hours. It might be mentioned, as one of the symbols of equality, that people of all ranks were crowded together in the same carriage without distinction. The clothing of some of the travellers (or the want of it) did not seem to be of any moment, neither did it appear necessary to consider the amount of accommodation afforded by the conveyances; and I could not help noticing, here as elsewhere in the United States, the good temper that prevailed, and the politeness exhibited towards one another by some very wild specimens of the human race.

Amongst these there were several individuals who hailed from the mining districts, and were ushered into the carriage, of which I was one of the occupants, when it was already apparently full —one in his shirt-sleeves, not remarkable for cleanliness, with a gaudy velvet waistcoat and fustian trousers, the waistcoat bedecked with gold chains that appeared to be of value, and his hands—such hands!—loaded with really costly rings. I made way for him, and, beyond squeezing me rather more than was pleasant, I suffered no inconvenience from his contact. Opposite to us (I speak in the plural number as there was no space between) sat a poor woman, with a child in her arms. The little thing was attracted by my double's jewellery, and was made very happy by being allowed to play with it.

The other miners shook themselves into places somehow or another, and, although I certainly should not have selected this journey as a specimen of pleasant travelling, it was by no means so disagreeable as many I underwent whilst in the States. I was very glad upon my arrival at Ogden to meet my former fellow-travellers from New York—Mr. and Mrs. Richards, and, remaining there until the following day, started upon the wearisome journey homeward.

The line of country through which the train passed was different from that by which I had come. We stopped at Kansas City and Denver, both having sprung up to their present dimensions with that rapidity which seems characteristic of all American undertakings. Of the journey I can record nothing new—the same abominable substitute for victuals, and wretched sleeping berths— violent rapidity, creative of an expectation of being thrown off the line, contrasting with an occasional dawdling, as if the very engine itself had fallen into a doze.

At last on Sunday we were disgorged from our prison, at the station in New York, arriving in the middle of the day—a broiling sun overhead (notwithstanding the season)—not a vehicle of any kind to be obtained, and so the passengers had to handle their own luggage, and get to their respective destinations in the best way their cramped legs would enable them. Fortunately my old rooms were not far off, and heartily glad I was to find myself once more in such comfortable quarters.

I have not, I think, mentioned before that in long journeys the system appears to be, that travellers take with them only such luggage as they require upon the way, and the heavier articles are despatched by what is called express; and it is quite necessary to remember this, as there are no porters upon the line specially to assist in the conveyance of packages, although there are many loafing negroes who will do so 'for a consideration.'

I cannot find much to praise in a Sunday in New York. As in London, it seems a sort of penitential day; and even the 'barbers' shops,' a great institution in all American cities, are closed after mid-day, and although upon the highest authority 'cleanliness is allied to godliness,' an American citizen must get up early if he wants a clean chin upon what they as well as we call the Sabbath. I do not think anyone shaves himself in New York; large barbers' shops are attached to the principal hotels, and a dozen shaving-brushes seem always at their work of preparation for the razor, which is most skilfully handled at a quarter-dollar per face.

How often it happens that the living are reminded of those they have known and valued by learning that they are no more! In the obituary of the 'Times,' a few days back, the announcement appeared that Sir Edward Archibald, late Consul-General at New York, had terminated his useful and honourable career at Brighton. When I first arrived in the States he had been amongst the earliest to bid me welcome. He performed that kindly office, as he was wont to do to all his fellow-countrymen not entirely unknown who visited the city in which he had for so many years represented his Government and its interests.

He might have known that I had been a friend and old circuit companion of his brother, a lawyer of unwearied industry and great legal attainments, rewarded by a judgeship too late for its comparative leisure to amend the strain that had attended a slow but conscientious intellect at the Bar. He died shortly after his elevation to the Bench, much beloved and regretted.

I dined with Sir Edward at New York, and remember talking to him of his brother, and referring to my last meeting with him in a railway carriage, whilst travelling in Switzerland the year before his death. He was younger than the consul, who, although attaining a ripe age, seemed when I saw him in the States to be commencing a new youth.

I found, upon my arrival at New York from Salt Lake City, that my kind friends Colonel and Mrs. Morse had left for England, and that 'Iolanthe' had ceased to captivate Lord Chancellors. I was too much knocked up by the journey to seek any pleasure but that afforded by entire rest. I obtained letters at the post office that had been lying there for some time—and, by-the-by, I may here say that for excellent arrangement, punctuality, and civility on the part of the officials, no institution could be better conducted.

After undergoing a lengthened and suspicious investigation at a bank upon which I held a bill, I sought the offices of the Guion Packet Line, and secured a berth in the famous Atlantic steamer 'Arizona,' advertised to start for Liverpool upon the following Tuesday, the 20th of March, at three o'clock in the afternoon.

At this hour, after taking leave with much regret of Madame Galliard and her accomplished daughter, I deposited myself on board for the voyage home. The vessel was not so large as the Cunard boat in which I had gone out, the 'Servia.' That was 8,000 tons, and the 'Arizona' but 5,000, still a very imposing ship. I did not think it so trim, nor generally so neatly and cleanly kept, as the 'Servia;' but it had a fine crew, and the captain presented the appearance, and under circumstances of much anxiety exhibited all the qualities, of a thorough seaman.

The vessel itself was, I believe, the quickest of the passenger-boats crossing the Atlantic with the exception of the 'Alaska,' belonging to the same company. It had not been long upon the station, and was unfortunate in its first trip, having encountered an iceberg, which very seriously damaged its fore-part. No blame was attached to the officers, and the resisting power of the vessel was said to have exhibited itself in a remarkable degree.

From what I have already said of the voyage across the ocean, my readers will conclude that I did not commence my journey back with any pleasurable sensations, although the night-cars upon the American railways reconciled me to the comparative miseries of a sea-voyage, and made the berths appear positively luxurious.

I was singularly fortunate in my fellow-passengers. Amongst them was a lady, the wife of a gentleman of rank, Madame Macchetta, who had made her *début*, under the auspices of Mr. Gye at the Covent Garden Theatre, as *prima donna* in the opera of the 'Traviata' with marked success, but had quitted the stage upon her marriage. She possessed a lovely voice, was a first-rate musician, and most kind in the exhibition of her powers for the amusement of her fellow-passengers.

There was also an extremely well-informed major in the American service, who had seen much of the world and society in all parts of it; an eminent New York doctor, who did the best he could to allay a bad cough with which I had come aboard, and was, as distinguished medical men of all countries usually are, a charming social addition to our party.

There was also an engineer, with whom I struck up an acquaintance, and whose explanation of the minutiæ of the machinery working the enormous structure that was bearing us gave me the sort of feeling that too familiar a knowledge of the veins, muscles, and arteries of the human body sometimes causes to anyone at all anxious about his own structure.

We steamed on, then, in pleasant companionship and fair weather, at a rate of speed averaging twenty miles an hour, until Easter Sunday, when in the middle of our dinner the vessel came to a dead stop. The captain, who was at the head of the table, preserved an unmoved countenance, and did not immediately quit his place.

Something, however, was clearly wrong with the machinery. The officers were not communicative, and there we lay for five wearisome and anxious hours. Fortunately a dead calm prevailed. From the innermost depths of the ship came noises as of work going on—the crew could or would tell nothing of the cause. At the end of the above time, with two or three puffs, the huge machine toiled on, no longer with the inspiring speed which had attended its movements previously, but like an animal, after an injury, as if with pain and difficulty.

Naturally I sought my friendly engineer, to see

what light he could throw upon the subject. He, however, could only speculate upon the cause, which he attributed to an injury to one of the cylinders; and I gathered afterwards that a bar of iron connecting the main cylinder with the rest of the works had broken, and thus rendered it useless for the remainder of the voyage. He explained that, with fine weather and favourable winds, we might make port in safety.

In my 'Experiences' I have referred to two railway accidents occasioned by a similar cause, and it is one that no human foresight can guard against. It was very fortunate for our safety that it happened in calm weather, thus enabling certain temporary measures to be effected, the main cylinder, however, remaining useless.

I had determined to land at Queenstown, but we were unable to make for that harbour. Thick weather came on upon the Thursday following the accident, and the wind rose, blowing a gale. The captain, owing to the state of the weather, was unable to take any observation, and we saw nothing of him in the cabin. The wind continued to increase, and as it was impossible to ascertain our exact position, the captain thought it prudent to lie to, which we did the whole of Thursday night. We got on sometime on Friday, and reached Liverpool the following day.

N

Much anxiety was undoubtedly felt during the storm; those who crawled upon deck reported that the captain, clothed in a 'sou'-wester,' was upon the bridge with the principal officers, assisting practically in sounding, and striving to ascertain our position by any *débris* brought up by the line. The wind was howling around us, but I am not conscious that we shipped many seas. Everyone knew the danger there must be in lying to on a dark night, and, as we were within reach of the Irish and Welsh coasts, anticipations varied between being run into, and drifting upon the shore. The faces of all the passengers were grave, but neither men nor women displayed fear.

I believe that a light upon the Welsh coast informed the captain where we were, and with daylight and his admirable seamanship we were able with contented minds to enjoy our last meal on board, in the course of which much appreciation was shown of the conduct of captain, officers, and crew.

This experience naturally increased the interest that I have already alluded to in the proceedings of these ocean giants that traverse the waves, and during the last twelve months there has been much to keep it alive. Amongst many other notable incidents, the anxiety of the public in London and New York has been centred upon the adventures of two of the steamers belonging to the White Star Company—the 'Britannic' and 'Celtic'— one of them upon her passage to England, and the other upon the voyage to New York, the former drifting exposed to tremendous weather for nearly a month, the other for more than twenty days. In both the calamity occurred from damage to the machinery, and the records of such injuries, terminating like that on board the 'Arizona' without any sensational result, are endless. Some of the conclusions are satisfactory, although by no means pleasant during their continuance.

It may, however, be truly said that these Atlantic steamers are built with the utmost attention and skill, and when through some accident to the machinery they are left with little motive power, they stand magnificently against the assaults of the ocean in its greatest fury; and this they could only do by the fact of being navigated by most efficient captains, officers, and crew. Indeed, too great praise cannot be extended to all the companies for the selection of those in whom so important a trust is reposed.

But is there not a dangerous rivalry which is being carried out at the risk of human life? And is not machinery, however fine, tried unnecessarily by the tremendous speed exacted from it?

There is another reflection that has presented

itself to my mind in reading some of the recent accounts, that during the encounter by these disabled vessels with the winds and waves, assistance is constantly offered, and refused. By it in some instances the lives of passengers might be saved and their suffering at all events shortened. This would, however, involve a question of salvage, and a black mark to the captain's name.

It was the pride of the old 'Cunarders' (I believe they were not at first starting a company) that the first and foremost duty enforced upon those entrusted with their command was consideration for the passengers, their comfort, and above everything their safety. Such ought to govern every other thought.

I know no fact that would justify me in charging any one of the companies, or any individual, with neglecting this paramount duty, but it cannot be denied that upon both sides of the Atlantic there have been murmurs to the effect that it has not (apparently at all events) been taken into sufficient account. But I firmly believe that those of my readers who have laboured through my above attempt at being useful, and suggesting warnings, would, as probably I should myself, if thinking of a voyage to the United States, find out what steamer had been advertised as having made the quickest passage ever known, and forthwith engage a berth on board it.

CHAPTER XXV.

HOME AGAIN.

The Mersey—Adelphi Hotel—London—Sir James Paget—State of health—Reflections—Politics—Gladstone—The clergy—Bishops—Curates—Science—Vivisection—Oxford Convocation—The Law - Lords Justices—Court of Appeal—Literature—Mudie—Philosophy—Science—Travels—Lyndhurst—Lytton—Biographies—Espinasse—Pomposity of—Anecdote of Lyndhurst—Traits of Lord Lytton—Gambling anecdote—Superstition of gamesters—Anecdotes of—Hope-Scott—Her Majesty.

March 31, 1883.—It was with a feeling of relief and thankfulness that I awoke this morning to find myself upon the calm waters of the Mersey, the stately vessel moving in dignified repose amongst the smaller craft, upon which a bright sun was casting its rays. It was England again, and although the hopes with which I left it had not been realised, and the fatigues I had undergone had greatly shaken my health, even after so short an absence I was able to appreciate the feelings so often described by travellers upon their return to their own shores.

We soon arrived at the quay at Liverpool; no trouble was created by the Customs, and we quickly got possession of our luggage. The captain had changed the tarpaulin in which he had last presented himself to my eyes, the look of anxiety had passed from his face, and as he went out his pleased expression showed a consciousness not only of his having performed his duty well, but also that we all felt that he had done so. The Adelphi Hotel received me amongst other passengers, and a good wash upon a steady floor, a comfortable English dinner, and a bed that one could turn round in, were events.

I reached London the following day, and under the advice of Sir James Paget left it again almost immediately. This is all I need say about my own life, and it is probably more than many of my readers will think worth recording, but it will account for the delay that has intervened between my return and the publication of my impressions of America and its people.

During my absence in the States two biographies had appeared, not only well worthy of a place in the library, but peculiarly interesting to me—those of Lords Lyndhurst and Lytton, the former by Sir Theodore Martin, and the latter by his lordship's son.

I had ventured, amongst the slight sketches that some time ago were kindly received by the public, to refer to the knowledge I had of both these noblemen, and, judging from the contents of the volumes in question, with no incorrect opinion.

Sir Theodore Martin, however, does not possess personal knowledge of his subject, and seems to have thought more of sustaining its character for political consistency than other great qualities that he possessed—to show that the slanders poured upon him by Lord Campbell were unfounded in truth—and in many respects he succeeded. But who, except members of his own family, or some unfortunate junior at the Bar, ever cared for what Lord Campbell either said or thought? No sane person will believe that one who was received, admired, and courted to the time of his death by the most renowned and honourable of men (as was Lord Lyndhurst) had been guilty of mean and dirty actions. Can the same eulogy be pronounced of his maligner?

Lord Lyndhurst was admired for his statesman-like qualities, and beloved for his social ones. Before he became one of the law officers of the Crown he had never received emolument, nor, as far as I know, expressed a leaning to either party; and before he accepted the Solicitor-Generalship he took the opinions of Mr. Denman (afterwards Lord Chief Justice) and Mr. Reynolds, a well-known Liberal, both upon his circuit, and who considered that he had not previously done any act disentitling him to accept office. Subsequent charges have been fully dealt with by his biographer.

What, I confess, interests me much more, and which I should have liked having had dwelt upon with greater particularity by an author so well able to do so, are the qualities which rendered him so popular with the profession, and also in private life.

I remember at the very commencement of my career a gentleman named Espinasse, who was a briefless barrister, hanging on the skirts of Messrs. Clarkson and Bodkin, and doing a variety of services for them, including a stray brief in a hopeless case. Somehow or another he got appointed to a small debts court at Rochester, and when the county courts were created he had the good fortune to be transferred to one of them. He was always pompous enough, and with his appointment his pomposity increased. He insisted upon barristers coming before him in forensic costume. The court, upon the occasion I am speaking of, was held in a country pot-house, and a young fellow to whom, as in those days to most of us, 1*l.* 3*s.* 6*d.* was no small boon, without being aware of the rule arrived minus the necessary apparatus. 'Who are you, sir?' said my lord. Name given. 'I do not know you, sir!'

He was not heard, and thus gross injustice was done that a punctilious judge might gratify his vanity.

My readers must begin to wonder why a ridiculous creature like this should be introduced into a reference to one of the greatest lawyers that ever lived. I will tell them. It is because I witnessed a scene before Lord Lyndhurst (it was, I believe, at Maidstone), and he as Lord Chief Baron was presiding in the Crown Court, when a juvenile barrister appealed to him to put off a case, as his wig had miscarried. 'Well!' said his lordship, 'I do not think your wisdom consists in your wig, but if it does not inconvenience anyone it can be postponed, or try your luck without one if it does.'

The interesting biography of Lord Lytton, by his son, has afforded proof that I was not wrong in the estimate I formed of some of the traits of his character, and that the presence of superstitious feeling at times developed itself in his actions and writings. In the notice I ventured to offer of him, an anecdote may be remembered strongly illustrative of this, in his absolute refusal to play whist in the same room as a gentleman named Townend, who, as he considered, always brought him bad luck. The circumstance related by his biographer of his early gambling adventure, and his viewing with horror the expression of his countenance afterwards, is most characteristic of the man. He had no meanness, and much vanity.

I suppose that amongst those with whom the turf and games of chance are the principal employments of life, and who pride themselves upon their successful powers of calculation, there is no class of mankind more strongly imbued with a spirit of superstition. At a whist-table, a stranger ignorant of the game would be lost in wonder to notice the anxiety of the finest players upon the subject of seats and cards; and there are gambling bouts upon record where discarded packs have nearly reached the ceiling. Some players there are who openly profess to despise luck, and who, when they think themselves unobserved, turn their chairs round some supposed magic number of times. A friend of mine, an excellent player, contemned in scornful language those who believed in such puerilities, but one day, when playing 'piquet,' refused to continue because I, having bad luck, betted upon him.

This is a subject I need not dwell upon; the reference I have made to it will bring plenty of examples to the minds of such of my readers as may, however occasionally, be present at a card-table.

The relatives of a great lawyer—Hope-Scott—have presented a life to its readers, including a singular mixture of religious devotion and legal subtlety, these two qualities not altogether separated from each other. I remember their possessor well; he was a fine advocate in Parliamentary committees, although not, I think, so successful as his great rival Austin, whose advocacy was not aided by any devotional assistance.

Another work, emanating from Her Majesty, has made the great body of the public, who thoroughly appreciate her pleasing style, regret that State reasons should confine her to the comparative trivialities of her most important and interesting life. Still we catch a glimpse of a mind which, whilst weighted by heavy responsibility and natural anxiety, and exhibiting deep sympathy with her subjects, their misfortunes and struggles, can nevertheless enjoy with keenness the simple pleasures of a country existence. Long may it be before anyone else is called upon to record the history of a reign of which she takes herself the lowest estimate.

CHAPTER XXVI.

MEN OF MARK.

A dinner-party—Editor of the 'Times'—Abraham Hayward—His appearance—Occupation—Bernal Osborne—His characteristics—Last meeting—Sir George Jessel—His ability—Self-confidence—Good-nature—Mr. Justice Byles—A Unitarian—Election failure—Anecdote of.

Amongst a large party comprising many brilliant and well-known characters, at a dinner given some two years ago by Mr. Alfred Rothschild, I observed seated near me a man who seemed engrossed in thought, and scarcely joined in the conviviality of the party. There was, however, something about him that demanded attention. His was a fine intellectual head and face. I learnt afterwards that this gentleman was Mr. Chenery, editor of the 'Times.' His qualities have been enlarged upon by most of his contemporaries. How much I regretted having lost the opportunity of even a few words with the representative of such a power!

Occasionally in the afternoon, walking down Pall Mall, a personage was to be seen who could not fail to attract attention. He was a man of advanced age, with a bent figure, walking rapidly, and apparently occupied by his own thoughts. His face indicated a Hebrew origin, and possessed much intelligence. Another marked character this, which has recently passed from the scene. Abraham Hayward was by profession a barrister, by rank a Queen's Counsel, although I am not aware that he ever conducted a cause.

He was a literary man, although he could scarcely be called an author, and his highest ambition seemed to be to deal with the works of others, his treatment of which was much coloured by the politics of the author, for Hayward, although never seeking office, was a bitter politician and unmerciful adversary. If one can judge by the numerous invitations that attended his career, he was a courted and popular guest in circles whose favour he was said greatly to value. Although promoted to the rank of Q.C., he was not elected a Bencher of the Inn to which he belonged—a circumstance not attributable to his having been briefless, as Hallam the eminent historian, and the agreeable author of 'Tom Brown's School-days' both received that compliment. I fancy (but here I speak without authority) that, as he inherited the bitterness of 'Croker,' so he succeeded to him in the pages of the 'Quarterly Review.' I have been in his company upon two or three occasions. The last was at Mr. Lionel Lawson's, when he was paying much attention to Mrs. Langtry. It recalled a fairy-tale to my memory.

Another brilliant light of society has been extinguished, one who even in an assembly so critical as the House of Commons always caught the Speaker's eye—Mr. Bernal Osborne. He was full of fun, and really possessed much natural humour, occasionally spiced with somewhat bitter sarcasm, and, up to a year or two before his death, high animal spirits, as well as much genuine wit, were his characteristics. It was said that Hayward would never meet him if he could help it, and I can well imagine that a *raconteur* of the weight (1 will not say heaviness) of the former's calibre would be disconcerted at the probably inopportune hilarity of the latter. The last time I met Osborne was shortly before I went to America. He was about to enter the Reform Club—death stamped upon his countenance.

I was not intimate with the lawyer whose name I regret having to add to the obituary of those who have in more or less degree been connected with my career. The legal profession sustained a great loss in the death of Sir George Jessel. He was a man possessing a singular grasp of mind, and was one of the few Chancery barristers whom I ever met with capable of dealing skilfully and powerfully with facts. Probably no man ever thought so much of his own powers, with so much justice. At the same time, his conceit extended to matters where undoubtedly it was not justified. He imagined himself to be a first-rate whist player, an opinion not joined in by the members of clubs at which he played. He frequented two to which I belonged, one at Brighton, and the well-known Portland Club at the corner of Stratford Place, Oxford Street; and he would not have hesitated to tell the late James Clay or Johnny Bushe what they ought to have played, any more than he would have done to snub a junior at the Bar, or for that matter a leader either. He was, however, essentially goodnatured and kindly, was a great sufferer from illhealth, which he bore bravely, and with him the Bench lost one of its most distinguished members.

Another legal worthy has recently disappeared from this mundane scene—Mr. Justice Byles. He had long quitted the Bench, but was still a character in and about the neighbourhood of London—he and his white horse—both of such grave temperament that, although moving slowly upon this world, their thoughts were apparently occupied with another. Both of them disappeared at the same time, but the death of the former only has been recorded.

Sir Bernard Byles was a very old man, and his

origin was somewhat obscure. He came originally from Norfolk or Suffolk. Mr. Veasey, the banker of Huntingdon, remembered him well. Although possessing much dry humour, he was habitually serious, and a most rigid attendant at a Unitarian Chapel. At the Bar his competition was by no means to be despised. Such men as Wilde, Talfourd, and, later on, Fitzroy Kelly, were formidable antagonists, and they did not despise him. He was an acute and subtle advocate, and although springing from the ranks was a Tory, and a warm supporter of the Corn Laws, in defence of which he wrote a book, and as an advocate for which he made an appearance, cheered by the solemn support of country parsons and by the voice of the squirearchy, as candidate for Aylesbury.

Upon this occasion an amusing incident occurred which put a premature end to his Parliamentary ambition. He was addressing a meeting with his accustomed plausibility, when he was interrupted by a stalwart farmer in somewhat the following terms: 'Muster Byles, do you go to that ere chapel in Essex Street?'[1] 'My dear friend,' answers the candidate, 'religious belief'—he was not allowed to proceed further. The question was repeated. Again he attempted to evade an answer, but his questioner insisted, and a neighbouring parson, one of his

---

[1] A well-known Unitarian Chapel.

supporters, suggested to him the necessity of answering. 'Well,' he said, 'certainly I do, but——' The remainder of his reply was drowned in howls and hisses. He was staying at an hotel, opposite to which was a dead wall, and which the first thing the next morning was covered with placards, somewhat to the following effect, but in varied and by no means complimentary phraseology: 'Brother Christians, will you vote for the scoffer of your Saviour?' A post-chaise consigned the unfortunate candidate to his chambers and to clients, indifferent to his place of worship and keenly appreciative of his book upon 'Bills.'

He made a good, useful judge, and was quick at taking his notes in shorthand; but latterly his memory failed him in a remarkable manner, and he resorted to unusual means to conceal its failure. Mr. Baron Huddleston will remember an instance of this in a case where he and I were opposed to each other, in his requesting us, after all the usual forms had been gone through, to repeat our arguments to the jury. This intellectual failure obliged his retirement, which took place many years ago, and was no doubt a loss to the Bench.

CHAPTER XXVII.

SIR ALEXANDER COCKBURN.

Russell Square—Former days—Talfourd's house—Mr. Gill—Cockburn—His doctor—Latter days—Letters—His career—Medical knowledge—Symptoms—Description of—Performance of duties—Sir William Jenner—Visit to Spa- November 1880—Cockburn resumes his duties—Sudden death—His judicial character—The Queen's Bench—Extinction of name—Mellor—Lush—Anecdote of Cockburn—Kindheartedness—Anecdote of Lush—The 'Traviata'—Sir Nicholas Tindal—Erle—Sir John Jervis—Bad health—Anecdote of—Gossip—Consequences—Maule.

The fields in the neighbourhood of Bloomsbury, in which the gallants of a former age were wont to ruffle their plumes, and where the easily given offence so often terminated in sanguinary encounters, appear to be suffering under the names of Bloomsbury, Bedford, and Russell Squares for their iniquities of those times, and are now clad in a garb of preternatural dulness. Sundays are apparently the only days upon which the inhabitants are permitted to enjoy themselves, when, to the music of the several steeples, they disport themselves in purple and fine linen. This is the last locality in which I should have expected to meet with an interesting incident, and yet it was in the very heart of it that I met the one which I hope will interest my readers as it did me.

Fifty years ago judges and successful barristers occupied some of the houses, and retarded its dulness; amongst them Mr. Serjeant Talfourd. How I love to dwell upon his memory! His house might be compared to the bright flicker of a candle in a surrounding darkness. If he was proud of himself, as he might fairly have been, he was still prouder of giving others the opportunity to shine. I have before feebly attempted to describe his guests, and his entertainments. The last that I remember, or at all events the one remaining pictured most vividly upon my memory, peopled the square one early May morning with the departing guests from a fancy-dress ball, many of whom have left honoured names behind as artists, actors, authors, and lawyers—none, however, more courted and beloved than that of their host.

Well, it was to this house, in the present year of 1884, that business conducted me. A gentleman of position as a solicitor now occupies it. After the conclusion of our conversation, in which I was very glad to receive his advice, I found myself in Russell Square, and, having some little time upon my hands, my mind reverted to Mr. Serjeant Simon, a gentleman for whom I entertain a great affection. I knew he lived in the neighbourhood, and thought that I would call upon him. I cast about to find someone who could give me his address. I stopped an impatient butcher-boy and a surly baker ineffectually. At last, in a bye-street, a courteous crossing-sweeper suggested the idea of my inquiring at the house of a medical man in the square.

Availing myself of the suggestion of the 'lady of the broom,' I rang the bell at the residence pointed out to me of Mr. Gill, and, whilst asking the question of the servant, he himself appeared in person. I fancy he knew me, and, inviting me into his study, he gave me what information he could. But to make a long story short, I found that he had been the medical attendant of Sir Alexander Cockburn during the latter days of his life, and he related to me some of the details. He had in his possession many letters from that distinguished man, and was kind enough to ask me to a *tête-à-tête* dinner, which I partook of some weeks afterward, and read with great interest the epistles he had previously mentioned.

I have already amongst my 'Experiences' given some account of Sir Alexander, who is worthy of a biographer more capable of the task, and with more extensive means of knowledge. He possessed great versatility, and his life was one of singular changes and great adventure. Belonging to a family of considerable position, he finished his education at Trinity Hall, Cambridge, taking, I believe, high honours. Originally his mind tended to a diplomatic career, and he was attached to his uncle's mission at Florence. He was a splendid modern linguist, as well as an accomplished scholar. It was strange that, considering the variety of his attainments, he should have found time to get into debt and embarrassment, but so it was, and his earlier days at the Bar were marked by struggles in which was mingled no small dash of adventure.

I have, in my former work, referred to the principal features which distinguished his professional career, and also mentioned his sudden death. My readers will not be surprised that I was interested to learn through the medium of a gentleman of great intelligence, and in whom he evidently placed unbounded confidence, some of the circumstances relating to that event.

The late Lord Chief Justice, like many men of mark in our profession, had made medical research the subject of study, and applied the knowledge thus obtained to his own feelings. He seems, during the many years that Mr. Gill was his confidential attendant, to have had a languid circulation, his pulse never exceeding sixty-two, and a letter received by that gentleman, which I will venture to quote, shows how fully he realised the fact. Great men, however, filling distinguished positions, are obliged to wear masks, and, indeed, few of those who saw Sir Alexander Cockburn take his seat and preside upon the Bench at Exeter on July 20, 1879, and witnessed his performance of his duties, could have imagined that he had learnt a circumstance which to him must have been a sentence of death :—

[*Private and Confidential.*]

Exeter: July 20, 1879.

'My dear Doctor,—Something serious is, I believe, the matter with me, though I don't know what. I had a disturbed night, last night. To-day I have not felt unwell, otherwise than I have suffered from shortness of breath, but my pulse gives warning that something is amiss—instead of being at sixty, its normal state, it is down to forty. I conclude something must be wrong about the heart. Don't breathe a syllable about this to a soul. I will write again to-morrow—if all goes well. 'Yours very truly,

'A. E. C.'

From this period down to his death he watched his symptoms with scrupulous care, and related them to Mr. Gill, never, however, shrinking from work or exhibiting signs upon the Bench that he was affected by a heavy trouble. He continued his duties without interruption, presiding every day during the Assizes. Subsequently the circuit adjourned to Wells, whence he wrote giving a minute account of his symptoms, which had not improved.

It would be of little interest to my readers to trace the course of the disease during the next twelve months. In August 1880 he was visited by another medical man, passed some time on board his yacht, and in November, being then at Spa, wrote a letter to Mr. Gill, in which he describes his feelings in the following lines:—

'For an hour it amounted to real agony. The sensation was as if some giant hand was pressing an iron weight or heavy stone against my breast-bone from within with the intention of crushing it; and, strange to say, the sense of pain extended, only in a lesser degree, into the arm-pit, down the arm, and into the hand. Much of it would make life a fearful thing to bear.'

Sir William Jenner saw him in the same month. He was then very ill, but the sense of his position did not prevent his paying that distinguished physician a well-merited compliment. On the 19th of November Mr. Gill dined with him.

He was in good spirits, enjoyed his dinner, his cigar after, and was full of fun and stories.

On Saturday, the 20th, he went to court. I am not aware that any circumstance signalised this from other occasions on which he presided. It will be very long before those who practised before him will forget that calm, powerful forehead, and the somewhat studied but musical tones in which his observations were addressed, nor his habitual courtesy. Upon this day, being Saturday, he rose early, and afterward walked home to Hertford Street from Westminster. Mr. Gill dined with him on this as upon the preceding day. He seemed pretty well, enjoyed his dinner, and drank two glasses of a favourite port that I had been fortunate enough to procure for him. He then went upstairs, intending to undress, leant upon the bed, ejaculated 'Help me!' and expired.

Before quitting the subject of Sir Alexander Cockburn, let me recall the time when the court over which he presided was something distinctive, not part of a modern amalgam. There was a dignity in the name, it carried with it consideration and respect. 'The Queen's Bench' is no more, and there is nothing now to prevent a lawyer from the ranks of Equity wielding the sceptre that once represented in grandeur the Common Law and liberties of the land.

I linger over a topic which brings back to my mind the recollection of early struggles, of successes beyond my hopes, and of kindnesses that certainly distinguished members of the profession in their intercourse with one another. Cockburn was popular in his court. Mellor and Lush were unfailing and serviceable lieutenants. Persecution and bigotry, that had defaced the court in former days, were matters of past history.

I remember when Sir Alexander Cockburn was pursuing the career that he loved best upon the benches of the House of Commons, and had made a speech in favour of marriage with a deceased wife's sister, Shiel, the Irish orator and a Romanist, in one of his speeches described Cockburn as reminding him of a military phrase, 'A Christian unattached.' Bigots are very apt to describe those who are more merciful than themselves towards the failing of others as wanting in religion. What Cockburn's views might have been upon dogma I cannot tell, but I am acquainted with many acts of his kindheartedness, and, amongst others, I was told the other day of his having quite recently before his death witnessed a poor cripple knocked down, and, picking him up, sent him to Mr. Gill to be properly treated and attended to.

A rather amusing incident either really took

place, or, to borrow the sense of the Italian proverb, 'which if not true is well invented,' related to Mr. Justice Lush. It is well known that he was a member of the Baptist community, not in name only, but truly and conscientiously. His intellect and genius belonged to the law, his belief and conscience to his pastor and church. His position, however, required, so he was told, that he should give some sort of social gathering. He naturally asked the advice of his chief, who, himself a fanatic in music, at once suggested a concert, undertook its arrangement, and the opera of the 'Traviata' delighted his numerous guests, the story unsuspected by their host. I am not entitled to disclose the effect of the discovery in a meeting of the serious friends of his persuasion, some of whom had been unconsciously exposed to the terrible pollution.

Mr. Justice Mellor has retired from the Bench. I always entertained a great respect and affection for him. He also belonged to a serious community, differing indeed in his views from those of his brother puisné, although, it is to be hoped, leading to the same end.

Another decease I have to record is that of the 'Court of Common Pleas,' with the succession of splendid lawyers and scholars who for ages have adorned its Bench. This also has become

an ingredient of what I will venture to call
'Palmer's Elixir.' The first of its Chief Justices
that I remember was Sir Nicholas Conyngham
Tindal. When I was a boy he occupied the house
at Hampstead once belonging to one more famous
as a consummate advocate than afterwards in his
position of Chancellor, Lord Erskine. Tindal was
still upon the Bench when I was called to the
Bar, and amongst the many from whom I met
with marks of welcome and kindness, Erle, of
whom I have already given to the public my
recollections, was the last.

Intermediately came a character worthy of a
few words of notice—Sir John Jervis. From the
earliest date that I knew him when at the Bar,
down to the day of his death, he existed in a continual struggle with disease—asthma. He fought
against it manfully, but I have seen him nearly
suffocated, and he ultimately died at a comparatively early age. He was not eloquent, his
person was not imposing, and he had a weak
voice, but nevertheless he was a profound and
most successful advocate. He knew human nature
apparently by intuition, his quickness was marvellous, and certainly his education seemed to
have drifted into channels not usually traversed
by the most investigating of lawyers.

I remember an illustration of this when he

was presiding at a criminal trial at Lewes. I think it was that of a man named Broome and some others for swindling, and a constable in the witness-box was professing to give an explanation of the 'thimblerig trick,' which, however, whatever might be his natural powers in that direction, he was doing very clumsily. The Chief, who had long exhibited signs of impatience, at last said to the constable, 'Give me the thimble,' which being done, he faced the jury and squared his arms. 'Look here, gentlemen,' he said, and proceeded to perform the trick three or four times in a manner that would certainly have acquired for him a distinguished character at a fair or race-course.

He was, I am afraid, a somewhat reckless talker, and apt to repeat gossip. He found himself one day in an unlucky scrape in consequence of his indulgence in this propensity. It was reported of the late Lord Chelmsford, who I should have thought had never committed a social irregularity in his life, that he was head over ears in debt, and the bailiffs were in his house. Jervis had got hold of it, and repeated the story. He received a letter from his lordship demanding his authority. 'How the d——, Jack, am I to answer this?' said he, addressing his son. 'I have not the slightest notion from whom I heard the story.' His son could not assist him. Just at this moment a member of the Bar sent him up the following message: 'Poor Godson died this morning.' 'I have it,' said the Chief; 'it was from him I heard it!'[1]

I suppose no man ever practised at the Bar, or became a member of the Bench, who possessed a greater appreciation of, and confidence in, his own powers than Jervis, and it would have been difficult to discover an assemblage of persons with any one of whom he would have felt himself to be an intellectual inferior, and yet certainly in his own court he evinced far less confidence in himself in the presence of Maule, a puisné judge, than he did upon any other occasion. Is it not Dr. Johnson who says that 'no two men were ever for an hour in each other's society without one of them tacitly acknowledging the superiority of the other!' and it is not wonderful to me if the Chief Justice of the Common Pleas felt innately the intellectual power of his junior. It is noticeable that these two men, possessing such mental traits, should both have succumbed to the same physical disease. They belonged to the same club as myself, and I have often been delighted by their brilliancy.

[1] If this incident is of any higher origin than the mischievous invention of an occasionally idle section of the Bar, it probably occurred before Lord Chelmsford had obtained the rank of Chancellor,

CHAPTER XXVIII.

WELL-KNOWN PEOPLE.

Anthony Trollope—His life—His complaint—His own account of it—Angina pectoris—The chase—Trollope's opinion—Last meeting with him—Charles Reade—Early acquaintance—His writings—Marquis of Anglesey—A game at cribbage—Vice-Chancellor Bacon—A dinner—His caricatures—The Honourable Robert Grimstone—Westminster election—Petition—Mr. Smith—Baron Martin—Result.

SINCE I ventured to give my early experiences to the world, and sketched to the best of my ability the lives and characters of some of those with whom, in my passage through life, I have occasionally mixed, other and by no means unimportant personages have become the property of the biographer; amongst them one who creates a loss in literature, to which he was a prolific contributor, and to society, where he was always a welcome addition—Anthony Trollope.

An interesting autobiography of this gentleman has been published, and from it we learn that the disease which occasioned his death was probably the same as that which caused Sir Alexander Cockburn's. Certainly a great similarity is to be discovered in the philosophic temperament with which they were both able to contemplate their condition and impending doom. It may be interesting to quote from the biography of Trollope his account of his own state, which I do from an article that appeared in the last January number of the 'Temple Bar Magazine':—

'I have had a terrible verdict pronounced against me since I saw you last. They say I have got angina pectoris. I am to eat and drink, get up and sit down at my peril, and may drop down dead at any moment.'

This observation was made to one of his oldest friends in his ordinary tone. I should never have imagined him to have been the victim of ill-health. His appearance rather presented the idea of a gentleman from the country, his manner was energetic, and he was a vehement politician. He was fond of hunting, and indulged in some ideas on the subject which certainly would not have been participated in by the objects of his sport. He declared that the fox ought to be deeply obliged to the sportsman, as through his instrumentality it led a comfortable life during a great portion of the year, living in luxury upon the poultry of the surrounding farmers.

It was at the Garrick Club that I had the pleasure of meeting him, and in his company and that of many other distinguished men was frequently Charles Reade, another author of celebrity who has very lately died. He also was a man well worthy of remembrance. I had formed his acquaintance very early in my professional career, being consulted on his behalf upon the subject of a will. Mr. Teesdale was the solicitor, and I remember how much difficulty we had in persuading Reade that law did not always accord with justice. His character has been portrayed in a variety of quarters, and justice has been done to his intense feelings of humanity, and his chivalrous advocacy of those whom he deemed to be oppressed and persecuted. Perhaps his views were exaggerated, and thus their effect weakened, but my own experience and observation, if they do not fully confirm, very strongly support, his opinions about prison discipline and the laws relating to insanity.

The last time I saw these two eminent authors was some three or four years ago at the Garrick Club, and upon this occasion they, the late Marquis of Anglesey, and myself made up a party at cribbage. It is a melancholy thought that I alone of the party am left to record the fact.

Before making a final adieu to the Garrick Club, let me say a word or two about a member who belonged to it, and was very popular, when I first joined. He was a distinguished lawyer, and I believe at one time sub-editor of the 'Times' newspaper. (If I am wrong in this statement, it may induce a contradiction from that journal, which will decidedly improve the circulation of these memories.) He holds now a high judicial position.

Vice-Chancellor Bacon is the oldest judge upon the Bench, but has apparently lost none of his natural powers, and it is only a few weeks ago that an able judgment pronounced by him took up several columns of the newspaper. He is very accomplished, enjoys life thoroughly, and is to be heard of at many social gatherings. He had in his youth joined the Home Circuit, and was present at a dinner at which I had the honour of presiding, and he proposed my health in kindly terms. He was a clever draughtsman, with a strong tendency to humour in the exercise of his accomplishment. As a caricaturist his taste was once discovered in some of his notes sent up to the Court of Appeal, upon which were sketched figures which bore a farcical likeness to witnesses who had given evidence before him. His name still appears in the law reports, and it will always be not only associated with great legal attainments, but with invariable courtesy and good-humour.

I may be permitted to mention here an incident in my professional career, brought back to my mind by seeing the death of the Honourable Robert

Grimstone reported in the daily papers. This incident occurred upon the trial of an election petition before Mr. Baron Martin, against the return to Parliament of Mr. Smith, the eminent publisher. The Honourable Robert was a vehement politician of the high Tory type, and had been very active in his canvass for the Conservative candidate. He, determining that this gentleman's claims should not be unknown, circulated bills to each of the residents of a certain court, setting these claims out in glowing terms, and, to secure them being duly exhibited, distributed at the same time a trifling sum to those who undertook the task. This was imputed to the Honourable Member as an act of bribery by his agent, but no imputation was suggested against Mr. Smith personally. Baron Martin, however, was so much struck by the candour and innocence with which the Honourable Robert Grimstone explained the transaction, that he expressed his confidence that no underhand motive existed, and thus the services of one of the most able and practical men of business have been secured to the country.

Baron Martin was himself a vehement Liberal in politics, and probably his sympathies would have led him in another direction. He has passed from this life at an advanced age, having some time previous to his death been obliged to leave the Bench in consequence of deafness.

The Honourable Robert Grimstone was universally popular, and his well-known figure at Lord's and other resorts where his favourite game of cricket was indulged in, will be remembered and missed with a general feeling of regret.

CHAPTER XXIX.

CORRESPONDENCE.

Sir Robert Phillimore—Letter from—Smethurst case—Cresswell—His character—Sir James Wilde—Anecdotes—My early days—Letter from Whitehurst—Felix Whitehurst—His early days—His death—St. Paul's School—Its masters—Empress of the French.

I REJOICE to say that the following name is not entitled to a place in my obituary. It is that of a distinguished lawyer, advocate, and jurist, now retired from the Bench—Sir Robert Phillimore. In my former 'Experiences' I have referred to this gentleman in connection with a curious poisoning romance, and after their publication I received from him the following letter, which I am very pleased to have the opportunity of publishing:—

'The Coppice, Henley-upon-Thames:
'April 13, 1882.

'Dear Serjeant Ballantine,—We have just got your interesting book, and I am much gratified by your complimentary notice of my speech in the poisoning case. I well remember your saying about the same thing to me at the time of trial. Might I ask you in your next edition to correct the error in my Christian name, which is Robert, and not John?

'Yours very sincerely,
'ROBERT PHILLIMORE.'

The speech referred to in the foregoing letter was indeed a great effort of forensic eloquence. It lifted a case full of prejudice against his client, one of the most villainous of murderers, out of the difficulties that surrounded it, and obtained for him possession of the property of his murdered victim. Perhaps this may be considered by many of my readers a doubtful compliment; however, it was not only an example of legal oratory, but it secured a result in accordance with its principles.

I believe that Cresswell, who tried the case, was much disappointed at the result, and, in a conversation repeated to me, attributed it to his own failing powers with a jury. Such was not the case, for, although doubtless he entertained intense disgust for the wretch who propounded the will, his mind was so evenly balanced and naturally fair, and his powers of explanation so clear, that they absolutely defeated any prejudice that the character of an individual might have engendered. It is from no want of appreciation of his successor—Sir James Wilde, a truly great judge—that I venture to describe his predecessor's death as having been a serious loss to the court over which he had presided.

It must not, however, be supposed that the eulogium I have here passed upon Sir Creswell Creswell, and which is founded upon a large practice whilst he presided in the court, is intended to offer a justification for a rudeness of manner which disfigured him, and possibly might occasionally have worked injustice. My opinion of the importance of courtesy from the Bench has been sufficiently declared, and I am sorry to admit a blot upon otherwise so fair an escutcheon.

I remember one day, before he went to the Probate Court, he was presiding at the Old Bailey. Edwin James was defending a prisoner. 'Stop!' said the judge, who took notes slowly. The counsel proceeded. 'Stop!' again from the Bench. Still the examination continued. 'Did you not hear me say "stop," Mr. James?' 'I beg your pardon, my lord,' said that gentleman, 'I thought you were addressing the usher.'

A trifling incident, to which I was a party, does not illustrate badly what I conceive to have been a merely defective manner. One day at the same tribunal, when he took his seat, I made an application for a case to stand over until the following Friday. 'Do you expect, Mr. Ballantine, that Her Majesty's judges should come here for your convenience?' 'Oh, my lord!' I replied, 'I should not have ventured to think of such a thing, but as your lordship is kind enough to suggest it——' I paused. He smiled, spoke to his brother judge: 'Well, then, be it so,' he said. This occurred at a period of my existence when the natural innocence of my mind led me into an apparent want of deference to the tribunal.

Those who have read my former 'Experiences' (and I strongly advise those who have not, to amend their ways) will remember the sketch I gave of my miserable school-days.

Shortly after my book came out I received a letter from the brother of an early and intimate friend—Felix Whitehurst.

The latter days of this gentleman were spent as Paris correspondent to the 'Daily Telegraph,' which journal was indebted to him for many amusing articles, and to which, as I knew from his own lips, he was in turn indebted for much generous consideration. As his brother confirms my account of my early persecutions, I venture to transcribe his letter:—

'Treneglos, Gulval, Penzance:
'May 18, 1882.

'Sir,—It is almost a liberty for the reader of a book to address its author, but as on one occasion I was a client of yours, and, if I recollect rightly, you were acquainted with my brother, Felix Whitehurst, once well known as correspondent of the 'Daily Telegraph,' I will venture to intrude upon you.

'Thank you most sincerely for the effective manner in which you have gibbeted the memories of those whom you well describe as "cruel, cold blooded, systematic tyrants "—Durham and Bean, whom I knew forty-seven years ago. Sleath[1] affected the style of Dr. Johnson, whose shadow hung over his early days. Although he was no scholar, as men are accounted scholars now, he was, I believe, a good master, and certainly he did good-natured things. The present Master of Balliol (Jowett) owed much of his success in life to Sleath's kindness and patronage. Jowett's father was not in opulent circumstances, and as Jowett was not on the foundation, and therefore not entitled to any of the numerous exhibitions attached to St. Paul's, he had slight chance of getting to college ; but Sleath facilitated his competing for a Balliol scholarship, which he obtained, and this was the foundation of his successful career. Sleath did not anticipate the 'Essays and Reviews,' the dissertations on St. Paul's Epistles, and the reformed liturgy at Balliol.[2]

[1] This gentleman was head-master of St. Paul's School at the period alluded to.

[2] It is well known that this distinguished scholar was the author of one of the 'Essays,' and of other writings, which very much shocked the orthodoxy of the religious world of that day.

'You overrate, I think, the acquirements of Durham and Bean. I was under Durham some years; he was a man of coarse mind—in his late years he never read a book. He knew a few stock lessons, and could teach the very little he knew; but his temper, especially when suppressed gout or overmuch port wine affected him, was that of a maniac, and at other times morose, vindictive, savage. Why I never knew, but Bishop Blomfield[1] gave him the Rectory of St. Matthew's, Friday Street, where there were no parishioners, and therefore he could not do any harm.'

[Mr. Whitehurst gives a further account of this gentleman, which would not interest my readers. He then proceeds:—]

'Bean was equally ignorant, and in that respect, unlike Durham, could not impart to others the little he knew.

. . . . .

'I think he was a more continuous, and therefore worse, tyrant than Durham. His wife threw herself out of the window in St. Paul's Churchyard. His friends said that after that event his mind was affected—he certainly acted like one so afflicted, but I believe he delighted in inflicting suffering. I have seen him repeatedly belabour

---

[1] At the time here spoken of Bishop of London.

Sir James Hannen and the present Baron Pollock, both at that time sturdy young men.

. . . . .

'In later years he used to preach to a clerk, beadle, pew-opener, sexton, and organist in St. Mary's, Aldermanbury, on Sunday evenings. When he retired from St. Paul's School, 1853-4, some men (great fools they must have been) tried to get up a piece of plate for him. I was asked to attend a meeting for the purpose. I said I would attend, but should speak in the spirit of this letter. It was not held, and whether they got up the plate I never heard. Edwards had left before I went to the school, and his place was supplied by an ignorant Evangelical clergyman named Cooper. He was the *beau idéal* of Arnold's description of an Evangelical, " an ordinary Christian with the narrowest possible mind."

'Edwards used to come at times to visit the scene of his former pleasures, but he was then "a spiked cannon" and could do no injury to his fellow-creatures.

. . . . .

'I read with assent your remarks on Sam Warren, who used to puff unblushingly his " Lectures [1] on the Moral and Professional Duties of

---
[1] A work published by Warren.

Attorneys" while acting as Master of Lunacy. I am glad to see you speak kindly of that much injured man Lord Westbury, one of my kindest friends—but I must not trespass longer on your attention.

'You will see I date from one of the most remote villages in England, where literature is supplied intermittently; hence I have only just seen your first volume, and am looking forward to your second very eagerly.

'I remain, Sir,
'Your faithful, obedient servant,
'EDWARD C WHITEHURST.'

The above is only one of many that I received in a similar strain, confirmatory of the impressions I recorded of my days at St. Paul's. It proves also how indelibly savage cruelty brands its marks.

I know of no two objects whose appearance, gestures, and movements remain so clearly upon my memory as those of Durham and Bean, and, as I believe there is no crime can be committed upon youth more calculated to destroy the body and affect prejudicially the mind, I make no excuse for referring to my own experiences, and fortifying them by those of others.

I remember the writer of the above letter, not

however at school. With his brother Felix I was upon terms of some intimacy, and I think I am not wrong in saying that upon one occasion, either at the house of a Mr. Hulbert or a Mrs. Waley, I met him at a party, in which the present Empress of the French was a guest, and with whom he appeared acquainted. I know that subsequently he was very popular in the circle that surrounded the Court of the Second Empire. I was in Paris at the time of his death, and was able to be of some comfort to the widow, who lived to lament his loss.

CHAPTER XXX.

A RETROSPECT.

Numerous correspondents—An attack of illness—Major Bethune—
His letter—An old memory—Death of a murderer—Letter from
a lady—Benevolence—Lord Westbury—Anecdote of—Vivisection
—Ouida—Dinner with—Letter from—Editor of 'Spectator'—
Quotation from—Thurtell—Trial—Anecdotes—Forbes Campbell
— Letter from — Sir Robert Clifton — Alexander Mitchell—
Duke of Brunswick—Mr. and Mrs. Hodgson—Milner Gibson—
The 'World'—Quotation from—Dr. Elliotson.

THE letters which I have quoted in my last chapter were by no means the only ones that I received from correspondents, both strangers and acquaintances, after the appearance of my late work, some confirming the views I had expressed and the circumstances I had detailed, and others correcting, in a very kindly spirit, inaccuracies into which I had fallen.

I should have acknowledged gratefully the receipt of many of them, but a serious attack of illness prevented me from paying them the attention they deserved. Of some of these letters I am now availing myself, as they bring back to my memory incidents and people, a reference to whom may possess interest for my readers, and form part of my life.

Amongst my very early acquaintances was a Major Bethune. I forget what regiment he had belonged to, but at the time I knew him he was a country squire, and present at the trial of the Sussex murderer, the circumstances of which I have already related. The major in his letter writes of the murderer in the following terms:—'He became cad to an omnibus, running to and from Hastings, and for some time no end of people were attracted to see a live murderer.'

I regret extremely that I have mislaid a letter which I received from a lady, the wife of a clergyman, in whose parish this individual had ended his days. He appears to have been a great sufferer from rheumatic gout, which he bore with patience and resignation, receiving evidently from this lady (although the letter does not express it) comfort and hope administered in a truly Christian spirit. I shall be glad if these lines meet the sight of the lady in question, and that she will believe how much her conduct is appreciated by one, at all events.

Major Bethune also relates an incident in the career of Lord Westbury, not as illustrative of that gentleman's disposition, but as of one of the causes that rendered him dreaded and unpopular except amongst those who knew what a really kind heart he possessed. I relate it in my friend's own words, but must, however, prelude it by mentioning that his lordship had an idea in early life that he was a Conservative, and had become a member of the charming club of that name. His career was distinctly Liberal, and he was called upon to answer at a general meeting for his delinquencies:—

'Lord Westbury was speaking before a general meeting at our Conservative Club. A member said "Speak up, sir!" "Oh!" Lord Westbury replied, " is it you? I thought your ears were long enough for anything!"'

Another extract from the same letter, in reference to my remarks upon vivisection:—

'I wish you would publish them in a sixpenny pamphlet, or let us do so. Your clever vivisection article would do so much good. Lord Coleridge has benefited us greatly by his letters.'

I forget how many years ago it is (and as the reference is to one of the fair sex it is a sacred subject) that I was dining at the Langham Hotel with a lady, who, under the *nom de plume* of 'Ouida,' had recently flashed into literary fame, and who has since retained it by many charming works of fiction. From her I received the following kindly epistle:—

'Villa Farinda, Florence.

'Dear Serjeant Ballantine,—Allow me to congratulate you on the great success of your book.

I am so glad to see that you are with me on the subject of vivisection.

'I send you herewith an article of mine upon it—perhaps, as a minnow catches a salmon, it may get me the gift of your book in return.

'I suppose you never go over the Alps. I should like to show you this queer old house, and all my *bibelots*. Once more let me felicitate you on having proved that a brilliant talker can be also a brilliant writer, and believe me,

'Sincerely yours,

'OUIDA.'

Upon the subject of vivisection my opinion has received much support, but these pages are scarcely a medium through which a discussion between the alleged discoveries of science and the feelings dictated by conscience can be carried on, and I shall therefore confine myself to quoting a note to a letter that appeared in the 'Spectator' newspaper, and which cannot be despised upon the ground of its writer not being eminently qualified to form opinions unbiassed by prejudice:—

'We should deny altogether the right to put animals to torture, even in the confident hope of lessening human suffering. Would any humane man torture a man to obtain a remedy for the toothache? And if not a man, why a dog or a cat? Their lives are not nearly so valuable but their sufferings are just as severe, and count for an even larger proportion of their whole experience.—Ed. "Spectator."'[1]

A letter alluding to the account I have given of the murderer Thurtell, from a gentleman named Pearce, signalling from 'The Club, Bournemouth,' relates an amusing incident upon the trial. It may be remembered that the body of the murdered man, Wear, was thrust under a sofa in Probert's house. The cook was asked, 'Was the supper postponed?' She replied, 'No! it was pork!' The well-known definition of a 'gentleman' comes from the same source. 'What do you mean by gentleman?' a witness was asked. 'He keeps a gig' was the reply. Lytton Bulwer borrowed the main idea of his novel 'Pelham' from the details of this crime.

On the 10th of April, 1882, Forbes Campbell writes to me from 74 St. James's Street, *inter alia*, in the following words :—

'You will comprehend the interest with which I have read your book, when I mention that I have known, more or less, seventy-three of the personages mentioned in it. Your sketches are true to the life. There are, however, some figures

[1] *Spectator* newspaper, February 16, 1884.

wanting that I expected to find; *ex. gr.* Sir Robert Clifton, *alias* the 'Nottingham Pet'; Mr. T. A. Mitchell, M.P.; the Duke of Brunswick; the Emperor of China; and 'Pale Ale,' the better-half of 'Brown Stout.' You had doubtless your reasons for not introducing them, and for omitting female celebrities. As your store of anecdotes cannot be exhausted, I indulge the hope that you will favour the public with a sequel.'

I was well acquainted with Sir Robert Clifton, a man of good family and wild habits. He died many years ago. He had married an extremely beautiful and clever woman, the daughter of Barry O'Meara, who, as medical man, attended the Emperor Buonaparte when a prisoner in St. Helena, and wrote an account, the very reverse of complimentary, of his treatment by Sir Hudson Lowe, the governor. I believe O'Meara was prosecuted for libel.

Alexander Mitchell I am able to speak of as an old and much valued friend. He was member for Bridport. I made his acquaintance shortly after I became a member of the Union Club. At that time he had made a very decided mark in the House of Commons by some exceedingly lucid financial speeches, and was spoken of as by no means an impossible future Chancellor of the Exchequer. He was a first-rate whist and piquet player. Unfortunately his health broke down, and his latter years did not fulfil their early promise. He married late in life, and I, as one of the friends he most valued, was invited to welcome his wife to her new home. His death occurred whilst I was in India, and it appears that I was present to his mind almost to the end. Some weeks before he died, he said to Wakefield, the hall-porter of the club, 'Have you heard when the Serjeant will return? I want to give a dinner, but must wait for him.' He had distinguished himself in Parliament about the time that Milner Gibson, with whom I had a slight acquaintance, was coming to the fore, and there was a great similarity between the mental characteristics of the two men.

I have just read with great interest, in the 'World' newspaper, of parties and people that I so well remember meeting at them, at Milner Gibson's house. There is one omission of a gentleman, to whom I referred in a shorter but similar notice that I gave in my 'Experiences,' one well worthy to be associated in the phalanx of distinguished characters whose names are quoted in the article, Dr. Elliotson, an eminent physician. He was a much valued guest at Mrs. Gibson's, and had much influence over her mind. They were both greatly affected by mesmeric theories.

I hope that I may be excused for appending the few lines that I wrote upon the same subject :—

'Amongst the houses at which he (Dr. Elliotson) was a constant visitor was that of a lady. Mrs. Milner Gibson, who, at one time, gathered around her a large circle, comprising most of those famous in literature, arts, and the professions; and here also every foreigner possessing a grievance and an unhappy country, was always made heartily welcome.'[1]

But to proceed with the personages mentioned in Forbes Campbell's letter :—

The Duke of Brunswick was loathsome-looking in the extreme—painted and dyed—the mark for the foul libellists of those days, and meeting with little sympathy from the British public, who, without the slightest scintilla of evidence, attributed to him the cruel murder of a girl in Waterloo Road—one of those crimes that does not justify the proverb, 'Murder will out.'

'Pale Ale,' the better-half of 'Brown Stout,' was one of our 'mutual reminiscences' alluded to in Campbell's letter. Their mention, alas! can now inflict no pain. Both have departed. The latter I have before spoken of, and certainly he was a man entitled to a mark of British gratitude. Mr. Hodgson

[1] *Some Experiences of a Barrister's Life*, 5th edition, p. 194. *Vide* the *World* newspaper, March 5, 1884.

was the first brewer of 'bitter beer' exported to India. He was next-door neighbour to my father at Wapping, and obtained the sobriquet of 'Brown Stout' from his business and dark complexion. For his wife—a lady naturally fair, and whose charms it was suspected were enhanced in that direction—was reserved the title of 'Pale Ale.' The frequenters of Homburg and Baden, in their naughty days, will remember her, a dear, kindly, hospitable little woman, whose favourite number at the *roulette* was eighteen, possibly from the memories associated in her mind with that period of her existence.

CHAPTER XXXI.

EASTBOURNE, PAST AND PRESENT.

Eastbourne—Present appearance—Memories—A country mansion—Charles Manby—Letter from—Mrs. Manby—Major Willard—His property—Theatrical connections—Adelphi Theatre—Honorary Canon of Rochester—Letter from—Dr. Robinson—Zadkiel—Sir Edward Belcher—Miss Bigg—Letter from—Tawell—Trial for murder—An explanation.

ANYONE with a view of securing solemn respectability—a choice from a numerous body of clergy presenting every kind of doctrine—stuccoed houses little differing from Belgravian mansions—and hotels, the outward appearance of which make the economic mind shudder—will find themselves amply supplied at Eastbourne, the now well-known watering-place on the coast of Sussex. But if their lives have been long, and their memories carry them back to some forty or fifty years ago, they will marvel at the change that these years have effected in this now appropriate haunt of Belgravian and Tyburnian seekers for health or pleasure.

When first I remember it, it consisted of a terrace facing the sea, not comprising more than half a dozen unevenly constructed houses, almost washed over by the waves—one narrow street, populated by very humble tradesmen—a comfortable, unpretentious public-house, and at right angles with the beach, stretching inland, a row of magnificent trees bounded by cornfields, and enlivened by the music of many a bird. This walk led to an, even then, old-fashioned red-bricked mansion, the inhabitants of the elms around announcing in solemn cawings the antiquity of a long undisturbed occupation. The voices of these sable inheritors are no longer heard, and if their habitations still exist, civilisation has given notice to possessors for centuries to quit their domiciles.

From this house, my memory of which I have endeavoured to sketch, and in which I had passed many a happy day, a letter reached me from a dear and valued friend, Charles Manby. It is dated 'The Greys, Eastbourne, April 13, 1882.' This gentleman possessed a very extensive and highly appreciated scientific reputation, and was from the earliest period that I remember him secretary to the College of Civil Engineers. He writes *inter alia*:—'You were born in the year when I was packed off to a military college at St. Servan in France—a clear start of ten years over you!' Another extract:—'Mrs. Manby, whom you knew very early in life as Miss Willard, sends her kind regards, hopes you will pay us a visit, and see the change that has taken place since you visited this house as a boy with your father.'

This letter recalled to my mind the origin of my very early acquaintanceship with the Manbys. The lady's father was a Major Willard, an officer in the Tower Hamlets Militia, my father having been the chairman of the sessions then appertaining to this hamlet. Major Willard was possessed of property at Eastbourne and its locality, including the house I have mentioned, and his daughter succeeded to it. I never knew exactly how it came to pass that Charles Manby, whose reputation depended upon his intimate knowledge of the most important and gravest paths of the scientific world, became associated with the inner circles of the most brilliant theatrical society; but so it was, and thus much amusement was afforded to me in those days, when I worshipped the stage with empty pockets. I believe he was intimate with Mr. Yates, became his executor, and thus had for some time practically the management of the Adelphi Theatre, during periods of many triumphs. It was a stuffy little hole then, but how happy I was when I could get poked into any part of it!

I have in former memories referred to Reeves, Paul Bedford, Mrs. Honey (how beautiful she was!),

Miss Woolgar, one of the brightest of light comedy actresses, and O. Smith, whose delineation of a villain made my youthful blood curdle in my veins—the whole company admirably marshalled by Mr. and Mrs. Yates. This letter from Charles Manby brought back to my memory pleasant hours, and scenes of town and country life, and I am glad here to have the opportunity of expressing how much pleasure it gives me to recall the kindnesses of old friends.

I am pleased to insert the two following letters, as, although they point to inaccuracies on my part, the spirit in which they do so, coming from such sources, is most gratifying:—

'Brompton Vicarage, Kent:
'June 2, 1882.

'Dear Sir,—Permit me to draw your attention to a paragraph in your excellent work—" Experiences," &c., which I think is not strictly correct.

'In your second volume you state that my friend Dr. Robinson, late Master of the Temple, was a believer in the Crystal Ball, and you express your surprise. I remember Dr. Robinson telling me he had been to see it, and some friend of his believed in it, but that he did not, and was astonished that anyone could have any faith in such things. I have seen his widow on the subject, and she confirms this opinion.

'If this paragraph could be omitted or qualified in your next edition you would be conferring a great favour upon the late Master's relatives and friends.

'Believe me,

'Yours truly,

'DANIEL COOKE,

'Hon. Canon of Rochester.

The above has reference to a trial that took place before Chief Justice Cockburn, in the Common Pleas, brought by a personage bearing the pseudonym of Zadkiel against Admiral Sir Edward Belcher. The plaintiff professed that through the medium of a crystal ball he was able to prophesy events, and the curious positions in which some of the well-known men of the day were placed in reference to the heavenly bodies, created much amusement.

My readers will perhaps remember that some years ago a person named Tawell was tried before the late Mr. Baron Parke for the murder of his mistress, and the following letter is in relation to my account of the incident:—

'Sutors, Beds: 'April 21, 1882.

'Miss Louisa Bigg presents her compliments to Mr. Serjeant Ballantine, and ventures to call his attention to a paragraph in his "Experiences" which she is reading with great interest. On

p. 153 these words stand: "This was the case of Tawell, *a Quaker of eminent outward respectability*," &c. The Society of Friends always entertained suspicions of Tawell (who bore a questionable character long before his final crime), and on that account would never listen to his requests for membership, consequently he never was a Quaker, though the belief that he was one is general.

'Miss Bigg begs that Serjeant Ballantine will pardon her troubling him with this letter, but she is assured that he is only anxious for the truth, and that he would be most unwilling to give pain to any of the wide circle of readers who are gaining so much pleasure and information from his book. Miss Bigg is closely connected with the "Society of Friends," and her mother well recollects the circumstances concerning Tawell, and has often related them to her.

'Serjeant Ballantine will understand that Tawell had his own reasons for wishing to appear a Quaker.'

It is an additional pleasure to me, in inserting the above, to be able to refer to the great amelioration of our criminal code through the instrumentality of this body, and to their invariable humanity when called upon to administer it upon juries

CHAPTER XXXII.

EXPERIENCES VERIFIED.

Letters—Henry Spicer—Frank Burnand—Clement Scott—Watson Wood—General Marriott Letter from—Incidents mentioned—Maidstone—Rochester — Charles Dickens — His house — Falstaff and Prince Hal—Scene of their exploits—Alexander Knox—Letter from—His retirement — Confirmatory incidents — Mrs. Knox—His illness—Conclusion of my memories.

It would give me much personal gratification to quote many other letters that I received written in a very kindly and complimentary spirit, but I do not feel justified in taking up the time of my readers for what might fairly be charged as a mere gratification of my own vanity. I may, however, adopt this medium for a word of thanks to my dear old friend, Henry Spicer, and tell him how much I valued an opinion so generously expressed; and the note from Frank Burnand is no small compliment; whilst Clement Scott, although I cannot but feel that friendship has greatly exaggerated my merits, does much to encourage hopes in my present venture.

I should have been very glad to publish a communication from Mr. Watson Wood, giving very interesting particulars about Mr. Woolley, who it may be remembered brought an action against the insurers of Campden House with a successful result,[1] but am not sure that I should be justified in doing so, or that the writer would desire it.

In looking over the correspondence with which I was favoured, I came upon the following superscription :—

'Old Rectory House, Littlebourne, Wingham, Kent:
'April 5, 1882.'

Upon reading this, a hope took possession of me that some venerable member of the Church had furnished me with matter calculated for the improvement of my mind. As, however, I proceeded with the letter, I discovered that it came from a gentleman signing himself ' H. Marriott—General—Aged 70.'

I am indebted to the writer for a very amusing illustration of a story I had told, without having by any means pledged myself for the truth of it, and in order to make the application related by him intelligible, I must repeat mine.[2] 'A certain great prince was very poor, and he noticed that his horses were very thin, of which he complained

---

[1] This remarkable trial will be found in p. 215 of my *Experiences*, 5th edition.
[2] *Vide Some Experiences of a Barrister's Life*, 5th edition, p. 33.

to his intendant, whose explanation was that the corn-dealer had refused further credit. " Is there anyone who will trust us ? " asked the prince. After much thought the intendant said that they still had credit with the pastry-cook. " Feed them upon tarts," was the immediate suggestion.'

I give my correspondent's anecdote in his own words :—

'The anecdote of the prince, his exhausted credit all but the pastry-cook's, reminded me vividly of a like occurrence at Chatham—it is now thirty-five years ago. I was then quartered in that garrison. In the barracks was an officer, quite a youth, named K——. He was a fine, good-hearted young fellow, and only his own enemy. Well, I can hardly say that, for he ran into debt and would never pay. He, too, had exhausted the credit of all the bakers, and bread he could not get. But he got hold of a muffin-man, and induced him to supply muffins on " tick," and every morning K—— might be seen running up and down the corridors, offering muffins for a slice of bread. This officer got into the habit of spending his spare hours at " Tom-all-alone," a small public-house in the woods, on the hill, overlooking the Vale of Maidstone. Charles Dickens knew it well. You will remember he uses the name. The colonel preferred charges against him. He was tried by a court-martial. I was one of the members. We liked the boy, but did not much care for the colonel. My neighbour asked me who we were trying, for he thought it seemed the colonel, and not K——. Well, he got off, and straightway he took for a wife his tailor's daughter. What became of him afterwards I never knew.'[1]

Many are the recollections brought back to my mind by the above letter. Maidstone was my favourite circuit town, Rochester a favourite trysting-place, and although I cannot remember the little public-house, nor the reference to it in any of Dickens's works, I knew the hill well upon which it was situated, and can imagine that its quaint title would attract the attention of that observant author. Unless I am wrong, this hill was behind the well-known house occupied by him during the latter days of his life. In front of it, according to veracious report, Prince Hal and Falstaff used to rob the King's lieges, and a not unworthy successor to the poet, who has immortalised, if not created, these adventures of former ages, was the literary photographer who was able from his windows to view the scenes of that redoubtable knight's reputed exploits.

I am sure that I require to make no apology

[1] The general gives the name of the officer, but, as the tailor's daughter may have reformed him, I omit its insertion.

for publishing the following letter, for not only does it confirm incidents that I have related, but it comes from one popular in many circles, a most conscientious and efficient public officer, and beloved by a large number of private friends, who lamented the cause that obliged him to retire from active life. Alexander Knox, Esq., presided for some years as magistrate at Marlborough Street Police Court. In the early days of his life he enjoyed those advantages of St. Paul's School which were so lastingly impressed upon my memory. But let the letter speak for itself:—

'91 Victoria Street, S.W.:
'May 2, 1882.'

'My dear Ballantine,—It is simply owing to the negligence of Messrs. —— that I never got hold of your book until yesterday, and since then I have been devouring it as eagerly as ever I did a plate of roast mutton at Hancock's,[1] when I could get it and pay for it.

'This was in the good old days, when we were so unhappy.

'Oh! for the tears of former days!
Oh! for the men who shed them!

'Let me thank you most cordially for your kindly mention of me. I have always felt a very warm

[1] An eating-house in Rupert Street, Coventry Street, described in my *Experinces*, p. 26, 5th edition.

regard for you, and I am right glad to see that you have not non-suited me in the Court of Friendship.

'But more than this—did I not go down to Margate in one of those old steamers?[1]—my first clear recollection of life. Did I not live in a farmhouse near St. Peter's? Did I not snivel my time at St. Paul's—horribly and cruelly beaten by Bean? and were not my nails cut off by Durham? Did I not go through all the rigs of law-studentship and newspaper work? Did I not often wish to dine at Hancock's—and couldn't? Did I not live for years in Jem Wilde's house in Serjeants' Inn (2nd floor)? Don't I remember Prendergast and Kelly—same diggings? Was I not in with all the *Littery* set (as poor Leech's Major-General called them) from Douglas Jerrold and Dickens's days? Wasn't old Hamblet[2] my bosom-friend? and so on of Evans—Offley's old Garrick Club, and the rest of it?

'By the way, what has poor " Leonora " (Wigan) done to you that you should bracket her in that cruel note with the Veuve Keeley, æt. 75?[3] I

---

[1] Also described p. 4, 5th edition.
[2] Also described p. 181, 5th edition.
[3] This refers to a notice of the above ladies, whom I had the pleasure of meeting at a party at Mrs. Levy's, Grosvenor Street, Grosvenor Square. I regret to say that the former, who, although possessing some peculiarities, had excellent qualities, has recently died.

would not take any offer from her fair hand were
I you. I am getting on very nicely, thank you,
save that I can't dance a hornpipe, and must fight
my battles with one hand —otherwise I can't see
that I am a greater donkey than before my enforced retirement.

'Next Monday we go down to Malvern for a
month. We shall be in London for the whole of
June (on July 1—more or less--we start for the
Ardennes for our summer wandering). Now, in
June, will you fix your own day and hour, and eat
your dinner here one day? I will just ask Bruce
Seton (no one else), and we will talk over old times.
We have a good supply of poor dear Claridge's
" Dry "[1] and cook is still the same, and so empha-
tically is my heart towards you. Susie desires me
to give you her very kind regards.

'Always sincerely yours,
'ALEX. A. KNOX.'

In the work that I have already published, as
in the preceding pages of this, I have avoided
domestic matters as a rule, and although I could
have added largely to my book by the relation of
incidents within my knowledge, highly honourable
to the fair sex, I have, in accordance with what I

---

[1] A well-known brand of champagne, scarcely wanted to enhance the pleasant little dinners of the writer.

believe would be their own wishes, abstained from doing so. But upon this occasion I must be permitted to break through the rule.

There never was more perfect happiness conferred upon a man than the union with the lady Knox had the good fortune to marry. In health she was his companion and friend, adding to every enjoyment and pleasure, and it is owing to her bravery, nobility of mind, and deep affection that, after the terrible calamity he endured, he has been able to write the charming letter I have had so much pleasure in transcribing, and which will prove conclusively that those defects to which he refers are simply physical, and that he is in as complete possession of his powers as he ever was in his life. And it is through the acquaintanceship and consequent regard I feel towards his wife, as well as the friendship with which I am proud to believe I am honoured by both, that I am able with a pleasant recollection to conclude my memories of former days.

CHAPTER XXXIII.

A RÉSUMÉ.

THE task which I imposed upon myself when illness and other causes threatened to separate me from the active pursuit of my profession is completed, and to many kind and generous friends I may, in conveying my adieus, offer also grateful thanks.

In recording the experiences of a long and varied life, including a professional visit to a remote district in India, and a short acquaintance-ship with the surface of American society, I do not affect to be infallible in the opinions and views that I have presented, and only offer them for what my readers may consider them worth, coming as they do from a very unpresuming item amongst the world's workers and thinkers. I do, however, claim to myself the credit of correctly relating the facts upon which they are founded, and believe that I have been unbiassed by prejudice.

I may venture to observe that it is through the works of different observers, themselves affecting no special claims to distinction, and the habits and tastes recorded by them of individuals, that great historians condescend to reap the information which afterwards, published to the world, renders the names of themselves famous.

Macaulay upon pamphlets and writings, long since forgotten, founded his graphic description of the manners and habits of the clergy and squirearchy which in Great Britain preceded the advent of his hero to our shores. The tunes whistled by city *gamins* indicated to him public thought and feeling, and upon such materials he largely relied for his brilliant though somewhat romantic description of that period of England's career. Death, casting a gloom over the entire country, prevented the completion of his task, and it is to be fervently hoped that no Smollett will arise to disfigure his noble work by the prosaic dulness of a so called continuation.

Perchance it may be my fortune that some future Macaulay may find in my unpretending gossip materials to aid him in a work of solid benefit to the human race. Whilst, however, my ambition has not, through a great portion of my writing, soared beyond a desire to amuse, I have earnestly desired that my experiences upon some of the graver matters I have dwelt upon may not be entirely without advantage.

Upon one subject, that of the criminal law, I

feel justified in expressing them with the confidence created by intimate personal knowledge; and, indeed, I am not without hope that the opinions I have given in my former volumes have already borne fruit, for since their publication, where I expressed in strong and unhesitating language my opinion of the impropriety of translating Chancery barristers, without preparation or knowledge of its procedure, into presiding over criminal cases involving the issues of life and death, I have not noticed any continuation of this extraordinary practice. On the contrary, gentlemen of the highest claims have been selected to preside in such cases.

It may be vanity to suppose that words of mine have had any influence; perchance some of the current jokes of the circuit messes may have reached even the august ears of the Chancellor, and ridicule not unfrequently initiates reform where grave argument fails to produce an effect. In addressing my protest to Lord Selborne, I have acted upon the belief that he is not only one of the most eminent and learned of those who have occupied the woolsack, but who, in the exercise of the enormous powers attached to that office, is governed by conscientious motives, and I venture to address a few more words to him upon the subject.

The effect of the administration of the criminal

law, the intense interest excited in a circuit town, can only be thoroughly appreciated by those who have closely watched such proceedings. Long before the Assizes take place the names of the judges are known, and their characters canvassed. The principal crimes to be tried, the prisoners, and the circumstances are also common talk.

The court, within a few minutes of its opening, presents at every disposable space the faces of eager, attentive, middle-class country people, as well as a good sprinkling of the labouring element. This interest continues during the Assizes, and a pretty just estimate is formed in the county of the results and the performers in them upon the Bench and at the Bar.

I will not now consider the possibility of unjust convictions; these are rare, and I have never witnessed a trial presided over by an Equity judge who has not exhibited almost painful anxiety to give the defence fair play. The failure of justice is more frequently in the opposite direction.

The conflict between the practised advocate and the witness requires all the skill of an experienced judge to control and direct it. It simply bewilders the very learned and courtly gentleman who witnesses it for the first time; and the results, which are completely recognised by the audience, and the escape of a rogue, lead naturally to the belief in immunity for crime, and to a very humble opinion of judicial wisdom.

I myself witnessed a scene in which a most conscientious but very energetic counsel so astonished a learned judge fresh from the peaceful fields of Equity, that he appealed to another barrister who happened to be standing in the body of the court as to whether he had ever before witnessed such behaviour to a judge. The case in which this occurred was one of murder, of which the accused was convicted but not executed.

I am bound to say that, whilst in my opinion unjust convictions rarely occur, they certainly are not unexampled, and the question as to whether the infliction of death should render them irrevocable has been, and still is, worthy of the gravest consideration.

But one objection seems to me of magnitude: 'that the principle of its application is founded, not upon the atrocity of the crime, but upon its result.' Of this permit me to give a possible illustration. The brutality of a ruffian followed by the death of his victim may, and constantly does, consign him to the gallows, whilst if the same criminal had for the deliberate object of assassination employed secret poisoning for months, and accidentally failed to effect it, his life would not be forfeited.

Moreover, I have always been of opinion that the main justification for taking away life was by the example that a public execution afforded, and I do not believe that the somewhat melodramatic exhibition of a black flag carries with it the same amount of terror to the general public, or of shame and anguish to the relatives of the unhappy wretch executed, as was supposed resulted from the former practice.

My object in the above remarks is not to write an essay upon the principles of death punishment, but to strengthen those I have already made upon the danger and injustice of denying to the convict a power of appeal, especially under a system where execution follows sentence with comparative rapidity.

Those who give merely cursory consideration to this great social question, satisfy themselves by the belief that cases are considered by the Secretary of State, and reviewed in some mysterious and extra-judicial manner. Upon this subject I can partially enlighten my readers. A petition may be presented to the Home Office, and is submitted to the Under-Secretaries of State—and in the remarks I am making upon this subject I am bound to admit that more admirable and conscientious officers never filled any public post than the gentlemen who perform this task.

The Honourable Adolphus Liddell has for a great number of years been the principal adviser of the Home Office upon these occasions. Patient, painstaking, a thorough lawyer and conscientious gentleman, he does all that is possible with the imperfect machinery under his control, but no materials exist for a searching inquiry. Counsel are not heard, and what statements may be made adverse to the petitioner are not known. The case is remitted back to the judge who tried it, and his opinion must, and does usually, govern the decision. And thus, through an inquiry entirely private, the fatal dictum so often issues from the Home Secretary—' Her Majesty's advisers see no reason to interfere.'

The case of the S——s, to which I have already referred, is well deserving of attention, as illustrative of this state of things. Little assistance could be expected by the petitioner from the judge who tried it, but it happened that its circumstances created much attention. The facts became the property of a press unanimous upon it, and the reversal of the sentence a necessary answer to a storm of public indignation.

It was my misfortune a few years ago to be called upon to defend a very worthless, drunken fellow, who had become connected with a weak-minded woman possessing money, and it was imputed to him that he caused her death by violence and neglect. An excited and indignant coroner's jury ushered him to the Old Bailey, and he was tried for murder.

From the commencement of the trial several of the jurymen showed that they were impregnated with prejudice, which they most indecently exhibited. The violence charged was disproved, and the prisoner was found guilty of Manslaughter upon the following legal principle laid down by the judge, that a man was by *law* bound to support a mistress in all necessaries according to his means, and take every reasonable care of her.

The moral worth of such a doctrine I by no means desire to dispute, but I do not acknowledge its legal correctness, and if there had existed a court of appeal I believe that it would have been overruled. At all events, such a principle was worthy of being discussed.

In this particular case, however, I believe that the accused was perfectly innocent. I do not believe that he either acted with violence toward the woman, or wilfully neglected her, nor do I think that her death even was attributable to the causes imputed; and, moreover, I have a strong suspicion it was occasioned by the agency of another person.

Petitions have been presented in this case.

I presume that the usual formalities have been gone through, that the learned judge is quite satisfied with his own law and approves of the conviction, and although the law laid down was wrong, and the facts more than doubtful, an innocent man, if still alive, may be undergoing penal servitude for the remainder of his days.

It will be understood by my readers that in naming these examples I have done so with a view of calling attention to the broad question of a court of appeal in criminal cases, and intend no reference to the selection of Equity judges, none of whom presided in either of them.

I have read with much interest a letter that appeared in the 'Daily Telegraph' in connection with a person named George Hall, who had been recently released from a sentence of twenty years' penal servitude for shooting his wife. If the details of the crime are truly stated, I cannot but believe that in a court of appeal the sentence would have been much modified; but my principal reason for referring to the letter is the account given by the correspondent of the paper, of the circumstances attending his release.

'George Hall was met at New Street Station by thousands of people, amongst whom intense excitement prevailed. He was received with remarkable demonstrations of welcome, the crowd thronging the station and its precincts, and a detachment of police had to be called in to preserve order. When Hall alighted from the train vociferous cheers were given, and were continued until he had driven off in a cab with his relatives.' [1]

I quote this account to support the assertion I have made of the interest the public take in the result of a criminal trial. The effect evidently produced in this case was, that the accused had been dealt with hardly and unjustly. This may not have been so, but surely no one can deny that such a scene as described above carries with it an important warning.

In conclusion I assert that logic and justice both demand that a court of appeal should be established in all criminal cases, and in my former work I have pointed out a mode by which such a court might be constituted without additional expense, and secure at the same time a general improvement in the administration of the law applicable to the criminal classes; but I desire to protest most solemnly against the continuance of a system in which a capital sentence is permitted to be carried out within a comparatively few days, without the power being given to the

[1] *Daily Telegraph*, March 6, 1884.

convict to have his case reviewed publicly before a competent tribunal.

The letter published in the 'Daily Telegraph,' from which I have quoted, and inserted *in extenso* in the Appendix to this volume, conveys very much the ideas that I have formed theoretically upon the subject of imprisonment, and a little incident that occurred to myself not many years ago helps to illustrate my views.

Some occasion took me to visit a poor woman in one of the alleys turning out of the Seven Dials. It was at Christmas time. No pen could fully describe the misery of the wretched creatures crowded in that hovel. I performed my task as quickly as I could, and was startled by a remark falling from the lips of a young child to the following effect—'Well, Tom has plenty to eat!'

The allusion was to a brother in gaol, and thus amongst the population of St. Giles's, a prison is esteemed a place to be envied. Is it a place that effects amendment? and, if it does, what becomes of the released convicts? What employment can they obtain in their own country? Surely it is a question for the Legislature to consider very gravely.

It would tax the patience of my readers were I to attempt to develop my theories upon the entire question, but I repeat, as the result of my experience, that transportation when inflicted created the greatest terror in the criminal, and in those likely to be affected by his fate, and also, what ought to be the prominent object of the State, the existence of hope in the minds of those willing to reform gave them an opportunity to become good citizens.

APPENDIX.

TWENTY YEARS' PENAL SERVITUDE.

A CORRESPONDENT writes:—

'George Hall, who shot his wife through the head in Birmingham more than twenty years ago, and who has since been in prison under a sentence of penal servitude, was released from Pentonville Prison with a ticket of leave yesterday morning. He was promptly followed by the present writer to a little mission room in St. Giles's and induced to tell some of the most interesting parts of his remarkable story. He will, I believe, shortly start for an obscure part of America, to begin a new life under conditions which he hopes will shake him free from his old reputation and name. He was found sitting in the little chapel of the mission house, where he had been persuaded to go partly by religious ministrations within the prison walls, and partly by a promise of monetary help in the purchase of an outfit for the voyage. He was not unwilling to give the particulars sought for.

'"I was convicted," said George Hall, "when I was twenty years old, and now I am forty-one; so I've been in prison more than half of my life. I was a jewellery stamper when I went in, but they sent me to Chatham for five months and taught me bootmaking. After that I was at Dartmoor fourteen years.

S

'"No! I don't agree with anyone that says that it's a jolly life there. It's like being dead. You're starved, and cut to pieces with the wind, and you talk to nobody except a mate when you walk in pairs on Sunday afternoon. I was a good-conduct man for the best part of the time. I wore blue breeches and a drab coat, and they let me walk as far as the outer walls, else I should have died.

'"The rest of the time I spent in Pentonville Prison. There it's worse still. You mustn't talk to anyone from year's end to year's end. If you try to talk to the warder he reports you for insubordination. The chaplain is the only good sort in the prison, Mr. De Renzi; he's the only chap you can speak to, but he hasn't time. There ought to be ten chaplains, sir, and fewer warders; then the prisoners would get a chance of doing some good.

'"No! I don't consider my sentence was just. I ought to have had six months—that's what I ought to have had; but, you see, it's a very serious thing to take life."

'Here the brother interposed: "The woman he killed was a beast!" he exclaimed; "she would have druv any chap mad."

'"Well, well," said George, with a sigh of deprecation, "she was a bad 'un, but she is dead and gone. She was my wife, too. But, only think! She left me on the first night of the marriage. She said she felt ill. 'Let me go with you,' I said; but, no, she would go by herself. I didn't know where she went for a long time after. She came back next day, and we lived for some days together. Then she went away and never came back, and I flew to drink.

'"Soon after I saw her in a theatre with a man. They say I took out a knife and made for him; but I don't remember it, I was mad with rage and drink. Well,

I shot her through the head, and that's a fact. If I had shot the man I should have got off easy, but I shot her, and I'm a murderer I suppose, although I don't remember a bit about it. How I got the pistol I don't know. How I shot the woman I don't know. I was as drunk as a weazel. I might as well have been asleep.

'" I little thought I should ever come to such a thing. I thought she was a good girl, and maybe she was to start with. But she was tempted by a villain, and the pair of them together made me a drunkard and a murderer, all in a month! I don't bear any spite against the man. I think that the vengeance of God is upon him. If God forgives him so do I. I shall forget it all if the world will only give me a chance now. I reckon that I am beginning my life at the age of forty-one." '

A Birmingham correspondent telegraphs:—

' George Hall was met at New Street Station by thousands of people, amongst whom intense excitement prevailed. He was received with remarkable demonstrations of welcome, the crowd thronging the station and its precincts, and a detachment of police had to be called in to preserve order. When Hall alighted from the train vociferous cheers were given, and were continued until he had driven off in a cab with his relatives.' [1]

[1] *Daily Telegraph*, March 6, 1884.

S. & H.

LONDON: PRINTED BY
SPOTTISWOODE AND CO., NEW-STREET SQUARE
AND PARLIAMENT STREET

A CATALOGUE OF NEW AND STANDARD WORKS PUBLISHED BY RICHARD BENTLEY & SON.

THE FOURTH QUARTER OF

1884.

ORDER OF ARRANGEMENT.

HISTORICAL WORKS.

BIOGRAPHY & CORRESPONDENCE.

EXPLORATIONS, VOYAGES, AND TRAVELS.

POETRY, THE DRAMA, &c.

ART AND SCIENCE.

RELIGIOUS AND KINDRED WORKS.

MISCELLANEOUS WORKS.

WORKS OF FICTION.

MAGAZINES.

MISCELLANEOUS LISTS.

LONDON:

RICHARD BENTLEY & SON,

NEW BURLINGTON STREET,

PUBLISHERS IN ORDINARY TO HER MAJESTY THE QUEEN,

AND PUBLISHERS TO THE PALESTINE EXPLORATION FUND ETC.

All works are in one volume unless stated to the contrary.

ALTERATIONS

SINCE THE LAST ISSUE OF THE CATALOGUE.

ADDITIONS.

	PAGE
Jackson's Court of Francis I.	4
Bourrienne's Napoleon	6
Weise's Discoveries of America	8
Harris's Reminiscences of the Road	9
Hook's Archbishops of Canterbury. New edit. Vols. VIII. and XII.	13
Brabourne's Letters of Jane Austen	14
Yates' Fifty Years of London Life	14
Buchanan's Literary Career	15
Ballantine's Old and New World	15
Lucy's East by West	18
Hissey's Old-fashioned Journey	18
Wilde's Driftwood from Scandinavia	18
Speedy's Wanderings in the Soudan	20
King's Civilian's Wife in India	20
Letters from Hell. New edit.	29
Mallock's Literary Essays	29

SPECIAL NOTICE.

Information furnished to Shippers, or others, without any loss of time on enquiry by Telephone to number

3,730.

Attendance from 10 to 5 on Weekdays (Saturdays 10 to 2 only) general holidays excepted.

** *A Circular giving full information in regard to the sending of* MANUSCRIPTS *will be forwarded upon application.*

** *For the convenience of persons abroad referring to this Catalogue, a table of equivalent values of money will be found on page 46.*

September 24, 1884.

A List of Works

PUBLISHED BY

RICHARD BENTLEY & SON,

NOW IN PRINT.

HISTORICAL WORKS.*

The History of Antiquity.

From the German of Professor MAX DUNCKER, by EVELYN ABBOTT, M.A., LL.D., of Balliol College, Oxford. In Six Vols. demy 8vo. Each Volume can be obtained separately, price 21s.   I C D I

'Translator and publisher are alike to be congratulated on the completion of this standard work on ancient history, the last volume of which has just appeared. There is no need of describing the fullness of detail by which it is characterised, or the interesting style in which it has been written. Those of the public who care to know what was the origin of European culture and civilisation, or what has produced the Oriental world of to-day, are already well acquainted with the merits of Professor Max Duncker book. The translator has done full justice to both author and subject; the English is thoroughly idiomatic, and reproduces all the charms of the author's style.

'Duncker is learned as an historian should be; but his learning is not confined to the old classical sources of information which alone were open to the writers of the last century. He has made full use of those marvellous discoveries in Egypt, in Assyria, in Babylonia, and in other parts of the East which have swept away the fables of Greek and Latin compilers, and brought us face to face with the every-day life and history of the ancient Oriental world. He has gone to the latest and best authorities, venturing to differ from their inferences and conclusions only where these seemed to him to conflict with the principles of historical criticism.'—THE ACADEMY.

'Professor Max Duncker's "History of Antiquity" is a work which should be in the hands of every historical student, not merely as a book for passing reference, but to be carefully read and digested. In all the six volumes we may safely say that there is no chapter lacking in interest.'
                                                                            SATURDAY REVIEW.

The History of Greece,

From the Earliest Time down to 337 B.C. From the German of Dr. ERNST CURTIUS, Rector of the University of Berlin. By A. W. WARD, M.A. In Five Vols. demy 8vo. with Index, 90s.; or each Volume separately, price 18s.
                                                                                    C D I

'A history known to scholars as one of the profoundest, most original, and most instructive of modern times.'—GLOBE.

'We cannot express our opinion of Dr. Curtius' book better than by saying that it may be fitly ranked with Theodor Mommsen's great work.'—SPECTATOR.

---

* See also some Works under *Biography*.

A 2

The History of Greece,

From the earliest times to the overthrow of the Persians at Salamis and Plataea. From the German of Professor MAX DUNCKER, by S. F. ALLEYNE. In demy 8vo. (Uniform in size with 'The History of Antiquity.') VOL. I. is now ready, price 15s.

The History of Rome,

From the Earliest Times to the Period of its Decline. By Professor THEODOR MOMMSEN. Translated (with the Author's sanction, and Additions) by the Rev. P. W. DICKSON. With an Introduction by Dr. SCHMITZ. The POPULAR EDITION in Four Vols. crown 8vo. £2. 6s. 6d.; or sold separately—Vols. I. and II., 21s.; Vol. III., 10s. 6d.; Vol. IV., with Index, 15s.

Also, a LIBRARY EDITION, in Four Vols. demy 8vo. 75s. These Volumes not sold separately.

'A work of the very highest merit; its learning is exact and profound; its narrative full of genius and skill; its descriptions of men are admirably vivid. We wish to place on record our opinion that Dr. Mommsen's is by far the best history of the decline and fall of the Roman Commonwealth.'—TIMES.

'This the best history of the Roman republic, taking the work on the whole —the author's complete mastery of his subject, the variety of his gifts and acquirements, his graphic power in the delineation of natural and individual character, and the vivid interest which he inspires in every portion of his book. He is without an equal in his own sphere.'—EDINBURGH REVIEW.

The History of Roman Classical Literature.

By Professor BROWNE. A New Edition, in 1 vol. demy 8vo. 9s.

'Professor Browne is not only a classical scholar, but one of the most graceful of English modern writers. In clearness, purity, and elegance of style, his compositions are unsurpassed; and his sketches of the lives and works of the great authors of antiquity are models of refined taste and sound criticism. We esteem very highly the value of a work like this. It is the result of great research and profound study; but it is also popular and entertaining. It is designed for readers of every class, and cannot fail to be attractive to all. Even the classical scholar may derive from its enlightened criticisms a more familiar or more accurate acquaintance with the literature of the Roman World; and the more unlettered reader will certainly draw from its eloquent pages a very lively and faithful impression of those literary treasures which have survived the ruin of ages. Whatever has been done by former writers to elucidate this interesting subject has been skilfully woven by Professor Browne into the course of his narrative; and, without wearying the reader by any laborious disquisitions, he has availed himself with judicious discrimination of the untiring industry of the German critics. Such are the main features of a work which, for utility of design and excellence of execution, may challenge comparison with any which the present century has produced; nor can we hesitate to regard it as a very valuable instrument for the instruction of the national mind and the elevation of the national taste.'
MORNING POST.

Sketches of the Historic Past of Italy;

From the Fall of the Roman Empire to the Earliest Revival of Letters and Arts. By MARGARET ALBANA MIGNATY. In demy 8vo. 16s.

The Court of France in the Reigns of Francis I. and Henry II.

By CATHERINE CHARLOTTE, Lady JACKSON, Author of 'Old Paris,' 'The Old Regime,' &c. In two vols. large crown 8vo. with portraits.

[*In the press.*

The Old Régime.

By CATHERINE CHARLOTTE, Lady JACKSON, Author of 'Old Paris' &c. With Portraits of Louis XV., Marie Antoinette, Rousseau, Voltaire, Madame du Barry, Mademoiselle Clairon. In 2 vols. large crown 8vo. 24s.   R 2

The French Court and Society in the Reign of Louis XVI. and during the First Empire.

By CATHERINE CHARLOTTE, Lady JACKSON, Author of 'The Old Regime,' &c. With Portraits of the Empresses Josephine and Marie Louise, Necker, Talma, Contesse de Provence, and Charlotte Corday. In 2 vols. large crown 8vo. 24s.   O Z 2

The Court of the Tuileries from the Restoration to the flight of Louis Philippe.

By CATHERINE CHARLOTTE, Lady JACKSON, Author of 'Old Paris,' 'The Old Regime,' 'French Court and Society,' &c. In 2 vols. large crown 8vo. with Portraits of the Emperor Alexander, the Duchesse de Berri, the Duchesse d'Angoulême, the Duchesse d'Orleans, Madame Recamier, Mdlle. Mars, Mdlle. Rachel, Charles X., the Duc de Bordeaux and his Sister, 24s.

The History of the Great French Revolution, from 1789-1801.

By ADOLPHE THIERS. Translated by FREDERICK SHOBERL. With Forty-one Fine Engravings and Portraits of the most eminent Personages engaged in the Revolution, engraved by W. GREATBACH. In 5 vols. demy 8vo. 36s.
   O A 1*

LIST OF THE ENGRAVINGS,
Showing the Plates in each Volume.

VOL.
I. The Attack on the Bastile.
Portrait of the Duc d'Orleans.
Portrait of Mirabeau.
Portrait of Lafayette.
Orgies of the Gards du Corps.
Portrait of Marie Antoinette.
Return of the Roya Family from Varennes.
Portrait of Marat.
The Mob at the Tuileries.
Attack on the Tuileries.
II. Murder of the Princess de Lamballe.
Portrait of the Princess de Lamballe.
Portrait of Madame Roland.
Louis XVI. at the Convention.
Last Interview of Louis XVI. with his Family.
Portrait of Louis XVI.
Portrait of Dumourier.
Triumph of Marat.
Portrait of Larochejaquelin.

VOL.
III. Assassination of Marat.
Portrait of Charlotte Corday.
Portrait of Camille Desmoulins.
Condemnation of Marie Antoinette.
Portrait of Bailly (Mayor of Paris).
Trial of Danton, Camille Desmoulins, &c
Portrait of Danton.
Portrait of Madame Elizabeth.
Carrier at Nantes.
Portrait of Robespierre.
IV. Last Victims of the Reign of Terror.
Portrait of Charette.
Death of the Deputy Feraud.
Death of Romme, Goujon, Duquesnoi, &c.
Portrait of Louis XVII.
The 13th Vendémiaire (Oct. 5, 1795).
V. Summoning to Execution.
Portrait of Pichegru.
Portrait of Moreau.
Portrait of Hoche.
Portrait of Napoleon Bonaparte.
The 18th Brumaire (November 10th, 17

Lessons of French Revolution, 1789-1872.
By the Right Hon. Lord ORMATHWAITE. 8vo. 10s. 6d. 253

The Private Life of Marie Antoinette, Queen of France and Navarre.
With Sketches and Anecdotes of the Courts of Louis XIV., XV., and XVI., by JEANNE LOUISE HENRIETTE CAMPAN, First Lady in Waiting to the Queen. An entirely New and Revised Edition, with additional Notes, in 2 vols. demy 8vo. 36s. With Sixteen fine Illustrations on Steel.

Memoirs of the Court and Family of Napoleon.
By Mdme. JUNOT (the Duchesse d'ABRANTÈS). Embellished by Portraits, engraved expressly for this work, of the entire Bonaparte Family. A New and Revised Edition, in 3 vols. demy 8vo. 63s. (originally 36s.)

9 Z 1

'A wondrously fascinating history of the First Napoleon.'—ILLUSTRATED LONDON NEWS.
'Contains the fullest, the most interesting, and, on the whole, perhaps the truest particulars ever published about Napoleon.'—ST. JAMES'S GAZETTE.
'Some of the most interesting memoirs in existence.'—SATURDAY REVIEW.
'Portraits lend an additional charm and value to the volumes, which teem with natural description.'—DAILY TELEGRAPH.

Memoirs of Napoleon Bonaparte.
By LOUIS ANTOINE FAUVELET DE BOURRIENNE, his private Secretary. Edited, with Preface and Notes, by Colonel R. W. PHIPPS, late Royal Artillery. In 3 vols. demy 8vo. with Map and the following Illustrations (except one) on Steel:

VOL. I.	VOL. II.	VOL. III.
Napoleon I. (a)	Josephine (a).	Marie Louise (a).
Pichegru.	Lannes.	The King of Rome.
Moreau.	Macdonald.	Bessieres.
Desaix.	The Cuirassiers at Eylau.	Duroc.
Kléber.	Murat.	Caulaincourt.
Duc d'Enghien.	Napoleon I. (b)	Marie Louise (b).
Letitia Ramolino.	Josephine (b).	Prince Eugene.
Talleyrand.	Davoust.	Napoleon I. (c)
Hortense.	Lasalle.	The Abdication.
Junot.	Suchet.	Wellington.
Ney (a).	Gouvion St. Cyr.	Blucher.
Massena.	Soult.	Ney (b).

[*In the press.*

'Whoever wishes to know, not merely the General but the Emperor but what the MAN really was, will find him well pictured in these memoirs by the Private Secretary of Napoleon.'
THE TIMES.

The History of the Rise and Progress of the English Constitution.
By Sir EDWARD CREASY, late Chief Justice of Ceylon. A Popular Account of the Primary Principles, and Formation and Development of the English Constitution, avoiding all Party Politics. Fourteenth Edition. Crown 8vo. price 6s.

1 S 2*

The Lives of the Queens of England of the House of Hanover:

Sophia Dorothea of Zell (wife of George I.)—Caroline Wilhelmina Dorothea (wife of George II.)—Charlotte Sophia (wife of George III.)—Caroline of Brunswick (wife of George IV.)—Adelaide of Saxe-Meiningen (wife of William IV.). By Dr. DORAN, F.S.A., Author of 'Table Traits and Something on Them,' &c. Fourth, and Enlarged Edition. 2 vols. 8vo. 25*s*.

The Naval History of Great Britain,

From the Declaration of War by France, in 1793, to the Accession of George IV. By WILLIAM JAMES. With a Continuation of the History down to the Battle of Navarino, by Captain CHAMIER. 6 vols. crown 8vo., with Portraits of William James, Lord Nelson, Sir Thomas Troubridge, Earl St. Vincent, Lord Duncan, Sir Hyde Parker, Sir Nesbit Willoughby, Sir William Hoste, Lord Hood, Earl Howe, Sir Sidney Smith, Lord Dundonald, 36*s*.

'This book is one of which it is not too high praise to assert that it approaches as nearly to perfection in its own line as any historical work perhaps ever did.'—EDINBURGH REVIEW.

London in the Jacobite Times.

By Dr. DORAN, F.S.A., Author of 'The Lives of the Queens of England of the House of Hanover,' &c. In 2 vols. demy 8vo. 36*s*.

The Court of London, from 1819-1825.

By RICHARD RUSH, United States' Minister in London during that Period. Edited by his Son, BENJAMIN RUSH. In 1 vol. demy 8vo. 16*s*.

Old Court Customs and Modern Court Rule.

With some account of Westminster, Greenwich, the Palaces of Whitehall, Kensington, St. James', Buckingham Palace, Hampton Court, Windsor, &c. By the Hon. Mrs. ARMYTAGE. In 1 vol. demy 8vo. with Four Illustrations, 10*s*. 6*d*.

'As entertaining as it is instructive, the information regarding all the intricacies of etiquette being carefully authentic and exact.'—DAILY TELEGRAPH.

'... Contains in a comparatively small space a large amount of information which cannot fail to interest all ranks and classes in the kingdom.'—MORNING POST.

Memorials of the South Saxon See and Cathedral of Chichester.

From Original Sources, by the Rev. W. R. W. STEPHENS, Prebendary of Chichester, Author of 'The Life and Times of St. John Chrysostom,' &c. In demy 8vo. with Plan of the Cathedral, and Seven Illustrations. 21*s*.

Lives of the Archbishops of Canterbury.

See page 13.

The History of the Ottoman Turks,

From the Beginning of their Empire to Recent Times, 1250-1878. By Sir EDWARD CREASY, late Chief Justice of Ceylon. New and Revised Edition, being the fifth. In crown 8vo. 6s.

'Of all the histories of the Turks this is by far the best.'—SPECTATOR.

The Fifteen Decisive Battles of the World:

Marathon, B.C. 490; Defeat of the Athenians at Syracuse, B.C. 413; Arbela, B.C. 331; The Metaurus, B.C. 207; Defeat of Varus, A.D. 9; Chalons, A.D. 451; Tours, A.D. 732; Hastings, A.D. 1066; Orleans, A.D. 1429; The Spanish Armada, A.D. 1558; Blenheim, A.D. 1704; Pultowa, A.D. 1709; Saratoga, A.D. 1777; Valmy, A.D. 1792; Waterloo, A.D. 1815. By Sir EDWARD CREASY, late Chief Justice of Ceylon. Twenty-ninth Edition, with Plans. Crown 8vo. 6s.

Also, a LIBRARY EDITION. In 8vo. with Plans, price 10s. 6d.

'It was a happy idea of Professor Creasy to select for military description those few battles which, in the words of Hallam, "A contrary event would have essentially varied the drama of the world in all its subsequent scenes." The decisive features of the battles are well and clearly brought out: the reader's mind is attracted to the world-wide importance of the event he is considering, while their succession carries him over the whole stream of European history.'
SPECTATOR.

The History of the American Civil War.

By Colonel FLETCHER. In 3 vols. 8vo. separately, price 18s. each.

'The conception and execution of this History are most creditable. It is eminently impartial, and Colonel Fletcher has shown that he can gain reputation in the field of Literature as well as in the camp of Mars.'—TIMES.

A History of the Invasions of India.

In 8vo. 14s.

The Secret Service of the Confederate States in Europe.

By JAMES D. BULLOCH, late Captain in the Confederate Navy, and Naval Representative in Europe. In 2 vols. demy 8vo. 21s.

A History of the Discoveries of America down to the year 1825.

By ARTHUR JAMES WEISE, M.A. In one vol. demy 8vo., with numerous Maps reproduced in facsimile from the originals. [Immediately.

The History of the Indian Navy.

Being an Account of the Creation, Constitution, War Services, and Surveys of the Indian Navy between the years 1613 and 1863 (when it was abolished). From Original Sources and hitherto Unpublished Documents. By Lieut. CHARLES RATHBONE LOW, (late) Indian Navy, F.R.G.S. In 2 vols. demy 8vo. 36s.

Historical Records of the 93rd Sutherland Highlanders,

NOW THE 2nd BATTALION PRINCESS LOUISE'S ARGYLL AND SUTHERLAND HIGHLANDERS. Compiled and edited by Captain RODERICK HAMILTON BURGOYNE, late 93rd Highlanders. Being a history of the Regiment from its formation to the present time, and containing a notice of nearly every officer who has served in it, also including nominal lists of all ranks killed and wounded, and particulars of officers and soldiers who have specially distinguished themselves. With numerous Illustrations of dress, &c. In 1 vol. demy 8vo. 30s.
4 R 2

The History of the Honourable Artillery Company of London.

By Captain G. A. RAIKES, 3rd West York Light Infantry, Instructor of Musketry, H.A.C., &c. In 2 vols. with Portraits, Coloured Illustrations, and Maps, demy 8vo. 63s.
S I P

*** *Each Volume sold separately*, price 31s. 6d.

Historical Records of the First Regiment of Militia ;

Or Third West York Light Infantry. By Captain G. A. RAIKES, 3rd West York Light Infantry, Instructor of Musketry, Hon. Artillery Company, &c. With Eight full-page Illustrations. In 8vo. 21s.
S I P

The Stage :

Its Past and Present History. By HENRY NEVILLE. Demy 8vo. 96 pp. 5s.
S I P

In and about Drury Lane,

And other Papers. By the late JOHN DORAN, F.S.A. In 2 vols. large crown 8vo. 21s.
S S I

Reminiscences of the Road.

By STANLEY HARRIS, Author of 'Old Coaching Days.' With Sixteen Illustrations on Stone by JOHN STURGESS. In demy 8vo.
[*In the press.*

BIOGRAPHY AND CORRESPONDENCE.

The Autobiography of Prince Metternich.

Edited by his Son, Prince METTERNICH. The papers classified and arranged by M. A. DE KLINKOWSTRÖM. Translated by ROBINA NAPIER and GERARD W. SMITH.

1773–1815. In 2 vols. demy 8vo, with Portrait and two Facsimiles, 36s.   2 s 2†
1816–1829. In 2 vols. demy 8vo. 36s.   6 s 2
1830–1835. In 1 vol. demy 8vo. 18s.   7 B 2
1836–1848. In demy 8vo.

The Life of Henry John Temple, Viscount Palmerston.

With Selections from his Diaries and Correspondence. By the late Lord DALLING and BULWER. In demy 8vo.
Volumes I. and II. with fine Portrait, 30s.
Volume III. edited by the Hon. EVELYN ASHLEY, M.P. 15s.   7 A 1
Volumes IV. and V. by the Hon. EVELYN ASHLEY, M.P. with Two Portraits, 30s.   2 A 1

ANOTHER EDITION.

In 2 vols. crown 8vo. with Frontispiece to each volume, 12s.   1 s 1†

This work, although based upon the previous 'Life of Lord Palmerston,' has been entirely re-edited by Mr. ASHLEY, and contains considerable additional matter and alterations.

'Mr. Evelyn Ashley's volumes could not have been published at a more appropriate moment, for the opinions of Lord Palmerston upon Ireland and upon foreign questions generally have a soundness which recommends them to the perusal of all. Rarely has Mr. Bentley sent out a more fascinating work or one of greater European importance. We have a book with all the attractions of a romance and all the value of a biography of one who was an Englishman first and a statesman afterwards.'—WHITEHALL REVIEW.

The Correspondence of Prince Talleyrand and Louis XVIII,

During the Congress of Vienna. Edited by M. G. PALLAIN. In 2 vols. demy 8vo. 24s.   2 B 2†

Personal Reminiscences of Lord Stratford de Redclyffe; and the Crimean War.

By the Author of 'Frontier Lands of the Christian and the Turk.' In demy 8vo. 12s.
   4 B

Memoir of Earl Spencer (Lord Althorp).

By the late Sir DENIS LE MARCHANT, Bart. In demy 8vo. 16s.   2 L 2

A Diary kept while in Office,

By EDWARD LAW, EARL of ELLENBOROUGH. Edited by Lord COLCHESTER. Containing Anecdotes of George the Fourth, William the Fourth, the Dukes of Cumberland, Wellington, and Richmond, Lord Hardinge, Sir Robert Peel, Lords Brougham, Grey, Bathurst, Palmerston, Aberdeen, and Melville; Huskisson, Sir Wm. Knighton, &c. In two vols. demy 8vo. 30s.

The History of Lord Ellenborough's Administration in India.

Containing his Letters to Her Majesty the Queen, and Letters to and from the Duke of Wellington. Edited by Lord COLCHESTER. In 8vo. 18s.

Selections from the Official Writings of the Rt. Hon. Mountstuart Elphinstone, Governor of Bombay.

Edited, with a Memoir, by Professor FORREST. In demy 8vo. 21s.

Lord Beaconsfield: His Life, Character, and Works.

By GEORG BRANDES. Translated by Mrs. STURGE. In demy 8vo. 10s. 6d.

Historical Characters.

(Talleyrand, Mackintosh, Cobbett, Canning, Peel.)
By the late Lord DALLING and BULWER, G.C.B. Fifth and enlarged Edition. In crown 8vo. 6s.

Diaries and Letters of Sir G. Jackson.

From the Peace of Amiens to the Battle of Talavera. Edited by Lady JACKSON. 2 vols. 8vo. 30s.
The BATH ARCHIVES. A further Selection from the Letters and Diaries of Sir GEORGE JACKSON, K.G.H., from 1809 to 1816. Edited by Lady JACKSON. In 2 vols. 8vo. price 30s.

MEMOIRS OF THE DUCHESSE D'ABRANTÈS (MADAME JUNOT).

See particulars on page 6.

MEMOIRS OF MADAME CAMPAN.

See particulars on page 6.

MEMOIRS OF M. DE BOURRIENNE (Private Secretary and Schoolfellow of Napoleon).

See particulars on page 6.

The Life of Lord Wolseley.

By CHARLES RATHBONE LOW (late), Indian Navy, F.R.G.S. A New and Extended Edition, brought down to date. In 1 vol. crown 8vo. with a Portrait. 6s.

Memoir of Charles the Twelfth.

By His Majesty THE KING OF SWEDEN AND NORWAY. Translated with His Majesty's permission by GEORGE APGEORGE, Her Britannic Majesty's Consul at Stockholm. In royal 8vo. with Two Illustrations, 12s.   1 S 2

The Autobiography of a Seaman:

(Lord DUNDONALD). Popular Edition. With Portrait and Four Charts. In crown 8vo. 6s.   (*Reprinting.*)   5 A 2*

'Full of brilliant adventure, described with a dash that well befits the deeds.'—TIMES.
'Ought to be a classic in every library afloat or ashore.'—DAILY NEWS.

Memoirs of Celebrated Etonians.

Including Fielding, Gray the Poet, Horace Walpole, William Pitt, Earl of Chatham, Lord Bute, Lord North, Horne Took, Lord Lyttelton, Earl Temple, Admiral Lord Howe, &c. By JOHN HENEAGE JESSE, Author of 'Memoirs of the Reign of George III.,' 'Memoirs of the Court of the Stuarts,' &c. In 2 vols. 8vo. 28s.   2 A 2

Letters to a Friend.

By the late CONNOP THIRLWALL, D.D., Bishop of St. David's, and Edited by the late Dean STANLEY. A New and much Enlarged Edition, in one volume, crown 8vo. with a Portrait, 6s.   4 S 1

'A real gain to literature, and a specimen of the thoughts of one of the most interesting minds of this century.'—TIMES.

'One of the most interesting collections of letters in the English language. Its interest is profound; the range of the writer's sympathies was so wide, his knowledge was so great, the part which he played in life was so important, and his style is at once so clear, so strong, and so elastic, so equally well adapted either to anecdote or to the discussions of the greatest moral or metaphysical problems, that it is impossible to read the book without being both delighted and edified in no common degree.'—ST. JAMES'S GAZETTE.

Life and Letters of the Very Rev. Walter Farquhar Hook, D.D.

Late Dean of Chichester.

By the Rev. W. R. W. STEPHENS, Prebendary of Chichester, Author of the 'Life of St. John Chrysostom,' &c. In 2 vols. demy 8vo. with two Portraits. Fourth Edition. 30s.   I S 2 *

Dean Hook: His Life and Letters.

Edited by the Rev. W. R. W. STEPHENS, Vicar of Woolbeding, Author of 'Life of St. John Chrysostom,' &c. The Popular Edition, in one volume, crown 8vo. with Index and Portrait, 6s.   9 S 2*

Dean Hook: an Address delivered at Hawarden.

By the Right Hon. W. E. GLADSTONE, M.P. In demy 8vo. sewed, 1s., or in small crown 8vo. 3d.   9 S 9

The Lives of the Archbishops of Canterbury.

From ST. AUGUSTINE to JUXON. By the late Very Rev. WALTER FARQUHAR HOOK, D.D., Dean of Chichester. In Twelve Vols. demy 8vo. price £9; or the following volumes sold separately as shown :—Vol. I., 15s.; Vol. II., 15s.; Vols. III. and IV., 30s.; Vol. V., 15s.; Vols. VI. and VII., 30s.; Vol. VIII.. 15s.; Vol. IX., 15s.; Vol. X., 15s.; Vol. XI., 15s. ; Vol. XII., 15s.

'The most impartial, the most instructive, and the most interesting of histories.'—ATHENÆUM.

'Written with remarkable knowledge and power. The author has done his work diligently and conscientiously. We express our sense of the value of this work. We heartily like the general spirit, and are sure that the author has bestowed upon his work a loving labour, with an earnest desire to find out the truth. To the general reader it will convey much information in a very pleasant form ; to the student it will give the means of filling up the outlines of Church history with life and colour.'—QUARTERLY REVIEW.

'The work of a powerful mind, and of a noble and generous temper.'—GUARDIAN.

VOL. I. Anglo-Saxon Period, 597-1070.—Augustine, Laurentius, Mellitus, Justus, Honorius, Deusdedit, Theodore, Brihtwald, Tatwine, Nothelm, Cuthbert, Bregwin, Jaenbert, Ethelhard, Wulfred, Feologild, Ceolonoth, Ethelred, Plegmund, Athelm, Wulfhelm, Odo, Dunstan, Ethelgar, Siric, Elfric, Elphege, Limig, Ethelnoth, Eadsige, Robert, Stigand.

VOL. II. Anglo-Norman Period, 1070-1229.—Lanfranc, Anselm, Ralph of Escures, William of Corbeuil, Theobald, Thomas à Becket, Richard the Norman, Baldwin, Reginald Fitzjocelin, Hubert Walter, Stephen Langton.

VOL. III. Mediæval Period, 1229-1333.—Richard Grant, Edmund Rich, Boniface, Robert Kilwardby, John Peckham, Robert Winchelsey, Walter Reynolds, Simon Mapeham.

VOL. IV. Same Period, 1333-1408.—John Stratford, Thomas Bradwardine, Simon Islip, Simon Langham, William Whittlesey, Simon Sudbury, William Courtenay, Thomas Arundel.

VOL. V. Same Period, 1408-1503.—Henry Chicheley, John Stafford, John Kemp, Thomas Bouchier, John Morton, Henry Dean.

The New Series commences here.

VOL. VI. Reformation Period, 1503-1556.—William Warham, Thomas Cranmer (in part).

VII. Same Period.—Thomas Cranmer (in part).

VOL. VIII. Same Period, 1556-1558.—Reginald, Cardinal Pole.

VOL. IX. Same Period, 1558-1575.—Matthew Parker.

VOL. X. Same Period, 1575-1633. — Edmund Grindal, John Whitgift, Richard Bancroft, George Abbott.

VOL. XI. Same Period, 1633-1663.—William Laud, William Juxon.

Vol. XII. The Index.

A Memoir of the late Rev. John Russell, of Tordown, North Devon.

By the Author of 'Dartmoor Days,' 'Wolf Hunting in Brittany,' &c. A New and Revised Edition, brought down to date. In 1 vol. crown 8vo. with a Portrait, 6s.

Life in the Cloister, at the Papal Court, and in Exile.
By GIUSEPPE MARIA CAMPANELLA. In 8vo. with two Portraits of the Author, 10s. 6d.   S I P

Wives, Mothers, and Sisters.
By Lady HERBERT, Author of 'Three Phases of Christian Love,' 'Impressions of Spain,' &c. In 2 vols. large crown 8vo. 21s.   3 S 2

Life of Madame de Beauharnais de Miramion, 1629-1696.
By M. ALFRED BONNEAU. Translated by the Baroness DE MONTAIGNAC, and edited by Lady HERBERT. Large crown 8vo. 10s. 6d.   O B 2

Mary Russell Mitford's Life.
Told by Herself in Letters to her Friends. With Sketches and Anecdotes of her most celebrated Contemporaries. Edited by the Rev. A. G. L'ESTRANGE. With an Introductory Memoir &c. by the late Rev. WILLIAM HARNESS, her Literary Executor. In 3 vols. post 8vo. 31s. 6d. Second Series, edited by HENRY CHORLEY. 2 vols. 21s.   O A 2
   O A 3

Recollections of a Literary Life.
With Selections from my Favourite Poets and Prose Writers. By MARY RUSSELL MITFORD. A New Edition in 1 vol. crown 8vo. with Portrait, 6s.

Records of Later Life.
By FRANCES ANN KEMBLE. In 3 vols. crown 8vo. 10s. 6d.   7 K 1

Alaric Watts.
The Narrative of his Life. By his Son, ALARIC ALFRED WATTS. In 2 Vols. crown 8vo, with Two Etchings, 21s.

Unpublished Letters of Jane Austen to Her Relations, 1796-1815.
Edited, with Introduction and Notes, by the Right Hon. LORD BRABOURNE. In 2 vols. large crown 8vo. with Frontispieces.   [*Immediately.*

Fifty Years of London Life.
By EDMUND YATES. In 2 vols. demy 8vo. with Portraits and Vignettes.
   [*Immediately.*

The Life of the Rev. Richard Harris Barham
(Author of the 'Ingoldsby Legends'). By his Son, the Rev. RICHARD H. DALTON BARHAM. A New Edition in one volume, crown 8vo. with Portrait, 6s.   2 B 2 †

The Life of Theodore Edward Hook.
By Rev. RICHARD H. DALTON BARHAM. A New Edition in crown 8vo. 6s.

Henry Fothergill Chorley: Autobiography, Memoir, and Letters.
Edited by HENRY G. HEWLETT. 2 vols. crown 8vo. with Portrait, 21s.

Reminiscences of a Literary Career:
An Autobiography. By ROBERT BUCHANAN. In Two Vols., crown 8vo., with Portrait. [*In the press.*

The Literary Remains of the late Charles F. Tyrwhitt Drake, F.R.G.S.
Edited, with a Memoir, by WALTER BESANT, M.A. In 8vo. with Portrait, price 14s.

A Memoir of William Page Wood, Lord Hatherley.
By the Rev. W. R. W. STEPHENS, Rector of Woolbeding, Sussex, Author of 'The Life and Letters of Dean Hook' &c. In crown 8vo. with two Portraits. 21s.

Some Experiences of a Barrister's Career.
By Mr. Serjeant BALLANTINE. A New Edition (being the Tenth), in one volume, crown 8vo. 2s. 6d.

From the Old World to the New.
Being some Experiences of a Recent Visit to America, including a Trip to the Mormon Country. By Mr. SERJEANT BALLANTINE, Author of 'Some Experiences of a Barrister.' In demy 8vo. with Portrait.
[*Immediately.*

Some Professional Recollections.
By a Former Member of the Council of the Incorporated Law Society. 9s.

The Early Life of Sir William Maule.
By his Niece, EMMA LEATHLEY. Crown 8vo. 7s. 6d.

Letters and Correspondence of the late Edward Denison, M.P. for Newark.
People's Edition. Tauchnitz size, 2s.

The Wit and Wisdom of the Earl of Chesterfield.
Edited, with brief Notes, by ERNST BROWNING. Small demy 8vo. 6s.

Lives of the Princes of the House of Condé.
By the DUC D'AUMALE. Translated under His Royal Highness's supervision by the Rev. R. BROWN-BORTHWICK. 2 vols. 8vo. with Two fine Portraits, 30s.

The Lives of the Queens of England of the House of Hanover.
Sophia Dorothea of Zell (wife of George I.)—Carolina Wilhelmina Dorothea (wife of George II.)—Charlotte Sophia (wife of George III.)—Caroline of Brunswick (wife of George IV.)—Adelaide of Saxe-Meinengen (wife of William IV.). By Dr. DORAN, F.S.A., Author of 'Table Traits and Something on Them,' &c. Fourth, and enlarged Edition. 2 vols. 8vo. 25s.

'It is almost superfluous to do more than announce that a book is by Dr. Doran in order to ensure its eager welcome in every reading household.'—MORNING POST.

The Life of Mary Queen of Scots.
From the French of M. MIGNET, by ANDREW SCOBLE. With Two Portraits, in crown 8vo. 6s.

' The standard authority on the subject.'—DAILY NEWS.
' A good service done to historical accuracy.'—MORNING POST.

The Life of Oliver Cromwell.
From the French of M. GUIZOT, by ANDREW SCOBLE. In crown 8vo. with Four Portraits, 6s.

'M. Guizot has unravelled Cromwell's character with singular skill. No one, in our opinion, has drawn his portrait with equal truth.'—QUARTERLY REVIEW.
' An admirable narrative, far more candid than any from an English pen.'—TIMES.

The French Humourists, from the Twelfth to the Nineteenth Century.
By WALTER BESANT, M.A., Christ's Coll., Cam., Author of 'Studies in Early French Poetry,' &c. 8vo. 15s.

'The author's pages never flag. Narrative, verse, and criticism flow on, bright, sparkling, and pellucid, from the first sentence to the last, and they are as full of information as they are of wit.'—GUARDIAN.

The Lives of Wits and Humourists:
Swift, Steele, Foote, Goldsmith, the Colmans, Sheridan, Porson, Sydney Smith, Theodore Hook, &c. &c. By JOHN TIMBS, F.S.A. In 2 vols. crown 8vo. with Portraits, 12s.

The Lives of Statesmen:
Burke and Chatham. By JOHN TIMBS, F.S.A. Crown 8vo. with Portraits, 6s.

The Lives of Painters:
Hogarth, Sir Joshua Reynolds, Gainsborough, Fuseli, Sir Thomas Lawrence, Turner. By JOHN TIMBS, F.S.A. Crown 8vo. with Portraits, 6s.

The Life and Work of Thorvaldsen.
By EUGÈNE PLON. From the French by Mrs. CASHEL HOEY. In imperial 8vo. with numerous Illustrations, 25s.

'It would be difficult to produce a better book of its kind than M. Plon's "Thorvaldsen." The life of the great sculptor was essentially worthy of being put upon record.'—STANDARD.

The Great Tone Poets.
Being Brief Memoirs of the Greater Musical Composers—Bach, Handel, Gluck, Haydn, Spohr, Beethoven, Weber, Rossini, Schubert, Mendelssohn, Schumann, &c. &c. By FREDERICK CROWEST. Fifth Edition. In crown 8vo. 3s. 6d.

The Lives of Eminent Violinists.
By Dr. PHIPSON. In 1 vol. crown 8vo. 6s.

'We have no common pleasure in recommending this book to the particular attention of all who delight in the author's favourite instrument.'—GLOBE.

See also p. 26.

Our Old Actors.
By HENRY BARTON BAKER, Author of 'French Society from the Fronde to the Great Revolution.' With a Portrait of Peg Woffington. Popular Edition, revised. In 1 vol. crown 8vo. 6s.

Seven Years at Eton, 1857-1864.
Edited by JAMES BRINSLEY RICHARDS. Third Edition. In 1 vol. crown 8vo. 6s.

'We may say at once that a better book of its kind we have never seen.'—SPECTATOR.
'Upon all subjects the reader will find something interesting and generally amusing in this book.'—TIMES.
'A readable, graphic, and faithful picture of Eton life.'—PALL MALL GAZETTE.

[*Memoir of Thomas Love Peacock*, see p. 39. *Memoir of Jane Austen*, see p. 34. *Memoir of Sir Robt. Strange*, see p. 25. *Memoir of Dr. McCaws and*, see p. 27.]

EXPLORATIONS, VOYAGES, & TRAVELS.

Travels in the East.
Including a Visit to the Holy Land, Egypt, the Ionian Islands, &c. By His Imperial and Royal Highness the CROWN PRINCE RUDOLF. In royal 8vo. with numerous Illustrations. [*In the press.*

Recollections of My Life.
By the late EMPEROR MAXIMILIAN of Mexico. In 3 vols. post 8vo. 31*s*. 6*d*.

East by West.
A Record of Travel round the World. By HENRY W. LUCY, Author of 'Gideon Fleyce.' &c. In Two Vols., crown 8vo. [*In the press.*

A Diary kept during a Journey to Europe in 1878.
By the SHAH of PERSIA, and rendered into English by General SCHINDLER and Baron LOUIS DE NORMAN. In demy 8vo. 12*s*.

An Old-Fashioned Journey in England and Wales.
By JAMES JOHN HISSEY. In demy 8vo., with Frontispiece.
[*Immediately.*

The Cruise of the Reserve Squadron.
By CHARLES W. WOOD, F.R.G.S., Author of 'Through Holland,' &c. In crown 8vo. with 60 Illustrations, 6*s*.

Five Weeks in Iceland.
By C. A. DE FONBLANQUE. In small crown 8vo. 3*s*. 6*d*.

Round about Norway.
By CHARLES W. WOOD, F.R.G.S., Author of 'Through Holland' &c. In demy 8vo. with 63 Illustrations, 12*s*.

Driftwood from Scandinavia.
By FRANCESCA, LADY WILDE. In One Volume, large crown 8vo.
[*Immediately.*

Through Holland.
By CHARLES W. WOOD, F.R.G.S. In demy 8vo. with 57 Illustrations, 12*s*.

The Dead Cities of the Zuyder Zee.
From the French of M. HENRY HAVARD, by ANNIE WOOD. In crown 8vo. with 10 Illustrations. The New and Popular Edition. 6*s*.

Picturesque Holland:
A Journey in the Provinces of Friesland, Groningen, Drenthe, Overyssel, Guelderland, Limbourg, &c. From the French of M. HENRY HAVARD by ANNIE WOOD. In demy 8vo. with 10 Illustrations and Map, 16s.

In the Heart of Holland.
From the French of M. HENRY HAVARD, by Mrs. CASHEL HOEY. In demy 8vo. with 8 Illustrations, 15s.

In the Black Forest.
By CHARLES W. WOOD, F.R.G.S., Author of 'Through Holland,' 'Round about Norway.' In 1 vol. small crown 8vo. with numerous Illustrations, 6s.

Among the Alsatian Mountains.
By KATHERINE LEE. 1 vol. large crown 8vo. with 2 Illustrations, 9s.

Summer Days in Auvergne.
By Admiral DE KANTZOW. In crown 8vo. with 5 full-page Illustrations, 5s.

Azahar. A Tour in Spain.
By E. C. HOPE-EDWARDES. Crown 8vo. 7s. 6d.

Among the Spanish People.
By the Rev. HUGH JAMES ROSE, English Chaplain of Jerez and Cadiz, Author of 'Untrodden Spain,' &c. In 2 vols. large crown 8vo. 24s.

A Lady's Tour in Corsica.
By GERTRUDE FORDE. In two volumes, crown 8vo. 21s.

Diary of an Idle Woman in Sicily.
By FRANCES ELLIOT, Author of 'Diary of an Idle Woman in Italy.' In 2 vols. crown 8vo. 18s.

Word-Sketches in the Sweet South.
By MARY CATHERINE JACKSON. Demy 8vo. 10s. 6d.

The Fortunate Isles;
Or, the Archipelago of the Canaries. By M. PEGOT OGIER. Translate by FRANCES LOCOCK. 2 vols. crown 8vo. 21s.

Eau-de-Nil. A Nile Diary.
By E. C. HOPE-EDWARDES. Large crown 8vo. 10s. 6d. 2 B 2

'"Eau-de-Nil" is without exception the most amusing work on Egypt we have seen for a long while; it gives one a remarkably good idea of Egypt as it is to-day.'—MORNING POST.

Five Months in Cairo and in Lower Egypt.
From the French of GABRIEL CHARMES, by WILLIAM CONN. Crown 8vo. 7s. 6d. 7 K I

'One of the best works on Egypt that has been published, M. Charmes being not only a quick observer and an industrious hunter after information, but the wielder of a most graphic pen. The translation has been most carefully done, and is a model of painstaking workmanship.'—GLOBE.

My Wanderings in the Soudan.
By Mrs. T. C. S. SPEEDY. In 2 vols. crown 8vo. with numerous Illustrations. [*In the press.*

A Voyage up the Niger and Benueh.
By ADOLPHE BURDO. Translated by Mrs. GEORGE STURGE. With Illustrations. In demy 8vo. 10s. 6d. 6 S I

In the Land of Misfortune.
By Lady FLORENCE DIXIE, Author of 'Across Patagonia' &c. With numerous Illustrations by Major FRASER and Capt. C. F. BERESFORD, R.E., engraved by WHYMPER and PEARSON. Demy 8vo. 18s. 9 Z 2

Diary of a Civilian's Wife in India.
By Mrs. MOSS KING. In 2 vols. crown 8vo. with numerous Illustrations from Drawings by the Author. [*In the press.*

Japan and the Japanese.
By AIMÉ HUMBERT, Envoy Extraordinary of the Swiss Confederation. From the French by Mrs. CASHEL HOEY, and Edited by W. H. BATES, Assist.-Secretary to the Geographical Society. Illustrated by 207 Drawings and Sketches from Photographs. In royal 4to. handsomely bound, 21s.
4 C 2

Old New Zealand.
A Tale of the Good Old Times, and a History of the War in the North against the Chief Heke. Told by an Old Pakeha Maori. With a Preface by the Earl of PEMBROKE. In demy 8vo. 12s. 2 W 2†

'The best book ever written about a savage race.'—ATHENÆUM.

South Sea Bubbles.
By the EARL and the DOCTOR. Library Edition. 8vo. 14s.
POPULAR EDITION. Crown 8vo. 3s. 6d. [*Reprinting*] 2 S 3*

The Coral Lands of the Pacific.
Being an Account of nearly all the Inhabited Islands of the Pacific, their Peoples and their Products. By H. STONEHEWER COOPER. A New and Revised Edition, in crown 8vo. 6s. I B 2†

The Trottings of a 'Tender Foot' in Spitzbergen and British Columbia.

By CLIVE PHILLIPPS-WOLLEY, F.R.G.S., Author of 'Sport in the Crimea and Caucasus.' In crown 8vo. [*In the press.*

Ten Years on a Georgia Plantation, since the War.

By the Hon. Mrs. J. W. LEIGH. Demy 8vo. 10s. 6d.

Peru in the Guano Age.

By A. J. DUFFIELD. In crown 8vo. 4s.

Western Wanderings:

A Record of Travel in the Land of the Setting Sun. By J. W. BODDAM-WHETHAM. With 12 full-page Illustrations, engraved by Whymper. Demy 8vo. 15s.

A Trip to Manitoba.

By MARY FITZGIBBON. In large crown 8vo. 10s. 6d.

A Search after Sunshine:

A Visit to Algeria in 1871. By Lady HERBERT. Square 8vo. with Illustrations engraved by George Pearson, 16s.

'The whole volume is full of charm.'—MORNING POST.

A Journal Abroad in 1868.

By F. M. T. TRENCH. In post 8vo. 7s. 6d.

Sport in the Crimea and the Caucasus.

By CLIVE PHILLIPPS-WOLLEY, F.R.G.S., late British Vice-Consul at Kertch. Demy 8vo. 14s.

Savage Svânetia.

By CLIVE PHILLIPPS-WOLLEY, F.R.G.S., Author of 'Sport in the Crime and the Caucasus.' In 2 vols. crown 8vo. with Illustrations, 21s.

'Mr. Phillipps-Wolley is a devoted sportsman and angler. He has already written a capital book on sport in the wilds of Russia ; and now he treats us again to a thrilling record of bear and wild mountain sheep hunting, mixed with fragmentary observations of Svânetian life (in the heart of the Caucasus), which is equally satisfactory reading. The book is capitally written, and should be on every sportsman's shelves.'—DAILY TELEGRAPH.

Rock Inscriptions in the Peninsula of Sinai.

By GEORGE BENTLEY, F.R.G.S. Demy 8vo, sewed, 1s.

Heth and Moab.

A Narrative of Explorations in Syria in 1881 and 1882. By Captain CLAUD REIGNIER CONDER, R.E. In demy 8vo. with Four Illustrations, 14s.

'Captain Conder has already proved his capacity on more than one occasion to make the dry work of survey appear as interesting as a romance. . . . . His accuracy, in short, is as unimpeachable as that of an explorer should always be ; his peculiar merit is in showing that this can be obtained without any loss of interest. Captain Conder is one of those rare travellers who know exactly what people want to be told, and even when he narrates facts and events which every one ought to know, he has such a pleasant way of telling his story that it sounds almost new, and is certainly well worth hearing over again. We have been barely able within our allotted space to indicate some of the most prominent points in an interesting volume, but perhaps they will suffice to induce our readers to turn to the book for themselves, with the assurance that seldom have such research in out-of-the-way pages of history, and the partial failure of an enterprise, been made to assume so attractive a garb as they do in this record of an interrupted survey in the land of Moab beyond Jordan.'—THE TIMES.

East of the Jordan.

A Record of Travel and Observation in the Countries of Moab, Gilead, and Basha during the years 1875-77. By SELAH MERRILL, Archæologist of the American Palestine Exploration Society, and with an Introduction by Professor ROSWELL HITCHCOCK, D.D. In demy 8vo. with 70 Illustrations and a Map, 16s.

Tent Work in Palestine.

By Captain CLAUD CONDER, R.E. Second Edition, in 2 vols. demy 8vo. with Illustrations, 24s. Also a New and Popular Edition in crown 8vo. with Illustrations, 7s. 6d.

The Recovery of Jerusalem.

An Account of the Recent Excavations and Discoveries in the Holy City. By Captain WILSON, R.E., and Colonel WARREN, R.E. With an Introductory Chapter by Dean STANLEY. Third Thousand. Demy 8vo. with 50 Illustrations, 21s.

The Temple or the Tomb?

By CHARLES WARREN, Captain in the Corps of Royal Engineers, F.G.S., F.R.G.S., Assoc. Inst. C.E., late in charge of the Explorations in the Holy Land, Author of 'Underground Jerusalem.' In demy 8vo. with Illustrations, 10s. 6d.

An Introduction to the Survey of Western Palestine.

Its Waterways, Plains, and Highlands. Illustrating the Survey recently conducted by Captain CONDER, R.E., and Lieutenant KITCHINER, R.E., for the Palestine Exploration Fund. By TRELAWNEY SAUNDERS. In demy 8vo. 7s. 6d.

STATEMENTS of the PALESTINE EXPLORATION FUND.

Quarterly, price 2s. 6d. See page 45 for particulars.

POETRY, DRAMA, &c.*

The Ingoldsby Legends;

OR, MIRTH AND MARVELS. By the Rev. RICHARD HARRIS BARHAM.

'Abundant in humour, observation, fancy ; in extensive knowledge of books and men ; in palpable hits of character, exquisite grave irony, and the most whimsical indulgence in point of epigram. We cannot open a page that is not sparkling with its wit and humour, that is not ringing with its strokes of pleasantry and satire.'—EXAMINER.

THE ILLUSTRATED EDITION. With Sixty-nine Illustrations by Cruikshank, Leech, and Tenniel. Printed on Toned Paper. Crown 4to. cloth, bevelled boards, gilt edges, 21s.; or bound in the Ely pattern, same price.   1 C 1

Also in *white* cloth, in the Ely pattern, for presentation copies, 22s. 6d.   1 C

'A series of humorous legends, illustrated by three such men as Cruikshank, Leech, and Tenniel—what can be more tempting?'—THE TIMES.

THE CARMINE EDITION. In small demy 8vo. with a carmine border line around each page. With Twenty Illustrations on Steel by Cruikshank and Leech, with gilt edges and bevelled boards, 10s. 6d.   1 A 3*

THE BURLINGTON EDITION. A Cabinet Edition, in 3 vols. fcp. 8vo. 10s. 6d.   4 C 2*

THE EDINBURGH EDITION. A Special Edition, published in 1879, in large type, with Fifty Illustrations by Cruikshank, Leech, Tenniel, Barham, and Du Maurier, re-engraved for this edition by George Pearson. In crown 8vo. red cloth, 6s.

⁎ Also bound in gold cloth, with paper label, same price.   9 Z 2*

THE POPULAR EDITION. In crown 8vo. cloth, with Sixteen Illustrations by Cruikshank, Leech, Tenniel, and Barham. 3s. 6d.   9 E 1*

THE VICTORIA EDITION. A Pocket Edition, in fcp. 8vo. with Frontispiece, cloth, 2s.   4 D 2*

THE PEOPLE'S EDITION. In 64 large quarto pages, printed on good paper, with 40 Illustrations by Cruikshank, Leech, and Tenniel, with wrapper, price 6d.   9 A 8?

The Ingoldsby Lyrics.

By the Rev. RICHARD HARRIS BARHAM, Author of 'The Ingoldsby Legends.' Edited by his Son, the Rev. R. H. DALTON BARHAM   In one volume, crown 8vo. 3s. 6d.   2 R 2†

The Bentley Ballads.

Selected from 'Bentley's Miscellany.' Edited by JOHN SHEEHAN. In crown 8vo. 6s.   2 B 2*

Amongst the contributors are :—Dr. Maginn—Father Prout—Thomas Ingoldsby—G. E. Inman—Thomas Haynes Bayly—C. Hartley Langhorne—Thomas Love Peacock—Samuel Lover—Charles Mackay—Robert Burns—H. W. Longfellow—J. A. Wade—Albert Smith—Edward Kenealy—'Alfred Crowquill'—Mary Howitt—The Irish Whiskey Drinker—W. Cooke Taylor—William Jones—Tom Taylor—G. K. Gillespie—R. Dalton Barham, and many others.

* *See* also Peacock's Works on p. 39, also page 31.

The Poetical Works of Frances Anne Kemble.
In crown 8vo. 7s. 6d.

Notes upon some of Shakespeare's Plays.
By FRANCES ANNE (FANNY) KEMBLE. In demy 8vo. finely printed in brown ink, 7s. 6d.
ON THE STAGE. MACBETH. HENRY VIII. THE TEMPEST. ROMEO AND JULIET.

The Village Coquettes.
By CHARLES DICKENS. A few copies have been reprinted in fac-simile of the original Edition of 1836. In demy 8vo. sewed, 4s. 6d.

The Poet and the Muse.
Being a Version of ALFRED DE MUSSET'S 'La Nuit de Mai,' 'La Nuit d'Août,' and 'La Nuit d'Octobre.' With an Introduction by Walter Herries Pollock. 32 pp. sewed, 1s. 6d.

The Roman :
By SYDNEY DOBELL. A Dramatic Poem. Post 8vo. 5s.

Epistles, Satires, and Epigrams.
By JAMES E. THOROLD ROGERS. Crown 8vo. 6s.

The Token of the Silver Lily.
By HELEN MATHERS. In large crown 8vo. 6s.

Poems.
By ARTHUR BRIDGE. In crown 8vo. 7s. 6d.

Rhymes and Legends.
By Mrs. ACTON TINDAL. In crown 8vo. 5s.

Dorothy's Troth.
By E. RIDGEWAY. Crown 8vo. 5s.

The Stage :
Its History in Relation to Art. By HENRY NEVILLE. Demy 8vo. 5s.

Charles Reade's Dramas.
Edited by TOM TAYLOR. I. Masks and Faces. [II. Two Loves and a Life.*] III. The King's Rival. IV. Poverty and Pride. 1s. 6d. each.
* Out of print.

Four Unacted Plays.
By A. W. DUBOURG. In 1 vol. crown 8vo. 7s. 6d.
GREEN CLOTH. A Story of Monte Carlo. | 3. LAND AND LOVE. A Story of English Life
VITTORIA CONTARINI. A Story of Venice. | 4. ART AND LOVE. A Story of Artist Life.

ART AND SCIENCE.

The Masterpieces of Sir Robert Strange.

A Selection of Twenty of his most important Engravings reproduced in Permanent Photography. With a Memoir of Sir Robert Strange, including portions of his Autobiography. By FRANCIS WOODWARD. Folio, 42s.

S 1 P

The Life and Work of Thorvaldsen.

See page 17.

Portraits of the Children of the Mobility.

Drawn from Nature by JOHN LEECH. With a fine Portrait of Leech, and a Prefatory Letter by JOHN RUSKIN. Reproduced from the Original Sketches by the Autotype Process. 4to. 10s. 6d. S 1 P

Studies in English Art:

Gainsborough, Morland, Wheatley, Sir Joshua Reynolds, Stothard, Flaxman, Girtin, Crome, Cotman, Turner (in 'Liber Studiorum'), Peter de Wint, George Mason, Frederick Walker. By FREDERICK WEDMORE. In crown 8vo. 7s. 6d.

2 A 1

'Those who have read them will read them again, for they are the work of one of the most thoughtful and conscientious of contemporary critics.'—GLOBE.

The SECOND SERIES, containing Romney, Constable, David Cox, George Cruikshank, Meryon, Burne-Jones, and Albert Moore. In one volume, large crown 8vo. 7s. 6d.

1 P 1

Holbein and his Time.

From the German of Dr. ALFRED WOLTMANN by F. E. BUNNÉTT. 1 vol. small 4to. with Sixty beautiful Illustrations from the Chief works of Holbein, 21s.

2 C 3

The Heavens.

An Illustrated Handbook of Popular Astronomy. By AMÉDÉE GUILLEMIN. Edited by J. NORMAN LOCKYER, F.R.A.S. An entirely New and Revised Edition, embodying all the latest discoveries in Astronomical Science. Demy 8vo. with over 200 Illustrations, 12s.

1 Z 3

'If anything can make the study of Astronomy easy and engaging to ordinary minds, it will assuredly be a work of the attractive style and handsome—we may almost say sumptuous—aspect of M. Guillemin's treatise on "The Heavens." It deserves to be spoken of with all praise, as one towards which author, editor, illustrator, and publisher have equally done their best. Of the translation itself we cannot speak too highly. It has all the force and freshness of original writing.'—SATURDAY REVIEW.

Marvels of the Heavens.
From the French of FLAMMARION. By Mrs. LOCKYER, Translator of 'The Heavens.' Crown 8vo. with 48 Illustrations, 3s. 6d.   o z 2

The Sun.
By AMÉDÉE GUILLEMIN, Author of 'The Heavens.' Translated by Dr. PHIPSON. With 50 Illustrations. Crown 8vo. 6s.   2 z 2

A Treatise on Navigation and Nautical Astronomy.
By OLIVER BYRNE, Inventor of Dual Arithmetic, &c. In 4to. 700 pp. 42s.

The Day after Death;
Or, the Future Life Revealed by Science. By LOUIS FIGUIER, Author of 'The World before the Deluge.' A New Edition. In crown 8vo. with Illustrations, 3s. 6d.   5 D 2*

The Great Tone Poets;
Being Brief Memoirs of the Greater Musical Composers—Bach, Handel, Gluck, Haydn, Spohr, Beethoven, Weber, Rossini, Schubert, Mendelssohn, Schumann, &c. &c. By FREDERICK CROWEST. Fifth Edition. Crown 8vo. 3s. 6d.   3 B 2*

Biographies of Eminent Violinists:
I. Lulli (1633-1687).—II. Corelli (1653-1713).— III. The Bannisters (1640-1729).—IV. Tartini (1692-1770).—V. Leclerc Giardini, Pugnani (1697-1798).—VI. Viotti (1755-1824).—VII. Nicolo Paganini (1784-1840).—VIII. Charles Auguste de Bériot (1802-1870).- IX. Ole Bull (1810-1875).—X. Contemporary Violinists: Ernst, Joachim, Vieuxtemps, Wieniawski, Sivori, St. Leon, Sainton, &c.—XI. Fraulein Schmöhling. By Dr. PHIPSON. In crown 8vo. 6s.   2 B 3†

RELIGIOUS AND KINDRED WORKS.*

The Church and its Ordinances.
Sermons by the late WALTER FARQUHAR HOOK, D.D., Dean of Chichester. Edited by the Rev. WALTER HOOK, Rector of Porlock. In 2 vols. demy 8vo. 10s. 6d.　　　　　　　　　　　　　　2 S 1†*

Parish Sermons.
By the late WALTER FARQUHAR HOOK, D.D., Dean of Chichester. Edited by the Rev. WALTER HOOK, Rector of Porlock. In crown 8vo. 3s. 6d.　1 2 2†

Hear the Church.
A Sermon by the late Dean HOOK. Reprinted separately, in demy 8vo. sewed, 1s.

Essays: Classical and Theological.
By the late CONNOP THIRLWALL, D.D., Bishop of St. David's. Edited by the Rev. Canon PEROWNE. In demy 8vo. 15s.

Ely Lectures on the Revised Version of the New Testament.
With an Appendix containing the chief Textual Changes. By B. H. KENNEDY, D.D., Canon of Ely, Honorary Fellow of St. John's College, Cambridge, &c. In crown 8vo. 4s.　　　　　　　　　　　　　2 S 1

Works by the late Dr. M'Causland.
1. ADAM and the ADAMITE; or, the Harmony of Scripture and Ethnology. With Map. Crown 8vo. 3s. 6d.　　　　　　　　　2 B 2†
2. SERMONS in STONES; or, Scripture Confirmed by Geology. New Edition, with Memoir of the Author. Crown 8vo. 19 Illustrations, 3s. 6d. [Reprinting.]　　　　　　　　　　　　　　　　　　　　0 C 2*
3. The BUILDERS of BABEL; or, the Confusion of Languages. New Edition. In crown 8vo. 3s. 6d.　　　　　　　　　　　　　0 B 2*

Christianity and Islam:
THE BIBLE AND THE KORAN. By the Rev. W. R. W. STEPHENS, Author of 'The Life of St. Chrysostom,' 'Life and Letters of Dean Hook.' Crown 8vo. 5s.　　　　　　　　　　　　　　　　　　　　　　2 S 1

Modern Society.
A PASTORAL for LENT. By His Eminence CARDINAL MANNING. 1s.

Nigh unto the End.
By the Rev. Dr. BOYCE. In post 8vo. 3s. 6d.　　　　　　　　2 B 1

* See also 'The Recovery of Jerusalem,' 'Palestine Fund Exploration Statements,' 'The Lives of the Archbishops of Canterbury,' 'Life of Lord Hatherley,' 'Memorials of Chichester Cathedral,' 'Rock Inscriptions in Sinai,' 'Life of Dean Hook,' 'Bishop Thirlwall's Letters, Dr. Duncker's 'History of Antiquity,' &c.

Works by Dr. Cumming.

The FALL of BABYLON FORESHADOWED in HER TEACHING, in HISTORY, and in PROPHECY. Crown 8vo. 5s.   O A 3

The GREAT TRIBULATION COMING on the EARTH. Crown 8vo. 5s. Fourteenth Thousand.   O A 10*

REDEMPTION DRAWETH NIGH; or, the Great Preparation. Crown 8vo. 5s. Seventh Thousand.   O A 10*

The MILLENNIAL REST; or, the World as it will be. Crown 8vo. 5s. Fourth Thousand.   O A 10*

READINGS on the PROPHET ISAIAH. Fcp. 8vo. 5s.   O A 10*

Works by Lady Herbert.

THREE PHASES of CHRISTIAN LOVE. In Tauchnitz size, 3s. 6d.   1 W

The MISSION of ST. FRANCIS of SALES in the CHABLAIS. In post 8vo. 6s.   O K 2

LOVE or SELF-SACRIFICE. In crown 8vo. 10s. 6d.   O S 1

WIVES, MOTHERS, and SISTERS. In 2 vols. large crown 8vo. 21s.   3 S 2

GERONIMO. A True Story. In fcp. with Frontispiece, 4s.   2 C 3

See also pp. 14 and 21.

Hymns and Anthems.

Edited by the Rev. Dr. TREMLETT. New Edition. Cloth, 1s. 2d.   2 B 2*

The Sword and its Retribution—God's

WAY of ANSWERING PRAYER—VIVISECTION; or, the Duty of Christians with Reference to its Cruelty and its Abuses. Being Sermons preached at St. Peter's, Belsize Park, by the Rev. F. W. TREMLETT, D.C.L., Vicar. Each separately, price 6d.   S I P

What is Unity? The Praise of God.

Two Sermons preached by the Rev. ROBERT BROWN-BORTHWICK. Each separately, price 1s.   S I P

The Fourfold Message of Advent.

Four Sermons preached at Chiswick. Fcp. cloth, 2s. 6d.   S I P

    I. WATCHING (Vigilance). By the Rev. A. EUBULE EVANS.
    II. WORKING (Zeal). By the Rev. ROBERT BROWN-BORTHWICK.
    III. WAITING (Patience). By the Rev. and Hon. FRANCIS E. C. BYNG.
    IV. WISHING (Hope). By the Rev. JOHN ELLERTON.

MISCELLANEOUS WORKS.

The Girl of the Period, and other Essays upon Social Subjects.
By ELIZA LYNN LINTON, Author of 'Patricia Kemball,' &c. In 2 vols. demy 8vo. 24s.

Letters from Hell.
Newly translated from the Danish. With an Introduction by Dr. GEORGE MACDONALD. In 1 vol. crown 8vo. 6s. [*Immediately.*

Turning Points in Life.
By the Rev. FREDERICK ARNOLD, Author of 'Christchurch Days,' &c. A New Edition in 1 vol. crown 8vo. 6s.

Literary Essays.
By WILLIAM HURRELL MALLOCK, Author of 'Is Life worth Living?' &c. In 1 vol. crown 8vo. [*In the press.*

Social Equality.
A Short Study in a Missing Science. By W. H. MALLOCK, Author of 'Is Life worth Living?' &c. Second Edition, in crown 8vo. 6s.

Curiosities of Natural History.
By FRANK BUCKLAND. Popular Edition, with Illustrations. All the Series together, 14s. or separately as follows:—

    1st SERIES.—Rats, Serpents, Fishes, Frogs, Monkeys, &c. Small 8vo. 3s. 6d.
    2nd SERIES.—Fossils, Bears, Wolves, Cats, Eagles, Hedgehogs, Eels, Herrings, Whales. Small 8vo. 3s. 6d.
    3rd SERIES.—Wild Ducks, Fishing, Lions, Tigers, Foxes, Porpoises. Small 8vo. 3s. 6d.
    4th SERIES.—Giants, Mummies, Mermaids, Wonderful People, Salmon, &c. Small 8vo. 3s. 6d.

'These most fascinating works on natural history.'—MORNING POST.

Racecourse and Covert-side.
By ALFRED E. T. WATSON, with Illustrations by JOHN STURGESS. In demy 8vo. 15s.

'"Racecourse and Covert-side" is one of the most amusing books of the kind which we have taken up for many a day. Mr. Watson has not only some practical experience on which he writes, but also a vein of quiet humour peculiar to himself, and the knack of story-telling to no ordinary degree.'—STANDARD.

Doctors and Patients.
By JOHN TIMBS, F.S.A. A New and Revised Edition. In 1 vol. crown 8vo. 6s.

One of Mr. Timbs' most delightful works of gossip and research.'—WORLD.

Pen-Sketches by a Vanished Hand.

Being Selections from the Papers of the late MORTIMER COLLINS. Edited by TOM TAYLOR, and with Notes by FRANCES COLLINS. In 2 vols. crown 8vo. with Portrait, 21*s*.   3 U 1

Thoughts in my Garden.

Being Selections from the Papers of the late MORTIMER COLLINS. Edited by EDMUND YATES, and with Notes by FRANCES COLLINS. In 2 vols. crown 8vo. 21*s*.   2 B 1

The Modern Cook.

By CHARLES ELMÉ FRANCATELLI, late *Maître-d'Hôtel* to Her Majesty In 8vo. Twenty-seventh Edition. Containing 1,500 Recipes and Sixty Illustrations, 12*s*.   1 E 4*

'There's no want of meat, Sir ;
Portly and curious viands are prepared
To please all kinds of appetites.'—MASSINGER.

The Cook's Guide.

By the Author of 'The Modern Cook.' 49th Thousand. In small 8vo. containing 1,000 Recipes. With Illustrations, 5*s*.   9 A 3*

'An admirable manual for every household.'—TIMES.
'Intended mainly for the middle class. A cookery book from Francatelli is an authority. He has such a variety and choice of rare dishes that a table spread by him would be a nonpareil.
OBSERVER.

What to do with the Cold Mutton.

Fcp. 8vo. 2*s*.   [*Reprinting*.   5 A 1

Pamphlets &c.

By Sir BALDWYN LEIGHTON.

The FARM LABOURER in 1872. Second Edition. Demy 8vo. 6*d*.

AGRICULTURAL LABOUR ; being a Paper read before the Social Science Congress at Plymouth. Demy 8vo. 6*d*.

DEPAUPERISATION : its Cause and Cure. With an Appendix. Demy 8vo. 1*s*.

The LULL BEFORE DORKING. Third Edition. Demy 8vo. 6*d*.

The STRENGTH of the BRITISH ARMY, and RESERVE FORCES. By 'A Militia Officer.' Demy 8vo. 1*s*.

The NEED of PROTECTION—FREE IMPORTS NOT FREE TRADE. By ALEXANDER MCEWEN. Demy 8vo. 6*d*.

REASONABLE PROTECTION. A Revenue Tariff. By ALEXANDER MCEWEN. Demy 8vo. 3*d*.

Professor Yonge's Virgil.
With copious English Notes. Used at Harrow, Eton, Winchester, and Rugby. Strongly bound, crown 8vo. 6s.　　　　　s s 2°

Professor Yonge's English-Latin and Latin-English Dictionary.
Used at Eton, Harrow, Winchester, and Rugby. This Work has undergone careful Revision, and the whole work (1,070 pp.) is now sold for 7s. 6d. The English-Latin Part can be obtained alone for 6s. and the Latin-English Part alone for 6s.
　　　　　8 s 1°
'It is the best—we were going to say the only really useful—Anglo-Latin Dictionary we ever met with.'—SPECTATOR.

The Andromache of Euripides.
With copious Grammatical and Critical Notes; and a brief Introductory Account of the Greek Drama, Dialects, and principal Tragic Metres. By the Rev. J. EDWARDS M.A., Trin. Coll. Camb., and the Rev. C. HAWKINS, B.C.L. Ch. Ch., Oxon. Used at Eton. Post 8vo. 4s. 6d.　　o s 5

The Alcestis of Euripides.
Translated from the Greek into English for the first time in its original metres. With Preface, Explanatory Notes, and Stage Directions. By H. B. L. In demy 8vo. limp cloth, 2s. 6d.

The Captives.
From the Latin of Plautus. By H. A. STRONG, M.A. Limp cloth, 2s. 6d.
　　　　　s 1 p

The Haunted House.
Translated from the 'Mostellaria' of Plautus. By H. A. STRONG, M.A. Limp cloth, 4s.　　　　　o x 2

An Elementary Greek Grammar.
By the Rev. G. J. DAVIE, M.A. In small crown 8vo. 86 pp. 4s.　　s 1 p

Spenser for Home and School Use.
Edited by LUCY HARRISON. Small post 8vo. 3s. 6d.　　2　2

FICTION.
BENTLEY'S FAVOURITE NOVELS.

Each Volume can be obtained separately, in crown 8vo. cloth, 6s.

Mrs. Henry Wood's Novels.
The Uniform and Only Edition.

BENTLEY'S FAVOURITE NOVELS. — EAST LYNNE. — One Hundred and Twentieth Thousand. With an Illustration (on Steel) by Hughes. 6s.   o b 1*

BENTLEY'S FAVOURITE NOVELS. — The CHANNINGS. — Forty-fifth Thousand. With Two Illustrations. 6s.   o e 1*

BENTLEY'S FAVOURITE NOVELS. — Mrs. HALLIBURTON'S TROUBLES. With Two Illustrations. 6s.   o b 1*

BENTLEY'S FAVOURITE NOVELS.—The MASTER of GREYLANDS. With an Illustration. 6s.   o j 1*

BENTLEY'S FAVOURITE NOVELS.—VERNER'S PRIDE. With Two Illustrations. 6s.   o j 1*

BENTLEY'S FAVOURITE NOVELS.—WITHIN the MAZE.—With an Illustration. 6s.   o j 1*

BENTLEY'S FAVOURITE NOVELS.—LADY ADELAIDE. With an Illustration. 6s.   o h 1*

BENTLEY'S FAVOURITE NOVELS.—BESSY RANE. With an Illustration. 6s.   o j 1*

BENTLEY'S FAVOURITE NOVELS.- ROLAND YORKE. With an Illustration. 6s.   o j 1*

BENTLEY'S FAVOURITE NOVELS. — LORD OAKBURN'S DAUGHTERS. With Two Illustrations. 6s.   o b 1*

BENTLEY'S FAVOURITE NOVELS.—The SHADOW of ASHLYDYAT. With Two Illustrations. 6s.   o b 1*

BENTLEY'S FAVOURITE NOVELS.—OSWALD CRAY. With an Illustration. 6s.   o j 1*

BENTLEY'S FAVOURITE NOVELS.—DENE HOLLOW. With an Illustration. 6s.   o j 1*

Mrs. Henry Wood's Novels—continued.

BENTLEY'S FAVOURITE NOVELS.—GEORGE CANTERBURY'S WILL. 6s. o j 1*

BENTLEY'S FAVOURITE NOVELS.—TREVLYN HOLD. 6s. o n 1*

BENTLEY'S FAVOURITE NOVELS.—MILDRED ARKELL. 6s. o j 1*

BENTLEY'S FAVOURITE NOVELS.—ST. MARTIN'S EVE. 6s. o j 1*

BENTLEY'S FAVOURITE NOVELS.—ELSTER'S FOLLY. 6s. o n 1*

BENTLEY'S FAVOURITE NOVELS.—ANNE HEREFORD. 6s. o j 1*

BENTLEY'S FAVOURITE NOVELS.—A LIFE'S SECRET. 6s. o j 1*

BENTLEY'S FAVOURITE NOVELS.—RED COURT FARM. 6s. o j 1*

BENTLEY'S FAVOURITE NOVELS.—PARKWATER. 6s. o n 1*

BENTLEY'S FAVOURITE NOVELS.—ORVILLE COLLEGE. With an Illustration. 6s. o n 1*

BENTLEY'S FAVOURITE NOVELS.—EDINA. With an Illustration. 6s. o j 1*

BENTLEY'S FAVOURITE NOVELS.—POMEROY ABBEY. 6s. o j 1*

BENTLEY'S FAVOURITE NOVELS.—JOHNNY LUDLOW. First Series. With a Portrait of Mrs. Henry Wood. 6s. o b 1*

BENTLEY'S FAVOURITE NOVELS. — JOHNNY LUDLOW. Second Series. 6s. o b 1*

BENTLEY'S FAVOURITE NOVELS.—COURT NETHERLEIGH. With an Illustration. 6s. o j 1*

By Miss Austen.

(THE ONLY COMPLETE EDITION BESIDES THE STEVENTON EDITION. See page 40.)

BENTLEY'S FAVOURITE NOVELS.—SENSE and SENSIBILITY. With an Illustration (on steel) by Pickering. 6s. 8 s 1*

'I have now read over again all Miss Austen's novels. Charming they are. There are in the world no compositions which approach nearer to perfection.'—MACAULAY'S JOURNAL, May 1, 1851.

'What wonderful books those are! Miss Austen must have written down the very conversations she heard *verbatim* o have made them so like—which is Irish.'
FANNY KEMBLE'S REMINISCENCES.

BENTLEY'S FAVOURITE NOVELS.—PRIDE and PREJUDICE. With an Illustration (on steel) by Pickering. 6s. 8 s 1*

'The perfect type of a novel of common life; the story is so concisely and dramatically told, the language so simple, the shades of human character so clearly presented, and the operation of various motives so delicately traced, attest this gifted woman to have been the perfect mistress of her art.'—ARNOLD'S ENGLISH LITERATURE.

BENTLEY'S FAVOURITE NOVELS.—EMMA. With an Illustration (on steel) by Pickering. 6s. 8 s 1*

'Shakespeare has neither equal nor second, but among the writers who have approached nearest to the manner of the great master we have no hesitation in placing Jane Austen, a woman of whom England is justly proud.'—MACAULAY'S ESSAYS.

By Miss Austen—continued.

BENTLEY'S FAVOURITE NOVELS.—MANSFIELD PARK. With an Illustration (on steel) by Pickering. 6s.

'Miss Austen has a talent for describing the involvements and feelings and characters of ordinary life which is to me the most wonderful I ever met with. Her exquisite touch, which renders commonplace things and character interesting from the truth of the description and sentiment, is denied to me.'—SIR WALTER SCOTT.

BENTLEY'S FAVOURITE NOVELS.—NORTHANGER ABBEY and PERSUASION. With an Illustration (on steel) by Pickering. 6s.

'Read Dickens' "Hard Times" and another book of Pliny's "Letters." Read "Northanger Abbey," worth all Dickens and Pliny together. Yet it was the work of a girl. She was certainly not more than 26. Wonderful creature!'—MACAULAY'S JOURNAL, Aug. 12, 1854.

BENTLEY'S FAVOURITE NOVELS.—LADY SUSAN and THE WATSONS. With a Memoir and Portrait of the Authoress. 8s.

'Miss Austen's life as well as her talent seems to us unique among the lives of authoresses of fiction.'—QUARTERLY REVIEW.

Miss Broughton's Novels.

BENTLEY'S FAVOURITE NOVELS.—JOAN. With an Illustration (on Steel) by Calderon. 6s.

'There is something very distinct and original in "Joan." It is more worthy, more noble, more unselfish than any of her predecessors, while the story is to the full as bright and entertaining as any of those which first made Miss Broughton famous.'—DAILY NEWS.

BENTLEY'S FAVOURITE NOVELS.—NANCY. With an Illustration (on Steel) by Capt. Norrie. 6s.

'If unwearied brilliancy, style, picturesque descriptions, humorous and original dialogue, and keen insight into human nature, can make a novel popular, there is no doubt whatever that "Nancy" will take a higher place than anything which Miss Broughton has yet written. It is admirable from first to last.'—STANDARD.

BENTLEY'S FAVOURITE NOVELS. — GOOD-BYE, SWEETHEART! With an Illustration (on Steel) by Hughes. 6s.

'We are more impressed by this than by any of Miss Broughton's previous works. It is more carefully worked, and conceived in a much higher spirit. Miss Broughton writes from the very bottom of her heart. There is a terrible realism about her.'—ECHO.

BENTLEY'S FAVOURITE NOVELS.—COMETH UP as a FLOWER. With an Illustration (on Steel) by Calderon. 6s.

'A strikingly clever and original tale, the chief merits of which consist in the powerful, vigorous manner of its telling, in the exceeding beauty and poetry of its sketches of scenery, and in the soliloquies, sometimes quaintly humorous, sometimes cynically bitter, sometimes plaintive and melancholy, which are uttered by the heroine.'—TIMES.

BENTLEY'S FAVOURITE NOVELS.—RED as a ROSE is SHE. With an Illustration (on Steel) by La Monti. 6s.

'There are few readers who will not be fascinated by this tale.'—TIMES.

BENTLEY'S FAVOURITE NOVELS.—NOT WISELY, but TOO WELL. 6s.

BENTLEY'S FAVOURITE NOVELS.—SECOND THOUGHTS. 6s.

BENTLEY'S FAVOURITE NOVELS.—BELINDA. 6s.

'Miss Broughton's story, "Belinda," is admirably told, with the happiest humour, the closest and clearest character-sketching. "Sarah" is a gem—one of the truest, liveliest, and most amusing persons of modern fiction.'—'Atlas' in the WORLD.

By Mrs. Parr.

BENTLEY'S FAVOURITE NOVELS.—DOROTHY FOX. With Illustrations. 6s.

'We must thank the author for a charming novel...... Dorothy Fox herself is represent as charming all hearts, and she will charm all readers.'—THE TIMES.

BENTLEY'S FAVOURITE NOVELS.—ADAM AND EVE. 6s.

'It is a treat to take up such a capital novel as "Adam and Eve."'—WHITEHALL REVIEW

By Miss Helen Mathers.

BENTLEY'S FAVOURITE NOVELS.—COMIN' THRO' the RYE. 6s. Tenth Edition.

BENTLEY'S FAVOURITE NOVELS.—SAM'S SWEETHEART. 6s

By Mrs. Alexander.

BENTLEY'S FAVOURITE NOVELS.—HER DEAREST FOE. 6s.

'There is not a single character in this novel which is not cleverly conceived and successfully illustrated, and not a page which is dull.'—WORLD.

BENTLEY'S FAVOURITE NOVELS.—The WOOING O'T. 6s.

'A charming story with a charming heroine.'—VANITY FAIR.

BENTLEY'S FAVOURITE NOVELS.—WHICH SHALL it BE? 6s.

BENTLEY'S FAVOURITE NOVELS.—LOOK BEFORE YOU LEAP. 6s.

BENTLEY'S FAVOURITE NOVELS.—THE FRERES. 6s.

BENTLEY'S FAVOURITE NOVELS.—THE ADMIRAL'S WARD. 6s.

BENTLEY'S FAVOURITE NOVELS.—THE EXECUTOR. 6s.

[*In the Press.*

By Baroness Tautphœus (née Montgomery).

BENTLEY'S FAVOURITE NOVELS.—The INITIALS. With Two Illustrations. 6s.

BENTLEY'S FAVOURITE NOVELS.—QUITS! With Two Illustrations. 6s.

By Hawley Smart.

BENTLEY'S FAVOURITE NOVELS.—BREEZIE LANGTON. With an Illustration. 6s.

By W. Clark Russell.

BENTLEY'S FAVOURITE NOVELS—AN OCEAN FREE LANCE. 6s.

'The author compels us to speak of his *genius*, as the only word that fitly describes the quality that makes his romances of the sea both in form and in spirit second to none that have ever been written at any rate. The merchant service is no longer without its Homer.'—GLOBE.

By Miss Jessie Fothergill.

BENTLEY'S FAVOURITE NOVELS.—The FIRST VIOLIN. With an Etching from Calderon. 6s.   1 B 1*

'The story is extremely interesting from the first page to the last. It is a long time since we have met with anything so exquisitely touching as the description of Eugen's life with his friend Helfen. It is an idyll of the purest and noblest simplicity.'—STANDARD.

'A story of strong and deep interest, written by a vigorous and cultured writer. To such as have musical sympathies an added pleasure and delight will be given to what, judged by ordinary literary standards, is a novel of real excellence.'—DUNDEE ADVERTISER.

BENTLEY'S FAVOURITE NOVELS.—PROBATION. With an Etching from Collier. 6s.   1 Z 1†

'Altogether "Probation" is the most interesting novel we have read for some time. We closed the book with very real regret, and a feeling of the truest admiration for the power which directed and the spirit which inspired the writer, and with determination, moreover, to make the acquaintance of her other stories.'—SPECTATOR.

BENTLEY'S FAVOURITE NOVELS.—THE WELLFIELDS. 6s.
   1 Z 1†

'The talent shown by Miss Fothergill in her earliest ventures held out a promise of future excellence, which is to a very great extent realised in her latest effort, "The Wellfields." The authoress has produced a most attractive novel, and one for which it is easy to predict a deservedly large share of popularity.'—WHITEHALL REVIEW.

BENTLEY'S FAVOURITE NOVELS.—KITH AND KIN. 6s. 1 D 1*

'In speaking of "Kith and Kin," it is not necessary to say more in the way of praise than that Miss Fothergill has not fallen below her own mark. None of her usual good materials are wanting. The characters affect us like real persons, and the story of their troubles and their efforts interests us from the beginning to the end. We like the book—we like it very much.'
PALL MALL GAZETTE.

'Miss Fothergill writes charming stories.'—DAILY NEWS.

BENTLEY'S FAVOURITE NOVELS.—HEALEY. 6s.

Mrs. Edwardes' Novels.

BENTLEY'S FAVOURITE NOVELS.—LEAH: a WOMAN of FASHION. With an Illustration (on Steel) by Calderon. 6s. 2 B 1*

'"Leah" is the best, the cleverest, and the strongest novel that we have as yet had in the season, as it is certainly Mrs. Edwardes' masterpiece.'—WORLD.

BENTLEY'S FAVOURITE NOVELS.—OUGHT WE to VISIT HER? With an Illustration (on Steel) by Hughes. 6s.   5 B 1*

'Mrs. Edwardes has never done better than in her charming novel "Ought We to Visit Her?"'
VANITY FAIR.

BENTLEY'S FAVOURITE NOVELS.—STEVEN LAWRENCE: YEOMAN. With an Illustration (on Steel) by Hughes. 6s. 2 B 1*

BENTLEY'S FAVOURITE NOVELS.—A BALL ROOM REPENTANCE. 6s.   4 R 1†

By Mrs. Notley.

BENTLEY'S FAVOURITE NOVELS.—OLIVE VARCOE. 6s. 1 z 1†

By the Hon. Lewis Wingfield.

BENTLEY'S FAVOURITE NOVELS.—LADY GRIZEL. 6s.

By Anthony Trollope.

BENTLEY'S FAVOURITE NOVELS.—The THREE CLERKS. With Two Illustrations. 6s. 5 A 1*

'Mr. Trollope amply bears out in the work the reputation he acquired by "Barchester Towers." We regard the tenderness and self-sacrifice of Linda as one of the most graceful and touching pictures of female heroism in the whole range of modern novels.'—JOHN BULL.

By Miss Florence Montgomery.

BENTLEY'S FAVOURITE NOVELS.—MISUNDERSTOOD. With Illustrations. 6s.
BENTLEY'S FAVOURITE NOVELS. — THROWN TOGETHER. 6s.
BENTLEY'S FAVOURITE NOVELS.—SEAFORTH. 6s.

*** *See also next page.*

By Marcus Clarke.

BENTLEY'S FAVOURITE NOVELS.—FOR the TERM of HIS NATURAL LIFE. 6s. ■ M 1†

By Lady Georgiana Fullerton.

BENTLEY'S FAVOURITE NOVELS.—TOO STRANGE NOT TO BE TRUE. With Two Illustrations. 6s. 2 5 1*

'One of the most fascinating and delightful works I ever had the good fortune to meet with.'
EINONACH, in NOTES AND QUERIES.

BENTLEY'S FAVOURITE NOVELS.—ELLEN MIDDLETON. 6s.

By Mrs. J. H. Riddell.

BENTLEY'S FAVOURITE NOVELS.—The MYSTERY in PALACE GARDENS. 6s. 5 I P

By Mrs. Campbell Praed.

BENTLEY'S FAVOURITE NOVELS.—POLICY and PASSION. 6s. I B 1†

By Miss Rosa N. Carey.

BENTLEY'S FAVOURITE NOVELS.—NELLIE'S MEMORIES. 6s. 2 Æ 1*
BENTLEY'S FAVOURITE NOVELS.—WOOED AND MARRIED. 6s. 4 Æ 1²
BENTLEY'S FAVOURITE NOVELS.—BARBARA HEATHCOTE'S TRIAL. 6s. 4 2 1†
BENTLEY'S FAVOURITE NOVELS. ROBERT ORD'S ATONE- MENT. 6s.

By J. Sheridan Le Fanu.

BENTLEY'S FAVOURITE NOVELS.—IN A GLASS DARKLY. 6s.

By Ernst Werner.

BENTLEY'S FOREIGN FAVOURITE NOVELS.—SUCCESS, and HOW HE WON IT. From the German by Mrs. CHRISTINA TYRRELL. 6s. 2 z 1†

'"Success, and How He Won It," deserves all praise. The story is charming and original, told with a delicacy which makes it irresistibly fascinating and attractive.'—STANDARD.

BENTLEY'S FOREIGN FAVOURITE NOVELS.—UNDER A CHARM. From the German by Mrs. CHRISTINA TYRRELL. 6s.
1 2 1†

'Novel readers owe a debt of gratitude to the translator of this fascinating story. The translation is so well done that one would never suspect the book to be other than of English origin, and the narrative is so absorbing that few who take up the book will lay it down without finishing it.'—SPECTATOR.

BENTLEY'S FOREIGN FAVOURITE NOVELS. — NO SURRENDER. From the German by Mrs. CHRISTINA TYRRELL. 6s.
1 B 1†

'A new novel by the clever author of " Success " must always be welcomed. In each new work we find no diminution of talent or interest. There is always something fresh, vivid, and life-like and in " No Surrender" there is considerable power . . . and a vein of the most delightful humour running through the book.'—VANITY FAIR.

By Mrs. Augustus Craven.

BENTLEY'S FOREIGN FAVOURITE NOVELS.—A SISTER'S STORY. From the French by EMILY BOWLES. 6s. 5 s 1*

'A book which took all France and all England by storm.'—BLACKWOOD'S MAGAZINE.

By Hector Malot.

BENTLEY'S FOREIGN FAVOURITE NOVELS. — NO RELATIONS. 6s. 7 B 1†

Miss Montgomery's Stories.

MISUNDERSTOOD. New Edition, with 6 full-page Illustrations by George Du Maurier. Crown 8vo. 6s. 2 s 3
THROWN TOGETHER. Eighth Thousand. Crown 8vo. 6s. 7 s 2*
SEAFORTH. Popular. Edition, with Frontispiece. Crown 8vo. 6s. 2 E 2*
THWARTED. Sixth Thousand. Crown 8vo. 5s. 7 s 2*
The TOWN-CRIER &c. Fourth Thousand. Crown 8vo. 5s. 2 s 2*
A VERY SIMPLE STORY and WILD MIKE. Sm. cr. 2s. 6d. 6 s 2*
HERBERT MANNERS, and The TOWN CRIER &c. In small crown 8vo. 2s. 6d. 6 B 2*
THE BLUE VEIL. Fourth Thousand. Crown 8vo. 5s.

The Works of Thomas Love Peacock.

The COLLECTED EDITION, including his Novels, Fugitive Pieces, Poems, Criticisms, &c. Edited by Sir HENRY COLE, K.C.B. With Preface by Lord HOUGHTON, and a Biographical Sketch by his Grand-daughter. In 3 vols. crown 8vo. with Portrait, 31s. 6d. 2 B 3

'His fine wit
Makes such a wound, the knife is lost in it;
A strain too learned for a shallow age,
Too wise for selfish bigots; let his page,
Which charms the chosen spirits of the time
Fold itself up for a serener clime
Of years to come, and find its recompense
In that just expectation.'—SHIRLEY.

Past Hours.

By the late ADELAIDE SARTORIS (née KEMBLE). Edited with a Preface by her Daughter, Mrs. GORDON. In two volumes, small crown 8vo. 12s. 2 B 1

Pastorals of France.

A Last Love at Pornic—Yvonne of Croisic—The Four Bells of Chartres. By FREDERICK WEDMORE. In large crown 8vo. 7s. 6d. 2 P 1

'In their simplicity, their tenderness, their truthfulness to the remote life they picture, "Pastorals of France" are almost perfect.'—SPECTATOR.
'Of singular quaintness and beauty.'—CONTEMPORARY REVIEW.
'Very pathetic and exquisitely told.'—THE WORLD.

'Once More'—The Short Stories of Lady Margaret Majendie,

Reprinted from 'Blackwood' and 'Temple Bar.' In 1 vol. crown 8vo. 6s.
4 R

He would be a Soldier.

By R. MOUNTENEY JEPHSON, Author of 'The Girl he left behind him,' &c. Third Edition. In crown 8vo. with 4 Illustrations, 3s. 6d. 2 B 3
'A more amusing military novelette we have not read for some time.'—THE ATHENÆUM.
'A clever, rollicking sketch, which will be as popular as "Verdant Green."'—THE WORLD.

Flitters, Tatters, and the Counsellor.

By the Author of 'Hogan, M.P.' Sixth Edition. In small crown 8vo. 1s. S 1 F
'In this seemingly unworthy subject the author finds scope for a pathos that is almost thrilling in its unstudied intensity.—SCOTSMAN.
'We can honestly say that no work of fiction that we have seen for a long time has such splendid humour and deep pathos as this little shilling book.'—SPECTATOR.

Twelve Wonderful Tales

By W. KNOX WIGRAM, Author of 'The Justices' Note-book.' New Edition, with Frontispiece. In crown 8vo. 5s. 4 S 2

'An edition which all lovers of this delightful authoress should hasten to place upon their shelves.'—ST. JAMES'S GAZETTE.

A SPECIAL EDITION OF
JANE AUSTEN'S NOVELS.
(THE STEVENTON EDITION.) 152ᵒ

To meet a desire sometimes expressed for a superior edition of these Works, a small number of copies have been worked upon Dickinson's hand-made paper, in a special ink, by Messrs. Spottiswoode & Co., and chastely bound in white cloth by Messrs. Burn.

These copies are sold <u>in sets only</u>, in six volumes, large crown 8vo. at the published price of 63s.

'In his 'Steventon edition' of Jane Austen's novels, Mr. Bentley—though he prints in the now fashionable brown ink on old-fashioned paper, and binds quaintly—avoids the discomfort of recent *éditions de luxe* so humorously pointed out by Mr. du Maurier in *Punch*. The new edition can be easily held in the hand, and is meant for frequent use and reference rather than for mere show.'—THE WORLD.

☞ Messrs. BENTLEY'S are the <u>ONLY COMPLETE EDITIONS</u>
of Miss Austen's Works.

VOLUME I. *SENSE AND SENSIBILITY.*
VOLUME II. *PRIDE AND PREJUDICE.*
VOLUME III. *MANSFIELD PARK.*
VOLUME IV. *EMMA.*
VOLUME V. *NORTHANGER ABBEY,* and *PERSUASION.*
VOLUME VI. *LADY SUSAN, THE WATSONS,* &c.
(*With a Memoir and Portrait of the Authoress.*)

'All the greatest writers of fiction are pure of the sin of writing to a text—Chaucer, Shakespeare, Scott, Jane Austen ; and are not these precisely the writers who do most good as well as give most pleasure?'—MARY RUSSELL MITFORD.

*** *See also page* 33.

RICHARD BENTLEY & SON, NEW BURLINGTON STREET,
Publishers in Ordinary to Her Majesty the Queen.

A NEW LIBRARY EDITION OF
MISS FERRIER'S NOVELS.
(THE EDINBURGH EDITION.)
In Six Volumes small crown 8vo.   1 z 2†

The Set 30s., *or separately as under:—*

MARRIAGE	*2 Vols. 10s.*
THE INHERITANCE . . .	*2 Vols. 10s.*
DESTINY	*2 Vols. 10s.*

This Edition is printed from the Original Edition as annotated by the Author, of whom a short Memoir is prefixed in 'Marriage.'

'Edgeworth, Ferrier, Austen, have all given portraits of real society far superior to anything man, vain man, has produced of the like nature.'—SIR WALTER SCOTT.

'Miss Ferrier's novels are all thick set with specimens of sagacity, happy traits of nature, flashes of genuine satire, easy humour, sterling good sense, and above all—God only knows where she picked it up—mature and perfect knowledge of the world.'—NOCTES AMBROSIANÆ.

'Miss Ferrier is a Scotch Miss Edgeworth—of a lively practical penetrating cast of mind, skilful in depicting character and seizing upon natural peculiarities, caustic in her wit and humour, with a quick sense of the ridiculous, and desirous of inculcating sound morality and attention to the courtesies and charities of life. The general strain of her writings relates to the foibles and oddities of mankind, and no one has drawn them with greater breadth of humour or effect. Her scenes often resemble the style of our best old comedies, and she may boast, like Foote, of adding many new and original characters to the stock of our comic literature.'—CHAMBERS.

'I retire from the field, conscious there remains behind not only a large harvest, but labourers capable of gathering it in. More than one writer has of late displayed talents of this description, and if the present author, himself a phantom, may be permitted to distinguish a brother, or perhaps a sister shadow, he would mention in particular the author of the very lively work entitled "Marriage."'—SIR WALTER SCOTT.

'I assure you I think it ("Marriage") without exception the cleverest thing that ever was written, and in wit far surpassing Fielding.'—LADY CHARLOTTE BURY.

'On Wednesday I dined in company with Sir Walter Scott, and he spoke of the work ("The Inheritance") in the very highest terms. I do not always set the highest value on the baronet's favourable opinion of a book, because he has so much kindness of feeling towards every one, but in this case he spoke so much *con amore*, and entered so completely, and at such length to me, into the spirit of the book and of the characters, that showed me at once the impression it had made upon him. Every one I have met who has seen the book gives the same praise of it.'—JOHN BLACKWOOD.

'On the day of the dissolution of Parliament, and in the critical hours between twelve and three, I was employed in reading part of the second volume of "Destiny." My mind was so completely occupied on your colony in Argyleshire, that I did not throw away a thought on kings or parliaments, and was not moved by the general curiosity to stir abroad until I had finished your volume. It would have been nothing if you had so agitated a youth of genius and susceptibility, prone to literary enthusiasm, but such a victory over an old hack is perhaps worthy of your notice.'—MACKINTOSH (to Miss Ferrier).

'I am unable to return you adequate thanks for being the cause of my reading "Destiny." I have done this (and all with me) with delight, from the interest and admiration at the whole composition, the novelty and excitement of its plan, the exquisite and thrilling manner of its disclosure, the absence of all flat and heavy intervals, the conception and support of the characters, the sound and salutary moral that pervades it all—these make me love and honour its valuable authoress, and lament that I am not in the number of her acquaintance.'—GRANVILLE PENN.

To be obtained of all Booksellers.

RICHARD BENTLEY & SON, NEW BURLINGTON STREET
Publishers in Ordinary to Her Majesty the Queen.

Recent Works of Fiction,

IN LIBRARY FORM.

I
Keith's Wife. By Lady VIOLET GREVILLE, Author of 'Zoe: a Girl of Genius.' In 3 vols. crown 8vo. 31s. 6d.

II
My Heart and I. By ELLINOR HUME. In 1 vol. crown 8vo. 10s. 6d.

III
Wilfrid's Widow. By the Author of 'Mrs. Jerningham's Journal,' &c. In 2 vols. crown 8vo. 21s.

IV
Unspotted from the World. By Mrs. G. W. GODFREY, Author of 'Dolly,'&c. In 3 vols. crown 8vo. 31s. 6d.

V
Honest Davie. By FRANK BARRETT, Author of 'A Prodigal's Progress,' &c. In 3 vols. crown 8vo. 31s. 6d.

VI
The Admiral's Ward. By Mrs. ALEXANDER, Author of 'The Wooing o't,' &c. In 3 vols. crown 8vo. 31s. 6d.

VII
A Woman's Glory. By SARAH DOUDNEY, Author of 'Strangers Yet.' In 3 vols. crown 8vo. 31s. 6d.

VIII
Contradictions. By FRANCES M. PEARD, Author of 'Cartouche,' &c. In 2 vols. crown 8vo. 21s.

IX
Transplanted. By M. E. FRASER-TYTLER, Author of 'Grisel Romney.' In 2 vols. crown 8vo. 21s.

X
Hélène. By Mrs. ARTHUR KENNARD. In 2 vols. crown 8vo. 21s.

XI
A Fair Countrymaid. By EMMA FAIRFAX BYRNE, Author of 'Millicent.' In 3 vols. crown 8vo. 31s. 6d.

XII
Estcourt. By LORD JAMES DOUGLAS, Author of 'Royal Angus.' In 2 vols. crown 8vo. 21s.

XIII
A Struggle for Fame. By Mrs. J. H. RIDDELL, Author of 'The Senior Partner.' In 3 vols. crown 8vo. 31s. 6d.

XIV
Disarmed. By Miss M. E. BETHAM-EDWARDS, Author of 'Kitty,' &c. In 2 vols. crown 8vo. 21s.

XV
Put to the Proof. By Miss CAROLINE FOTHERGILL. In 3 vols. crown 8vo. 31s. 6d.

XVI
Juliet. By Miss M. E. CARTER. In 3 vols. crown 8vo. 31s. 6d.

XVII
Dr. Edith Romney. By a new writer. In 3 vols. crown 8vo. 31s. 6d.

XVIII
Belinda. By RHODA BROUGHTON, Author of 'Goodbye! Sweetheart!' &c. In 3 vols. crown 8vo. 31s. 6d.

XIX
Abigel Rowe. A Tale of the Regency. By the Hon. LEWIS WINGFIELD, Author of 'Lady Grizel,' &c. In 3 vols. crown 8vo. 31s. 6d.

XX
Ephraim: or, the Few and the Many. From the German of Auguste Niemann, by Mrs. CHRISTINA TYRRELL. In 3 vols. crown 8vo. 31s. 6d.

XXI
The Executor. By Mrs. ALEXANDER, Author of 'Which shall it be?' &c. In 3 vols. crown 8vo. 31s. 6d.

XXII
Winifred Power. By JOYCE DARRELL. In 3 vols. crown 8vo. 31s. 6d.

RICHARD BENTLEY & SON, NEW BURLINGTON STREET,
Publishers in Ordinary to Her Majesty the Queen.

BENTLEY'S EMPIRE LIBRARY.

The price of each volume is Half-a-Crown, bound in cloth.

The following Volumes are now published, and can be obtained separately at every Bookseller's:—

I
By HELEN MATHERS.
    The Land o' the Leal.   6 B 2*

II
By FLORENCE MONTGOMERY.
    A Very Simple Story, and Wild Mike.   6 S 2*

III
By Mrs. ALEXANDER.
    Ralph Wilton's Weird.   6 B 2*

IV
By Mrs. EDWARDES.
    A Blue Stocking.   6 R 2*

V
By HELEN MATHERS.
    As He Comes Up the Stairs.   6 B 2*

VI
By WILKIE COLLINS.
    A Rogue's Life.   6 B 2*

VII
By A GERMAN PRIEST.
    A Victim of the Falk Laws.   6 R 2*

VIII
By Mrs. EDWARDES.
    A Vagabond Heroine.   6 R 2*

By Mrs. G. W. GODFREY.
    My Queen.   6 R 2*

X
By JULIAN HAWTHORNE.
    Archibald Malmaison.   6 B 2*

XI
By RHODA BROUGHTON.
    Twilight Stories.   6 B 2*

XII
By CHARLES DICKENS.
    The Mudfog Papers, &c.   6 R 2*

XIII
By FLORENCE MONTGOMERY.
    Herbert Manners, and other Stories.   6 B 2*

XIV
By JESSIE FOTHERGILL.
    Made or Marred.   6 B 2*

XV.
By JESSIE FOTHERGILL.
    One of Three.   7 R 2†

(*See also back page.*)

The Temple Bar Magazine.

(With which is incorporated 'Bentley's Miscellany.')

Demy 8vo. 144 pages, monthly, of all Booksellers, price One Shilling. 4 A 8

'*One can never help enjoying* "TEMPLE BAR."'—GUARDIAN.
'*Who does not welcome* "TEMPLE BAR"?'—JOHN BULL.

THE BACK NUMBERS (with the following exceptions) can also be obtained, price One Shilling each.

NUMBERS OUT OF PRINT:—

No. 1, December 1860	No. 26, January 1863	No. 146, January 1873
,, 2, January 1861	,, 37, December 1863	,, 148, March 1873
,, 3, February 1861	,, 38, January 1864	,, 149, April 1873
,, 9, August 1861	,, 61, December 1865	,, 156, November 1873
,, 12, November 1861	,, 63, February 1866	,, 168, November 1874
,, 13, December 1861	,, 74, January 1867	,, 169, December 1874
,, 14, January 1862	,, 97, December 1868	,, 170, January 1875
,, 20, July 1862	,, 110, January 1870	,, 251, October 1881
,, 23, October 1862	,, 133, December 1871	,, 254, January 1882
,, 25, December 1862	,, 134, January 1872	,, 266, January, 1883

and No. 278 for January 1884.

THE VOLUMES (three in each year) can be obtained, with exception of Vols. 3, 4, 5, 6, 7, 10, 16, 25, 37, 38, 43, 63, and 64. Each Volume, 5s. 6d.

INDEX.—Annual Reference Tables will be found from time to time in the Advertisement Sheet of 'TEMPLE BAR.'

CASES for binding the Volumes can be had, price 1s. each.

TO CORRESPONDENTS.—All MSS. must be addressed, post-paid, to the EDITOR of TEMPLE BAR, 8 New Burlington Street, London, W. Every MS. should bear the Name and Address of the Writer (not necessarily for publication), and be accompanied by postage stamps for its return in case of non-acceptance. Every care will be taken, but the Editor or the Publishers cannot be responsible for any Articles accidentally lost. MSS. should be written in a clear hand on one side of the paper only, and the leaves should be fastened together and paged. POETRY.—From the large number of Poems received every month, it is impossible to return them. A copy should be kept, as rejected Poems are destroyed. CORRESPONDENCE.—All articles sent are carefully considered, but it is impossible to advise beforehand what subjects are likely to meet with acceptance.

TO ADVERTISERS.—All communications respecting Advertisements and Bills should be forwarded by the 17th of the month to Mr. RATCLIFFE, Advertising Manager, 8 George Yard, Lombard Street, London, E.C.

'The Temple Bar Magazine' will be published at One p.m. on the undermentioned days, unless unforeseen circumstances arise to cause any alteration :—

1884.
Tuesday, October 28
Wednesday, November 26
Friday, December 19

and copies can be obtained by the public on the following day.

THE ARGOSY MAGAZINE.

Edited by Mrs. HENRY WOOD.

Monthly of all Booksellers, 6d. (the December number, 1s.).

THE BACK NUMBERS, with exception of the undermentioned, which are out of print, can be obtained at the same price :—

Nos. 1 to 24, December 1865 to November 1867 No. 83, October 1872
No. 51, February, 1870   No. 74, January 1872   ,, 88, March 1873
,, 65, April 1871   ,, 75, February 1872   ,, 97, December 1873
,, 71, October 1871   And No. 135, for February 1877.

THE VOLUMES (of which there are two in each year) can be obtained, price 5s. each, with exception of Vols 1, 2 (for 1866), 3, 4 (for 1867), 7 (for 1869), 9 (for 1870), 11, 12 (in 1871), 13, 14 (for 1872), 15 and 16 (in 1873), which are out of print.

CASES for binding the Volumes can be had, price 1s. 6d. each.

To CORRESPONDENTS.—All MSS. and Communications must be addressed to the SUB-EDITOR of THE ARGOSY, 8 New Burlington Street, W. From the large number of Articles received, it is impossible to return them unless accompanied by stamps. The Publishers cannot be responsible for Articles accidentally lost.

To ADVERTISERS.—All Advertisements and Bills are requested to be forwarded to Mr. NELSON, Advertisement Contractor, 14 & 15 St. Swithin's Lane, Cannon Street, E.C., by the 10th of each month.

The Publication days are the same as shown on the previous page for ' Temple Bar.'

STATEMENTS of the PALESTINE EXPLORATION FUND.

Published Quarterly by the Committee of the Palestine Exploration Fund. Price 2s. 6d.

The earlier Numbers are now out of print. July, October*, 1874; January*, April*, July, October, 1875; January, April, July, October, 1876; January, April, July, October, 1877; January, April, July, October, 1878; January, April, July, October, 1879; January, April, July, October, 1880; January*, April, July, October, 1881; January, April, July, October, 1882; January* April, July, October, 1883; January, April, July, October, 1884. The Numbers to which an asterisk (*) is affixed are also out of print.

YEARLY CASES for binding the Statements can be had, price 1s. 6d. each.

The Statements are published about the 15th of the month they are dated.
See also page 22.

FOREIGN MONEY

The following Table has been prepared for the convenience of persons residing in this Catalogue will be found here, but the cost of carriage or

England, Australia, New Zealand, South Africa	India (and Ceylon?)	Canada, United States, Mexico	France, Belgium, Italy, Switzerland, Spain, Algeria	Germany	Austria	Holland, Dutch East Indies	Denmark, Sweden, Norway, Iceland	Portugal, Madeira	Russia
s. d.	r. a.	dols. c.	fr. c.*	m. pf.	fl. kr.	fl. c.	k. o.	m. r.	r. c.
1 0	0.10	0.24	1.25	1.00	0.38	0.61	0.91	0.230	
1 6	0.15	0.36	1.88	1.50	0.56	0.92	1.36	0.345	
2 0	1.04	0.48	2.50	2.00	1.15	1.22	1.81	0.460	
2 6	1.08	0.60	3.13	2.50	1.34	1.53	2.27	0.575	
3 0	1.13	0.72	3.75	3.00	1.53	1.83	2.72	0.690	
3 6	2.02	0.84	4.38	3.50	2.11	2.14	3.18	0.805	
4 0	2.07	0.96	5.00	4.00	2.30	2.44	3.63	0.920	
4 6	2.12	1.08	5.63	4.50	2.49	2.74	4.08	1.035	
5 0	3.01	1.20	6.25	5.00	3.08	3.04	4.54	1.150	
5 6	3.06	1.32	6.88	5.50	3.26	3.35	4.99	1.265	
6 0	3.11	1.44	7.50	6.00	3.45	3.65	5.45	1.380	
7 6	4.09	1.80	9.38	7.50	4.41	4.56	6.81	1.725	
8 0	4.14	1.92	10.00	8.00	5.00	4.87	7.26	1.840	
9 0	5.08	2.16	11.25	9.00	5.38	5.48	8.17	2.070	
10 0	6.02	2.40	12.50	10.00	6.15	6.08	9.08	2.300	
10 6	6.07	2.52	13.13	10.50	6.34	6.38	9.53	2.415	
12 0	7.05	2.88	15.00	12.00	7.30	7.30	10.89	2.760	
12 6	7.10	3.00	15.63	12.50	7.49	7.60	11.34	2.875	
14 0	8.09	3.36	17.50	14.00	8.45	8.52	12.71	3.200	
15 0	9.02	3.60	18.75	15.00	9.23	9.12	13.61	3.430	
16 0	9.12	3.84	20.00	16.00	10.00	9.73	14.52	3.660	
17 6	10.11	4.20	21.88	17.50	10.56	10.65	14.98	4.005	
18 0	11.00	4.32	22.50	18.00	11.15	10.95	16.34	4.120	
20 0	12.03	4.80	25.00	20.00	12.30	12.16	18.15	4.570	
21 0	12.13	5.04	26.25	21.00	13.08	12.77	18.60	4.800	

Owing to the paper currency the proportionate prices are frequently liable to variation.

NOTE.—*The accuracy of the above Tables is not guaranteed, and*

* *In Italy lire and centesimi, and in Spain pesetas and centesimos*

CONVERSION TABLE.

abroad when remitting to an English bookseller. The equivalent of all prices postage would have to be added or allowed for in each instance.

England, Australia, New Zealand, South Africa	India (and Ceylon?)	Canada United States Mexico	France, Belgium, Italy, Switzerland, Spain, Algeria	Germany	Austria	Holland, Dutch East Indies	Denmark, Sweden, Norway, Iceland	Portugal, Madeira	Russia
s. d.	r. a.	dols. c.	fr. c.	m. pf.	fl. kr.	fl. c.	k. o.	m. r.	r. c.
22 6	13.12	5.40	28.13	22.50	14.04	13.69	20.42	5.145	
24 0	14.10	5.76	30.00	24.00	15.00	14.60	21.78	5.520	
25 0	15.04	6.00	31.25	25.00	15.38	15.20	22.69	5.750	
26 0	15.14	6.24	32.50	26.00	16.15	15.81	23.60	5.960	
27 6	16.13	6.60	34.38	27.50	17.11	16.73	24.96	6.305	
28 0	17.02	6.72	35.00	28.00	17.30	17.04	25.41	6.400	
30 0	18.04	7.20	37.50	30.00	18.46	18.24	27.22	6.860	
31 6	19.03	7.56	39.38	31.50	19.42	19.16	28.59	7.205	
32 0	19.08	7.68	40.00	32.00	20.00	19.46	29.04	7.320	
35 0	21.06	8.40	43.75	35.00	21.53	21.30	31.77	8.010	
36 0	21.15	8.64	45.00	36.00	22.30	21.90	32.67	8.240	
40 0	24.07	9.60	50.00	40.00	25.00	24.32	36.30	9.140	
42 0	25.10	10.08	52.50	42.00	26.17	25.54	38.11	9.600	
45 0	27.08	10.80	56.25	45.00	28.10	27.38	40.84	10.290	
48 0	29.05	11.52	60.00	48.00	30.00	29.20	43.56	11.040	
50 0	30.08	12.00	62.50	50.00	31.16	30.40	45.36	11.500	
52 6	32.00	12.60	65.63	52.50	32.50	31.93	47.65	12.015	
60 0	36.10	14.40	75.00	60.00	37.32	36.48	54.45	13.710	
63 0	38.07	15.12	78.75	63.00	39.25	38.31	57.18	14.400	
70 0	42.12	16.80	87.50	70.00	43.46	42.60	63.52	16.000	
75 0	45.12	18.00	93.75	75.00	46.55	45.60	68.05	17.150	
84 0	51.04	20.16	105.00	84.00	52.34	51.08	76.23	19.200	
90 0	55.00	21.60	112.50	90.00	56.20	54.76	81.67	20.580	
100 0	61.01	24.00	125.00	100.00	62.32	60.80	90.75	22.850	
105 0	64.02	25.20	131.25	105.00	65.40	63.86	95.30	24.000	

Owing to the paper currency the proportionate prices are frequently liable to variation.

trifling changes constantly take place through the fluctuations of Exchange,
but practically of the same value as the figures shown above.

'One can never help enjoying "Temple Bar."'—*Guardian.*

One Shilling Monthly, of all Booksellers in the United Kingdom;
Fourteen Shillings and Ninepence Yearly, by post, in the United Kingdom,
Europe, North America, Egypt, or Cyprus.

'Who does not welcome "Temple Bar"?'—*John Bull.*

PRICE ONE SHILLING.

'"TEMPLE BAR" is sparkling and brilliant. It might command a constituency by its fiction alone, but it takes so much care of its more solid matter that, if there were no stories at all, there is enough to interest the reader.' *English Independent.*

'A Magazine for the Million.'—*Standard.*

NEW SERIAL STORIES
NOW APPEARING in TEMPLE BAR:—

I.

'A PERILOUS
SECRET.'

By CHARLES READE,
Author of 'Christie Johnston,' &c.

II.

'PERIL.'

By JESSIE FOTHERGILL,
Author of 'The First Violin,' 'Kith
and Kin,' 'Probation,' &c.

BESIDES ESSAYS AND SHORT ARTICLES.

For further information see page 44.

www.ingramcontent.com/pod-product-compliance
Lightning Source LLC
Chambersburg PA
CBHW030750230426
43667CB00007B/911